The Holy War
in Los Altos

THE H✝LY WAR

A REGIONAL ANALYSIS O

N LOS ALTOS

MEXICO'S *Cristero* REBELLION

JIM TUCK

UNIVERSITY OF ARIZONA PRESS
TUCSON, ARIZONA

About the Author...

JIM TUCK has won the Francisco Zarco Prize for the best reports on Mexico in the foreign press. He has contributed to books on Mexico and was named Regional Editor for Mexico by Fodor Guides in 1970. He graduated from Princeton University in 1951 with a degree in history, and in his parallel careers as professional writer, editor, and lecturer he has maintained a lively interest in historical reading and research, particularly on Mexico.

THE UNIVERSITY OF ARIZONA PRESS

Copyright ©1982
The Arizona Board of Regents
All Rights Reserved

This book was set in 11/12 V-I-P Palatino.
Manufactured in the U.S.A.

Library of Congress Cataloging in Publication Data

Tuck, Jim.
    The holy war in Los Altos.

    Bibliography: p.
    Includes index.
    1. Cristero Rebellion, 1926–1929.   2. Jalisco
(Mexico)—History.   I. Title.
F1234.T9   1982   972.08'2   82-8587

ISBN 0-8165-0779-1   AACR2

To my daughter

Contents

A Word
From the
Author

THIS ACCOUNT OF THE HOLY WAR IN LOS ALTOS is presented within
the framework of a larger event—Mexico's *cristero* (soldier for
Christ) rebellion of 1926 to 1929. It examines in detail the effect
of this conflict in one of its key geographic sectors, the Los
Altos plateau of northern Jalisco. Except for a fertile southern
strip, Los Altos is barren, red-clay and mesa country. It is the
Republic's most fervently Catholic enclave, and a Caucasian
enclave as well. The inhabitants are largely of European stock,
descended from both Spanish Creoles and from Maximilian's
troops quartered in the area during his campaign against
Juárez. In this region of fair-skinned folk, many with blond
hair and blue eyes, the original Indian population became a
minority.

Most Mexicans of predominantly European origin gravi-
tated to cities and became leading exponents of secular and
liberal doctrines. A reverse process took place in Los Altos.
Isolated in their harshly beautiful homeland, the *alteños* clung
to a European peasant Catholicism undiluted by the pagan
influences prevalent among the Indian populations in Mexico.

This faith, always strongly held, was heated to fanatic intensity by the repressive policies of an unfriendly central government.

Though the *cristero* war was fought in a 115,000-square-mile area that comprised all of five Mexican states and large parts of several others, nowhere else was it waged with the genocidal intensity that it reached in this Vermont-sized sector of rolling cattle country. The *cristeros* of Los Altos were such skilled and motivated fighters that—in what was basically a guerrilla war—they held off the Mexican Army for three years on open terrain remarkably unsuited to guerrilla operations. This feat can be credited partly to the fighting qualities of their homegrown militia, the *Brigada de Los Altos*, and partly to the extraordinary devotion of the *alteño* civilian population. Their stoicism in the face of executions, disease, starvation, and mass deportations was exceptional.

To view the entire *cristero* conflict as a holy war is to accept a propagandist explanation. In other theaters of the rebellion—notably coastal Michoacán and southern Jalisco—the "soldiers of Christ the King" were often *caciques* (political bosses) out to extend their influence or malcontents eager to avenge a grudge. In the sierra of southern Durango, an Indian enclave, the war took on a tribal aspect. There semi-pagan hill dwellers, who mingled Christianity with ancient peyote rites, joined the *cristeros* mainly because other tribes, who were their traditional enemies, had sided with the government.

In Los Altos, however, the rhetoric about crusades and holy wars had unassailable validity. Whatever one may think about the primitive faith of the *alteños*, their devotion to it was unquestionable. Though *la cristiada* (*cristero* war) has been described as Mexico's Catholic counterrevolution, in Los Altos it was a people's war in the truest sense. The tiny minority of *alteños* (including a Federal governor of Jalisco) who supported the government were fiercely despised as traitors.

This study also focuses on the peasant and proletarian aspect of the *cristero* movement in Los Altos and on how greatly that movement suffered because of episcopal vacillation and the perfidy of many wealthier Catholics. In addition, it examines one of the rebellion's strangest anomalies: the fact that the *cristero* leadership in Los Altos became subject to liberal and Masonic influences at the very time that the Church was moving toward accommodation with the anti-clerical central government.

The discussion of military operations keeps the focus on the *Brigada de Los Altos*. Other *cristero* fighting units are mentioned only in the interest of general exposition or to the extent that their activities relate to those of the *Brigada*. Recording casualties has presented a problem. Since the archives of the Mexican Defense Department are off limits to researchers, I have relied as much as possible on contemporary U.S. military and diplomatic reports. Rebel statistics must be approached with caution. Most of them derive from *DAVID*, the veterans' publication, and have been recorded by men whose appraisals of *cristero* successes may have tended to improve with the passage of time. When citing this material I have always been careful to identify its origin.

The last chapter covers the role of Los Altos in *la segunda*—the second *cristero* rebellion of 1934 to 1937 or, as some chroniclers maintain, 1932 to 1940. It also examines *alteño* resistance to the so-called "socialist education" program, during which the idealism of the *cristiada* became corrupted and lapsed into some of the worst excesses of sadism and banditry ever committed by self-proclaimed defenders of religion.

ACKNOWLEDGMENTS

This work owes its existence both to individuals who figured personally in the events it covers and to later observers whose interest in the *cristiada* led them to assemble vital material that previously had been overlooked. The late René Capistrán Garza was an early leader of the *cristero* movement. Though not directly involved in the events of Los Altos, he was intimately acquainted with the *alteño* leaders, and his unique relationship to the *cristiada* equipped him with special and invaluable perceptions. He was kind enough to furnish me with previously unreleased file material relating to his controversy with the anti-*cristero* faction of the Mexican hierarchy.

Antonio Ríus Facius, noted student and chronicler of Catholic activism in Mexico, supplied me with useful documents from his extensive collection. Of particular value were papers relating to the early life of Father Aristeo Pedroza, *cristero* brigade commander in Los Altos. Through the assistance of Nieves Acevedo, I was able to obtain a body of indispensable source material: seven of the eight existing volumes of *DAVID* (the *cristero* veterans' monthly that ran from 1952 to 1968).

Work on the first chapter was facilitated by the cooperation of Ethel Brinton—a keen student of *alteño* culture and folklore—of the Anglo-Mexican Cultural Institute. I also wish to thank Ronald E. Swerczek and Timothly K. Nenninger of the U.S. National Archives and Records Service, who assisted me in obtaining vital diplomatic papers and military reports. These coldly analytical documents, prepared by foreign diplomats and military attachés, saved me from having to rely on dubious claims made by rival Mexican factions in the heat of civil war.

Among direct participants in the *alteño* struggle, Rafael Martínez Camarena was particularly generous with his time. Though intermittently stricken by illness, the former *cristero* interim governor of Jalisco allowed me to copy important file material and consented to make a tape recording detailing his role in the rebellion. Heriberto Navarrete, S.J., an ex-*cristero* combat officer in Los Altos, was another important witness to these events. A controversial figure who has come under sharp attack from other ex-*cristeros*, he provided valuable information in a number of interviews.

My greatest debt is to the late Father Salvador Casas, indefatigable archivist of the movement in Los Altos. As a young priest he clandestinely exercised his ministry in combat areas, operating exclusively in the *alteño* region. Father Casas devoted much of his later life to assembling a massive archive relating to these events. In this collection are the Gómez Loza papers, documents deriving from the brief but energetic tenure of Miguel Gómez Loza, first *cristero* governor of Jalisco. Thanks to Father Casas, I was able to obtain insights of incalculable value into the *cristero* civil infrastructure. He was also instrumental in enabling me to secure hitherto unconfirmed information about the legendary *cristero* guerrilla leader, Victoriano Ramírez. This material, previously denied to researchers, is stored in the parochial archives of the *alteño* community of San Miguel el Alto. For his painstaking efforts in locating this evidence, I wish to thank San Miguel's parish priest, Father J. Guadalupe Becerra.

An acknowledgment of deep gratitude goes to the late Luz María Mendoza for her research assistance in the early stages of this work.

I wish to add a final expression of thanks to Clare Chamberlain Spera for her diligent and insightful editing and to the University of Arizona Press for effecting publication of this book.

JIM TUCK

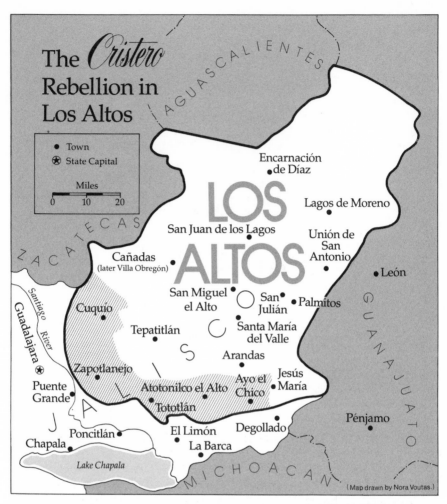

The *Cristero* Rebellion in Los Altos

- Town
⊛ State Capital

Miles
0   10   20

Encarnación de Díaz

Lagos de Moreno

San Juan de los Lagos

Unión de San Antonio

León

Cañadas
(later Villa Obregón)

San Miguel el Alto

San Julián

Palmitos

Cuquio

Tepatitlán

Santa María del Valle

Arandas

Zapotlanejo

Ayo el Chico

Jesús María

Puente Grande

Atotonilco el Alto

Pénjamo

Tototlán

Poncitlán

El Limón

Degollado

Chapala

La Barca

Lake Chapala

Santiago River

Guadalajara

ZACATECAS

AGUASCALIENTES

LOS ALTOS

GUANAJUATO

MICHOACAN

(Map drawn by Nora Voutas.)

Location of major events during the *cristero* rebellion in the Los Altos region of northeastern Jalisco. Hatching shows area historically and culturally belonging to Los Altos, but arbitrarily detached in 1970 and assigned to the Centro district. Small map below shows the location of Los Altos in the state of Jalisco and of Jalisco in Mexico.

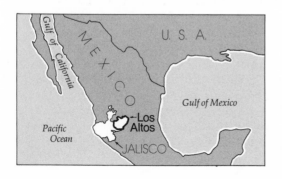

The
Lean Lands

A Profile

LOS ALTOS DE JALISCO IS A REGION that played a central part in the *cristero* rebellion, a major twentieth-century civil conflict in Mexico. As an entity, the region presents problems of definition as well as demarcation. Literal translation conveys the impression that these are the "high lands" of the west-central state of Jalisco. Yet the area is more plain than mountain and completely dwarfed by sections of the Sierra Madre Occidental found in the southern and western parts of the state.

The region did not exist officially until 1970, when Jalisco, for administrative purposes, was divided into five major districts—Norte, Centro, Sur, Costa, and Altos.[1] Until then Los Altos had been simply a cultural and historic unity, as one thinks of the "Deep South" and "Far West." Instead of eliminating confusion, the change heightened it. In giving Los Altos official status, the Federal planners inexplicably took five municipalities that are *alteño* to the core and arbitrarily assigned them to the Centro sector. These communities, forming the southern and western fringe of Los Altos, are Cuquío, Zapotlanejo, Tototlán, Atotonilco, and Ayo el Chico. In this

[1]

study they have been restored to Los Altos. This rectification can be justified on cultural, ethnic, and historical grounds. It is also warranted on grounds of precedent. Not only did these communities play a leading role in *alteño* history, but no chronicler of the *cristero* rebellion, past or present, has ever placed them outside Los Altos.

In the simplest terms, Los Altos is all of Jalisco north and east of Guadalajara with the exception of a strip of fertile black loam country (100 miles long and 10 to 30 miles deep) that begins at Chapala and Juanacatlán and runs east through Zapotlán, Poncitlán, Ocotlán, Jamay, and La Barca until it reaches the village of Degollado. This is where Jalisco ends, at a point where it meets the converging borders of Guanajuato and Michoacán.

Las tierras flacas (the lean lands) is what novelist-politician Agustín Yañez called his native Los Altos. It is also the title of one of his books. Strictly speaking, Yañez erred in describing all of Los Altos as lands that are lean and infertile. Of a total of about 9,650 square miles, there is an 855-square-mile southern strip of rich, black soil where tropical fruits and vegetables grow in profusion. This is a region comprising four of the five communities assigned to the Centro sector in 1970: Ayo el Chico, Atotonilco, Tototlán, and Zapotlanejo. These locations, like the Guadalajara-Lake Chapala area, have altitudes ranging from 5,000 to 5,200 feet. The fifth municipality, Cuquío, joins the rest of Los Altos in forming the lean lands. There altitude ranges between 5,800 and 7,400 feet. The lean lands enjoy one of the world's finest climates. Though that honor has been claimed by the Atemajac valley, where Guadalajara is located, there is really no comparison. In April and May, the end of the dry season, the valley is afflicted with stifling heat—an unpleasantness that vanishes as one reaches the bracing *alteño* plateau, where the air is marvelously pure, and there are ghostly white clouds, the clearest of blue skies, rolling hills of dark purple, and soil so bright red that uncultivated stretches look like open wounds. The *alteño* countryside is perhaps even more impressive on an overcast day. Then it looks like a stormy sea. The rolling beauty of Los Altos is enhanced by the fact that at no point are the hills steep enough to create those high, vision-blocking valleys found in more mountainous regions.

Notwithstanding scenic and climatic attractions, the lean lands live up to their name. Life is hard on this red-clay plateau, whose thin soil yields few of the succulent comestibles found in the rich region to the south. Principal agricultural products are corn, beans, and sorghum, with agriculture playing a subordinate role to livestock raising. This is cattle country, with a profusion of ranches and dairy farms. Pigs, chickens, and—to a lesser extent—goats are also raised here.

In addition, Los Altos plays an important role in Mexico's liquor industry. There are only two areas in the world suitable for cultivation of the blue maguey (*agave tequilana*), the sole source of tequila. One surrounds the town of Tequila, about forty miles west of Guadalajara, and the other is centered on Tepatitlán, about the same distance away in a northeasterly direction. Tepatitlán, the largest population center in Los Altos, is considered the region's unofficial capital.

The people of this austere land belong to one of Mexico's most unusual subcultures. They and the blacks of the Costa Chica, a strip along the Pacific shore of Guerrero and Oaxaca, are the only sizable ethnic groups found outside the Republic's prevailing Indo-Hispanic mix. (Though blacks and mulattoes are found all along the Gulf, it is on the Costa Chica alone that they are concentrated densely enough to form a distinct enclave.) *Alteño* heritage is Spanish Creole, Basque, French, and probably Germanic. The non-Iberian element derives from 35,000 troops under Marshal Bazaine who were quartered in the region during Maximilian's campaign against Juárez.[2] The fact that many *alteños* are blond and blue-eyed would suggest the presence of German and Austrian contingents among the French forces. Of four regiments under Bazaine, three of them—the 3rd Zouaves, the 3rd Chasseurs d'Afrique, and the Tiralleurs Algériens—were colonial units open to foreign enlistment.[3] Yet one encounters few French or German surnames in Los Altos. Since almost all unions between Bazaine's soldiers and local women were irregular—and many forced—children invariably took the mother's Spanish name.

There is also an Indian minority in Los Altos, descendants of aboriginal Otomís, Tecos, and Tecuexes.[4] Since Mexico's Statistical Agency classifies only Indian-speaking members of national minorities as indigenes, all Spanish speakers are considered Mexican regardless of ethnic background. Into this second category fall all the Indians of Los Altos, so it is difficult to state exactly what percentage of the population they form. From observation, it is doubtful that the total exceeds 20 percent, and even this figure may be high. On market days in such pure *alteño* communities as San Juan de Los Lagos and Arandas, the few Indians present are highly conspicuous, standing out amid a sea of ruddy complexions and blond mustaches. White and brown *alteños* live together harmoniously, but there is little evidence of intermarriage; thus, a *mestizo* culture has not been established.

Indian *alteños* were as ardently *cristero* as their Creole brothers. The village of Moya, an indigenous community near Lagos de Moreno, contributed the only infantry contingent to fight in Los Altos during the rebellion (an interesting throwback to colonial days, when Indians were forbidden to use horses).[5]

How did Los Altos come to be the heartland of the *cristero* rebellion? The roots of *alteño* resistance to a centralizing and anti-clerical revolutionary government in Mexico City are historic, religious, cultural, and economic.

Usually the term *patria chica* (little fatherland) is applied to territory occupied by isolated indigenous groups. Huicholes, Coras, and Lancandons may be legally Mexicans, but they live completely outside the Republic's cultural mainstream and many never learn Spanish. Whites, mestizos, and Hispanicized Indians, on the other hand, are too assimilated to identify with a *patria chica*. Mexico is their *patria grande* and they haven't the slightest desire to be associated with some lonely and primitive backwater. Whatever concessions they make to localism are strictly within a Mexican context. They are *jarochos* (natives of Veracruz) or *tapatíos* (inhabitants of Jalisco); they are not quaint natives to be studied by anthropologists and photographed by tourists.

Los Altos furnishes the exception. True, curious outsiders with notebooks and cameras have not overrun the lean lands to the extent that they have the Indian enclaves. But an attempt at cultural penetration was made in the 1930s, when a corps of teachers descended on the red-clay country to educate the *alteños* out of their "fanaticism." The reaction of the *alteños* against this ill-advised mission was so violent[6] that the experiment was never repeated.

Los Altos is a *patria chica* in every way but linguistically. *Alteños* are clannish, suspicious of outsiders, and conservative in an anarchistic, non-Hamiltonian way. They detest central authority of any kind, whether federal, state, or local. This feeling has made them traditionally prone to the leadership of *cabecillas* (ringleaders). During the *cristiada* some were rebels fighting oppression, but many were bandits fishing in troubled political waters. Cattle thieves yesterday, "generals" today, the *cabecillas* placed their bands at the service of whatever faction suited their convenience.

POLITICS, HISTORY, AND HERITAGE

The only consistent political behavior pattern exhibited by the *alteños* was unflagging support of the Church. Their shifts in allegiance were almost always in line with those of the hierarchy and clergy. In the early days of the Independence War, Los Altos was royalist; *alteños* were doubtless swayed by anathemas pronounced against the rebel leader, Father Miguel Hidalgo y Costilla, by such dignitaries as the Bishop of Guadalajara. As the eleven-year struggle dragged on, the picture changed. An anti-clerical faction forced Ferdinand VII of Spain to accept a liberal constitution in 1820. To the Mexican hierarchy, previously opposed to independence, it was shocking heresy for the mother country to become infected with liberalism. It was now the duty of Mexicans, as a conservative priest-historian wrote, to "achieve our necessary and highly desirable separation from corrupt Spain."[7] With this reversal the *alteños* became such champions of independence that Felix Calleja, the royalist governor, advocated burning San Juan de Los Lagos to the ground for "addiction to the bad cause."[8]

During the War of Reform, the liberal-conservative struggle that raged from 1857 to 1861, Los Altos was uncompromisingly on the clerical side. Promulgation of the 1857 Constitution under President Benito Juárez set off an explosion of violence in the lean lands that was not again matched until the *cristiada*. The Reform War launched the careers of such renowned *cabecillas* as Zermeño, Larrumbide, Soto, and

Cuellar.[9] These chieftains lent enthusiastic support to the conservative stalwart, General Miramón, who set up headquarters at Lagos de Moreno in June, 1860.[10]

Though Juárez marched into Mexico City on New Year's Day of 1861, his troubles were far from over. The clericals called on France for help, and Napoleon III responded by pouring French troops into Mexico. The Franco-conservative goal was to oust Juárez and set up a monarchy. Casting about for a candidate, they finally settled on the ill-fated Maximilian von Habsburg. Duped into thinking that the majority of Mexicans wanted him as emperor, the gullible Archduke came to his rendezvous with death.

During this period Los Altos was a hive of anti-*juarista* activity. The peak year of *alteño* service to the clerical cause was 1863. On 25 April a new *cabecilla*, Angel Manzo, joined his forces with those of General Tomás Mejía.[11] (The latter, like his enemy Juárez, was a full-blooded Indian.) In mid-July the *cabecilla* Larrumbide defeated a liberal force under Colonel Alvarelli. On 21 and 28 July the *juaristas*, under Colonel Mójica, made two abortive attacks on Tepatitlán. On 11 October Mójica was repulsed at Atotonilco and, two days later, again at Tepatitlán. The persistent Mójica made a fourth try against Tepatitlán on 11 November. Though he had strengthened his forces, this attempt proved no more successful than the others.[12]

The liberals scored only two successes in that disastrous year. On 27 July Cuellar, Zermeño, and Soto rode on Lagos de Moreno with a 500-man force. The *juarista* garrison, under Major Prudencio Topete, turned them back after a six-hour fight. On 8 October a Zermeño-led force of conservatives attacked again; this time they were successful. The other liberal victory took place near Atotonilco on 26 November, when Colonel Serapio defeated a 200-man force led by the *cabecilla* García.[13]

Alteño fervor for Maximilian's cause cooled perceptibly between 1864, the year the French entered Los Altos, and 1867, when the luckless Austrian was executed. Bazaine's men were not decorous guests. *Alteños* resented not only their romantic ardor but such senseless acts as the wanton destruction of Tepatitlán's municipal archive.[14] Maximilian himself also proved a disappointment. The *alteños* had expected a flaming defender of the faith, but their paladin turned out to be a mild liberal who believed in freedom of worship and refused to return the Church's confiscated holdings. Maximilian's death caused little grief in the red-clay country.

Religious warfare next broke out in 1873, during an uprising launched by a group known as *religioneros*, Catholic rebels outraged by the anti-clericalism of Juárez's successor, Sebastián Lerdo de Tejada. It was under President Lerdo, in September of 1873, that the Reform Laws were officially made part of the 1857 Constitution. The rebellion broke out in Michoacán and spread to a region that would be solidly *cristero* half a century later. This region included the Sierra Gorda in Guanajuato, southern and western Jalisco, and, of course, Los Altos. Ironically, a prominent *religionero* was Eulogio Cárdenas, grandfather of Mexico's most radical president.[15] The *alteños* performed with their usual zeal, attacking federal garrisons at Atotonilco, Arandas, and Lagos de Moreno. One band, led by Felix Vánegas, got to the outskirts of Guadalajara before being stopped.[16] The insurrection died out in 1876, following Lerdo's overthrow by Porfirio Díaz. Díaz, seeking a national consensus, quickly reached a modus vivendi with the Church. Though the Reform Laws remained on the books, they were simply not enforced. This policy worked so well that in 1900 Bishop Montes de Oca of San Luis Potosí noted with the greatest satisfaction that "although the [Reform] laws are still in effect, we have enjoyed over twenty years of absolute peace thanks to the prudence...of the superior man who governs us."[17]

Los Altos played only a minor role in the chaotic revolutionary decade between 1910 and 1920. Neither Porfirio Díaz nor his successor, Francisco Madero, was a foe of the Church, so *alteños* were not pushed to any fiercely partisan position during their struggle for power. Moreover, a considerable number of the clergy had embraced the social gospels of Pope Leo XIII. Such theory caused them to tilt toward Madero and away from an aging liberal-turned-reactionary like Díaz. Don Porfirio was too friendly with the big industrialists and *latifundistas* (big landowners) to win the affection of country priests ministering to impoverished campesinos.

Victoriano Huerta, the hard-drinking military adventurer who overthrew President Madero in 1913, had been an admirer and supporter of Díaz. Longing for the golden days of the *porfiriato*, he ardently courted the Church. Though he made inroads among the hierarchy, the lower clergy remained *maderista*. As Huerta's fortunes declined, the hierarchs also turned against him. Josephus Daniels wrote: "[He] thought he had won their favor, but later the influential leaders of the Church came to the conclusion that peace would not come to Mexico, except by the withdrawal of Huerta."[18]

So detached was Los Altos from events of the decade of revolution that only one high-ranking *cristero* officer figured in them. All others who rose to top command positions in Los Altos had civilian backgrounds. Two were priests, one a veterinary student, one a sewing machine salesman, and the rest ranchers. Why didn't such an ardently Catholic region as Los Altos fight against the revolutionaries, even after the promulgation of the harshly anti-Catholic constitution of 1917? This quiescence may be attributed to the fact that not one of the revolutionary leaders—Francisco Villa, Emiliano Zapata, Venustiano Carranza, or Alvaro Obregón—ever moved against the Church in the potentially explosive region.

For Villa and Zapata, such action would have been an impossibility. Zapata—as parochial as any *alteño*—was mainly concerned with obtaining social justice for the Indians of his native Morelos. Neither he nor Villa was ever president (which would have given them jurisdiction over Los Altos) and neither man was particularly anti-clerical. Zapata carried a saint's relics during a hometown procession and one of Villa's generals was a parish priest.[19] Both Villa's and Zapata's men displayed banners of the Virgin of Guadalupe, and Villa, in an angry letter, accused Carranza of "having profoundly outraged the religious sentiments of the people."[20] This accusation is doubtless a reference to excesses committed by the forces of Carranza and Obregón. Both men were anti-clerical and their 1913 to 1914 march on Mexico City against Huerta was characterized by incidents of terror and vandalism. Priests were killed, soldiers destroyed images of saints and clothed their horses in religious vestments, and a famous ecclesiastical library in Monterrey was burned.

At the same time both leaders had the saving grace of pragmatism. Their policy was one of selective anti-Catholicism. In states with a strong anti-clerical tradition, like Tabasco and Veracruz, Carranza and Obregón went to great lengths in applying the restrictive provisions of the 1917 Constitution. But in regions like Los Altos they stopped short of such provocations. Doubtless aware of the *alteños'* toughness and devotion to their faith, they shied away from the specter of religious war.

No such prudence was shown by Obregón's mulish successor, Plutarco Elías Calles. He and others doubtless accepted the prevailing stereotype of Los Altos as a land of strong tequila, lusty ranchers, and fair-skinned women of surpassing beauty. Ignored or underestimated was the intensity of *alteño* Catholicism. Misinterpreting inaction for cowardice, Calles read the semi-dormant role of Los Altos—and of all Jalisco—during the Revolution as a sign that *jalisciences* were not fighters. He was to learn better.

To grasp the essence of *alteño* Catholicism, it is first important to understand what it is not. Much has been written about Mexican Catholicism as a religion of idols behind altars. In colonial times the Church demonstrated remarkable flexibility in adapting to indigenous cultures. In many instances Indians were allowed to keep their local deities on condition that they give them the names of saints and acknowledge the Virgin and Trinity. This flexibility has led to astounding doctrinal deviations. Some Indians in Chiapas believe in a "wicked" Christ (who was chained to a tree for his sins by four good saints), while blacks on the Costa Chica fear the "evil" St. Martha.[21] What passes for Catholicism in much of Mexico is actually a pagan polytheism under a Christian veneer.

Idols-behind-altars Catholicism forms no part of the religious tradition in Los Altos. With their French, Spanish-Basque, and Germanic antecedents, the *alteños* are ethnically as well as ideologically related to the narrow country clericalism that prevails in the Vendée, Navarre, and highland Austria. Theirs is a European Catholicism, but it is a back-country variety far removed from ecumenism and modernization. Another salient feature of *alteño* Catholicism is that it is fanatic without being in the slightest degree puritan. The *beato* (literally, beatified person, but used here to mean prude) is almost always an urban type, usually a chaste young man who spends his spare time at meetings of Catholic discussion groups. While the *beata* is tolerated in Los Altos (especially if she is old and ugly), the *beato* is a stereotype figure of fun. Having the "right" attitude toward such hated enemies as Freemasons and anti-clericals is far more important than prissy concerns about temperance and chastity. Sunday morning at Mass is invariably preceded by a Saturday night of drinking, brawling, and demonstrating machismo to willing cantina girls.

European, peasant, clannish, uncompromising about faith, tolerant about morals—these are the characteristics of *alteño* Catholicism and of the people who became standard bearers of the *cristiada*. Nowhere else in Mexico is Catholicism so deeply and strongly rooted. Here is a community with ancestral roots in the most Catholic parts of Western Europe which has resisted all assimilative pressures and maintained itself intact on a red-clay plateau in upland Jalisco. Mexico's tribal Indians have a Catholicism that was imposed from above and is heavily adulterated with paganism. Other Mexicans—assimilated Indians, mestizos, whites—may be devout, but they are still Catholics living in a secular society, while *alteños* belong to a culture which is distinctly Catholic. As a priest, a non-*alteño* who spent many years in Los Altos, has said, "You can't imagine how it is in those little villages, how set in their ways these people are. Even today they'll tell you to your face, 'If you're not Catholic, get out of town.'"[22]

ALTEÑO SOCIETY

If Catholicism is the religious fact of life in Los Altos, machismo is the cultural one. As befits this hard-bitten community, there is a tradition of extravagant machismo in Los Altos. Facial hair as a status symbol is nothing new here. While pencil line mustaches are the Latin norm, in Los Altos the style runs to luxurious handlebars. Quite possibly, this custom may be an unconscious belittlement of the more sparsely whiskered Indians and *mestizos*.

Though *alteños* pride themselves on their lovemaking, the machismo of Los Altos is not just sexual. Other important components are physical toughness, bravery, and an ingrained contempt for intellectualism, prissy virtuousness, dandyism, and putting on airs. Long before the term became part of the popular jargon, the *alteños* were masters of intimidation. Intimidation is inseparable from contempt, and during the *cristiada* the *alteños* perfected the technique of harassing the Federals with daring acts of defiance. Lone riders would gallop through government-held towns shouting the *cristero* slogan "Viva Cristo Rey! (Long live Christ the

King!)," and a rebel band, on capturing a village with a telephone, would place an insulting call to the nearest Federal commander.

The contempt expressed by the *alteños* for their enemies may at first have been bravado. Later, it became genuine. In the early days of the rebellion the *alteños* were themselves intimidated by enemy superiority in numbers and weaponry and by their own inexperience. During that period they referred to the Federals as *sardos* (a term deriving from the soldiers' rust-colored uniforms). As the war progressed, and the *cristeros* began winning battles, they more often referred to their enemies as *changos* (apes).

In the early 1980s the chief outlet for *alteño* physical machismo has been the *charreada*. These events, similar to Wild West rodeos, are competitive on a nationwide basis. Though the local team, Alteña de Charros, represents a rural backwater, the Los Altos *charros* (cowboys) have consistently held their own against rivals from such metropolises as Mexico City, Guadalajara, and Monterrey.

The *alteño* is a lover and a fighter, but his machismo has a third face. This is the face that looks with scorn on the egghead, the dandy, the poseur, and the puritan. This prejudice has its roots in the *cristiada*. During the rebellion a group of educated young men, mostly of urban background, came to Los Altos to join the fighting forces. Though well intentioned, many of these youthful Catholic activists had been too softened by city life to make good soldiers. The *alteños* resented them and called them *catrines* (swells). They were *catrines* not only for their uselessness in combat but also for their education (most of the *alteños* were illiterate), their correct diction, and their unfamiliarity with *alteño* dialect. Some, though not all, of the *catrines* were *beatos;* this characteristic earned them an extra measure of contempt.

In fairness, it must be acknowledged that the *alteños'* animosity did not extend to the minority of these newcomers who displayed soldierly qualities. An educated man who could fight was not only respected but considered a candidate for high command. One of them (raised in Guadalajara but *alteño*-born) ended the rebellion a general.

For all their narrow conservatism, it would be an error to dismiss the *alteños* as fascists or racists. This conservatism is social, not ideological, and their anti-intellectualism pre-disposes them against political sophistry of any ideological shade. It is noteworthy that western Guanajuato, which borders on Los Altos, was a stronghold of the clerical-fascist Unión Nacional Sinarquista (UNS; later reborn as the Partido Democrático Mexicano [PDM]). Yet the *sinarquistas* never gained a toehold in Los Altos. Their mystic rhetoric about *Hispanidad* struck the earthy, apolitical *alteños* as pretentious blather. They—and other *cristeros* of campesino origin—were completely turned off by the urban, middle-class leadership of the *sinarquistas*. Only one prominent *cristero* ever joined the movement and Aurelio Acevedo, the Zacatecas *cabecilla*, went so far as to say that *sinarquismo* was "invented for the express purpose of extinguishing the *cristero* spirit."[23]

Any suspicion of *alteño* racism is dispelled by the record of friendly relations between the Caucasian majority and Indian minority in Los Altos. This lack of prejudice was also apparent during the *cristiada*. There were a number of Indians and mestizos among the young men who came to Los Altos to fight in the rebellion. Only the *catrines* among them were looked down on. The services of talented nonwhites were highly valued, and those who showed military ability rose quickly in the ranks. Of seven regimental commanders in the Los Altos brigade, two were non-*alteño* mestizos, as was the brigade commander himself. This color blindness was not limited to the *cristiada*. During the 1930s Los Altos was terrorized by bandits. Claiming to be *cristeros*, they robbed Catholics and anti-clericals alike. Leading one of these bands, composed mostly of whites, was the dreaded Indian *cabecilla* "El Pinacate."[24]

One might think that such a machismo-oriented society as Los Altos would be a stronghold of male chauvinism, but this is not the case. *Alteña* women are cut from the same abrasive cloth as their fiercely mustachioed menfolk. The expression "proud beauty" could have been invented with these viragos in mind. Tall, arrogant, many with striking green eyes, they completely live up to the popular localism *"una alteña altañera* (a haughty *alteña*)."* Only in Tehuantepec, a matriarchal society, are women less submissive.

Augustín Yañez, whose novels have been acclaimed for their starkly honest *alteño* images, furnishes an unforgettable picture of one of these women in *Las tierras flacas*. In this work the essence of *alteña* characteristics is embodied by the terrible

Plácida, one of many illegitimate children of the *cacique* (political boss) of Clamores, don Epifanio Trujillo. When the old man dies, Plácida, by sheer force of will, succeeds in gaining control of his estate. Then she goes into action: "Once she was absolute mistress of the place...she settled herself in the saddle...raised her whip...and was off like a shot. Who is brave enough to stand up to her?"[25] Plácida first sent away her father's mistress and then lay down the law to her numerous siblings and half-siblings. Then she began running the estate, making economies and terrorizing all under her:

> Naturally she abolished the old custom of inviting all those who passed the Big House for a meal. She would not give a taco or even a drink of water to those who came to the novena of rosaries for the deceased and those who came from far away to express their sympathy. With the rations drastically reduced, the servants at Belén went hungry...and she never stopped from sunrise to sunset.... She kept an eye on everything, weighed and measured everything. Nothing escaped her notice, the badly milked cow, the hen badly placed on the nest, the furrow covered with weeds, broken tools. She went around giving out scoldings, curses, blows; making a fuss over trifles; inspiring fear as her eagle eye noted the smallest bit of carelessness. She forgave neither grownups nor children. She could not bear to see anyone doing nothing; she gave no one any rest.[26]

During the rebellion *alteñas* served as nurses, performed espionage missions in Federal-occupied communities, and smuggled arms and ammunition to their men in the sierra. And woe to any woman whose dedication to the *cristiada* was less than total. One unhappy girl, rejected by a *cristero* general, became the mistress of a Federal captain. Though blameless in the affair, her entire family suffered ostracism.

THE ROOTS OF REBELLION

Marxist dogma notwithstanding, it is probable that Los Altos would have risen for reasons that had nothing to do with economics. Still, the economic base of the *cristiada* in Los Altos should not be overlooked. The Soviet writer Nikolai Larin, in a polemical work, characterized the *cristeros* as "servants who executed the will of big business and the large landowners" and their rebellion as one "prepared and directed by Mexico's clerical-landowning reaction."[27] This portrait of the *cristero-as-white* guard is interesting because it furnishes an exact description of what the *cristeros* were not.

Let us first examine the premise that the rebels were at best pawns—at worst, hired gunmen—of the big landowners who opposed agrarian reform. In the interest of precision, we will define a big landowner as proprietor of a *hacienda* employing more than a thousand people.

When the war broke out Jalisco was divided into units called *cantones*. Los Altos was made up of the *cantones* of Teocaltiche, Lagos, and the northern part of La Barca. (Southern La Barca, outside the *alteño* area, forms the north bank of Lake Chapala.) In 1930, the year after the rebellion ended, the state average for land occupied by these big *haciendas* was 44.1 percent. In Los Altos the distribution was as follows: Teocaltiche, 16 percent; La Barca, 24 percent; and Lagos, 83.9 percent.[28] Thus, most of the big *haciendas* were concentrated in Lagos, which occupies the northeastern part of Los Altos.

What was the role of Lagos during the *cristiada?* Not only was it the quietest sector, but it was the only one that failed to furnish a regimental-size unit to the *cristero* fighting forces. Of the seven regiments raised in Los Altos by rebels, three came from the Zapotlanejo-Tototlán-Atotonilco-Ayo el Chico black-soil belt and four from the red-clay country south and west of Lagos. In both regions the number of large *haciendas* is negligible. The Los Altos *cristeros,* rather than armed guards in the pay of *latifundistas,* were in reality small ranchers, ranch-hands, tenant farmers, agricultural day laborers, and village artisans.

The big *hacendados* were, in fact, overwhelmingly pro-government. During the *cristiada* they either fled to the cities or paid the Army for protection. The only "white guards" in Los Altos were Federal troops defending the *latifundistas* against a revolutionary peasantry: the *cristeros.*

Nor was there any link between the rebels and big business; indeed, an unending cause of complaint was the parsimony and perfidy of rich Catholics. The term *acomodado* (literally, well-accommodated one) came to be as much of an epithet in Los Altos as *catrín.* When their pleas for aid were ignored the *cristeros* took to kidnaping Catholic merchants and businessmen. Several were executed when ransom was not forthcoming.

It is also wrong to suppose that the rebels were working at the direction of Mexico's Catholic hierarchy. The attitude of most bishops toward the rebellion ranged from tepid endorsement at the beginning to active opposition at the end.

If the *alteños* were not reactionary peasants or white guards, what was the reason for their violent opposition to the agrarian movement? The *agraristas*, a rural militia sponsored by the government, were hated even more than the Federal troops. Said Aurelio Acevedo, the Zacatecas *cabecilla:* "We don't judge the Federals and *agraristas* by the same standard. The first we consider brothers who fight because it's their duty, though they disgrace themselves by serving such an infamous government; the second are vile people who persecute a religion they learned at their mothers' breasts."[29]

Alteño military leaders, particularly Colonel Manuel Ramírez de Olivas, gave the *agraristas* no quarter. But animus against the rural militiamen did not mean that the *cristeros* were opposed to land reform. It is noteworthy that many *cristeros*—in Los Altos and elsewhere—were strong admirers of Zapata. Of forty-four former rebels who responded to a French writer's questionnaire, forty-three considered him a friend of the *campesino* and twenty believed he would have been a *cristero*. Only one judged him a bandit.[30]

Almost all the *cristeros* in Los Altos were rural folk who disliked big landowners and *acomodados* and who stood to gain from land reform. Their hatred of *agrarismo* was based simply on the fact that they considered it a fraud and a racket. They pointed to a cynical deal consummated in Ayo el Chico, where *ejido* (communal) land was administered for the benefit of a local *latifundista*. The *ejido's* "administrative committee" functioned openly as his advisers and servants.[31]

Agrarismo was also considered an instrument of the central authority viewed so suspiciously by *alteños*. A farmer living north of La Barca at first refused a plot of land offered by the government; he was sure there were strings attached. He was finally persuaded to accept, and a few days later he and some of his friends were issued rifles. "That's the price you have to pay," they were told. "You are now in the service of the government."[32]

In their anti-*agrarismo* stance the *alteños* found support from an unexpected quarter. *El Machete,* then the publication of Mexico's Communist Party, declared that "the campesino class is in large part led by lawyers and engineers, professional 'agrarians' who haven't been able to lead the campesinos to a single real victory."[33]

During the closing months of the rebellion the *alteños* were given an even more compelling reason to detest the agrarian establishment. Much of the Army was then tied up fighting a military rebellion in the north, so a large force of *agraristas* was mobilized to use against the *cristeros*. While the rural militiamen had once been used exclusively as regional self-defense units, they were now deployed as invasion troops. The chief target was Los Altos and the early days of April 1929 witnessed an 8,000-man incursion from neighboring San Luís Potosí.

Los Altos furnished the *cristiada* with two major heroes, whose names are as much revered among older *alteños* in the early 1980s as they were half a century ago. The first, Victoriano Ramírez, was the exemplar and archetype of *alteño* machismo. An illiterate ranch hand, he was famed even before the rebellion for his marksmanship, skill with the lasso, and sexual prowess. He was also endowed with natural military aptitude and enormous charisma. These qualities served him well during the war when he gathered a band of followers and became the most feared guerrilla in Los Altos. Victoriano was also known as "El Catorce," the name deriving from an incident in which he is reputed to have killed fourteen men singlehanded. (Though firmly ensconced in regional folklore, the story was an exaggeration.) Had he died fighting the Federals, Victoriano would have been martyr enough. His martyrdom was enhanced by the fact that he was treacherously murdered following a conspiracy by fellow *cristeros*, one of whom may have been a Federal spy.

The second figure in the *alteño* pantheon, Anacleto González Flores, was—curiously—an intellectual, but his humble birth, simplicity, and hatred of pretension saved him from any suspicion of being a *catrín*. Of all the Catholic activists in Los Altos, he was the only one to transcend regional boundaries and become a national figure in the rebellion. If the *cristiada* had a moral, spiritual, and intellectual director, it was this gifted man.

The
Maestro and
His Pupils

ANACLETO GONZÁLEZ FLORES, a leader and hero of the *cristero* rebellion, was an unusual man. Perhaps the most interesting aspect of his personality was that he had the happy faculty of exuding intellectual brilliance and personal sanctity without incurring animosity. Despite a towering mind and a lifestyle of forbidding rectitude, nobody was ever known to resent him for his cerebral and moral supremacy. This was as true of enemies as of friends. Though the former detested his political role and feared him as the most dangerous demagogue in Mexico, there was a curious absence of personal rancor. Even the soldiers who tortured and executed him did so with thinly disguised admiration for the man whose body they were brutalizing.

González Flores was born in Tepatitlán on 13 July 1888. Though his father, proprietor of a small tool shop, qualified as a petit bourgeois, there can never have been much money in a house that teemed with twelve children. From the beginning Anacleto showed signs of brilliance. Nicknamed "The Camel" because of a stoop-shouldered walk, he was a strange anomaly in Los Altos—an intellectual prodigy growing up in a region where machismo was ever esteemed over intellect.[1] "Cleto," as he was also known, was neither more nor less religious than his youthful companions until he reached the age of seventeen. At that time he was so moved by the sermon of a visiting Guadalajara priest that the experience proved his personal road to Damascus. Overnight he made the transformation from lukewarm communicant to fervent believer. He attended Mass daily, performed acts of charity, and began to develop his lifelong interest in Catholic social action.[2]

At the age of twenty Anacleto enrolled in the seminary at San Juan de los Lagos. There he found time to mingle ecclesiastical studies with recruiting work for the National Catholic party in Jalisco. Though he left the seminary in 1913, this move was not due to any flagging of religious zeal. He simply decided that he could advance Catholic interests more effectively as a lay leader. His only deviation from a lifelong career of Catholic militancy came in 1914 when he served as secretary to the *villista* General Delgadillo.[3] Afterward, with customary energy, he plunged into such diverse fields as teaching, political action, journalism, and law. Some of these activities were interrelated. To finance his legal studies he taught history and literature in private schools. Though he didn't take his law degree until the relatively late age of thirty-four, he was the only applicant ever to receive a perfect score on the tests.[4] González Flores was also active in the founding of five Catholic newspapers in Guadalajara—periodicals that regularly served as outlets for his writings.

His best-known role was that of political, intellectual, and spiritual mentor to the young Catholic activists who formed his following. They called him "El Maestro" (sometimes rendered as "Maistro"—an affectionate diminutive) and looked to him for guidance in all things. The apparent secret of his magnetism was that he was able to combine scholastic rigor with an appealing and unaffected sweetness of nature. An old pupil recalls his "iron discipline" in class but also "the happiness, almost infantile...reflected in his gaze" when, between classes, he amused himself by singing a ranchero song from his native Los Altos.[5]

The organization that served as González Flores's principal sounding board was the Asociación Católica de la Juventud Mexicana (Catholic Association of Mexican Youth). The ACJM was founded in 1913 and González Florers was an early

...nd enthusiastic member. In his teaching capacity he was in an ideal position to recruit new members among his students. One incident in particular highlights his proselytizing gifts. Not only does it demonstrate Anacleto's evangelistic powers but casts a revealing look into his concepts of human development, duty, and social action.

One afternoon in 1920 González Flores encountered five of his students on a street corner near the Plaza del Carmen in downtown Guadalajara. All the youths were preparing for university degrees in engineering. An informal discussion developed in which the Maestro first posed the question of what they would obtain after receiving their professional titles. Food? Clothing? Shelter? These were necessary, to be sure, but was a higher standard of living their only goal in life? One of the boys ventured that they would be in a better position as engineering graduates to advance science. A noble ambition, Anacleto agreed, but what was science? Was it not man's desperate effort to extract from nature the secret of her functions, to anxiously seek the meaning of her phenomena and the reason for the existence of things? Could this be the true mission of a being such as man? There was, he insisted, a higher calling, one that would cultivate the most exalted qualities of the human spirit. That mission was to love the only being worthy of love without measure: God.[6]

With perfect timing, González Flores switched from this lyric appeal to a more matter-of-fact one. There is within all of us, he said, a petty and cowardly spirit that works to diminish Christian faith. Persons animated by this spirit delude themselves that they are true Catholics just because they occasionally attend Mass or listen to a sermon. Such tepid observance is not religion but mockery of religion, and men of conscience should realize this. To love God is to live for Him, to suffer for all the offenses committed against Him. Love of God, especially for a young man, means boundless enthusiasm, the impassioned ardor of a saint, dreams of heroism, and reckless boldness.

The Maestro made no effort to conceal the difficulty of sticking to such a program. Just as life is a struggle, so is the true love of God. Every one of us is a soldier, and who is more idealistic than a young man who places love of God above his own life? He urged his pupils to banish all empty and irrelevant concerns from their young lives. Yet—even if they succeeded in doing so—he warned them that they would still encounter a great deal that seemed petty, routine, and far removed from the world of heroism they dreamed of. But they should not be discouraged. They must bear in mind that every humdrum task and obligation is part of an infinite scheme, just as every hour of the day is a small part of one's life.

This, then, is the duty of a Christian soldier: to plan activities based on the belief that love of Christ is the ultimate goal in life. Such activity will also develop one's own life, the life of one's family, and the life of one's community. These lives will then converge toward a holy ideal, one that González Flores described as "the glorious heroism of identifying the honor of God with one's own and placing this ideal ahead of one's own life."[7]

Anacleto concluded by inviting the young men to the ACJM center the following afternoon. All came and all joined the same day.

In this particular performance both method and ideology are revealed. With uncanny adroitness González Flores switched back and forth between passionate exhortation and sturdy common sense. His Socratic technique of questioning is also apparent. To the young men under his spell he was the perfect mentor—idealistic without being fanatical, practical without being mundane.

There was another, less appealing, side to Anacleto's personality: his obsession with martyrdom. Though it surfaced only twice in the "sales talk" to his students, it was a recurrent theme in his speeches and published works. Significantly, his only book was entitled The Plebiscite of the Martyrs.

Martyrdom, in his view, conferred a special sanctity on those who sought it. His admiration was not confined to Christian martyrs. Well-grounded in the classics, González Flores venerated Socrates, "who, in order to take a stand against the Athenian state, spoke his philosopher's words and serenely drank his cup of hemlock."[8] By contrast he looked down on Plato, who "never dared take a stand against those in power."[9]

Unlike more quixotic folk, Gonzáles Flores did not regard martyrdom as simply a glorious gesture or even as a ticket to salvation. These considerations were secondary. Sacrificial death had a concrete and clearly defined historical purpose, one which he raised to the level of a philosophical concept. It was best expressed in this passage from the Plebiscite:

What is written in blood, as Nietzsche says, is written forever. The offering of a martyr will never perish.... The sacrifice of martyrs has written pages in history that will remain there forever. He [the martyr] has gone further.... He has touched the living flesh of future generations and every day performs the miracle of reviving our spirits through the shedding of his blood and through his daring gesture of a gladiator who never surrenders. The martyr is and always has been the first citizen of a strange and unforeseen democracy who, in violent times, sacrifices his life so that his offering or his memory will never be extinguished.[10]

These are heady words; yet it would be wrong to dismiss González Flores as simply a death-obsessed fanatic. Part of his attachment to martyrdom was rooted in something highly praiseworthy: his lifelong detestation of violence. He was one of two prominent Jalisco Catholics, and the only layman among them, who consistently opposed armed rebellion. (The other was Guadalajara Archbishop Francisco Orozco y Jiménez.) An admirer of Gandhi and Daniel O'Connell, Anacleto deplored the brutalizing effects of violence and saw it as leading to tyranny. Corrupt and despotic systems should be overthrown by individual sacrifice (hence the emphasis on martyrdom) and a mass program of passive resistance.

THE UNION POPULAR

Though the least violence-prone of Mexico's Catholic militants, González Flores was also one of the most authoritarian. His social Catholicism tilted more to the clericalism of Engelbert Dollfuss than toward Western European Christian-Democratic doctrines. His more liberal colleagues saw political democracy and social Christianity walking hand in hand, but Anacleto rejected this view. Democracy had to be earned and must be withheld until society purged itself of secularism. Premature installation of democracy would result in the election of demagogues to office and a rebirth of tyranny.[11]

González Flores demonstrated less rigidity when the time came for him to found his own party. He had long been thinking of ways to broaden the base of the Catholic resistance movement in west-central Mexico. The ACJM was too youth-oriented and other groups—Knights of Columbus, Damas

Católicas (Catholic Ladies), and Catholic Workers—were lacking in universal appeal. Urgently needed was an organization that would reach all members of the faith.

Thus was born the Unión Popular. Founded in 1925, it was based on the ideas of two nineteenth-century German Catholics, Bishop Wilhelm von Ketteler and Ludwig Windthorst, leader of the Center Party. Ketteler, a politically active cleric who served a term in the Reichstag, resisted Bismarck's trend toward state centralism and supported Austria during the 1866 Austro-Prussian War. He was keenly interested in labor problems and his best-known book, *The Labor Question and Christianity,* advocates a Christian and humanitarian approach to labor-management relations that rejects both laissez-faire capitalism and socialist collectivism.

Windthorst, Bismarck's chief enemy during the anti-Catholic *Kulturkampf,* so infuriated the Iron Chancellor that he was driven to observe that "everybody needs somebody to love and somebody to hate. I have my wife to love and Windthorst to hate." Bismarck later made his peace with Windthorst and both united against the Socialists.

In organizing the Unión Popular (or UP, as it soon came to be known) along Center Party lines, González Flores had the good fortune to be guided by Father Neck, a visiting German priest with a background in Catholic action. Father Neck passed out pieces of literature dealing with the Windthorst-Bismarck controversy and these were avidly read by the Maestro's disciples.[12] "The Little Excellency," as Windthorst was known, was already something of a hero in the ACJM and a chapter was named for him. Anacleto's followers had no difficulty identifying the Maestro with Windthorst and President Calles (who unleashed a far more ruthless *Kulturkampf* than was ever dreamed of in Germany) with Bismarck.

Organizationally the UP was headed by a Directive Committee of five (with Anacleto as first chief) and was divided (in descending order) into parishes, zones, and blocks. There were no dues and the only condition for joining was that the potential member "be disposed to listen to us."[13] Bureaucratic functions were kept to a bare minimum and messages were transmitted, whenever possible, by word of mouth. The new party also put out a one-page newspaper. Entitled *Gladium,* it was so widely read that by the end of 1925, a hundred thousand copies were being published.[14]

The UP was entirely successful in its goal of giving a mass base to the resistance movement. Workers, campesinos, and women joined in droves and at one time there were two female members of the Directive Committee. Yet the party never became a national organization. Its influence was limited to the Catholic west-central enclave: Jalisco, southern Zacatecas, and bordering portions of Guanajuato and Michoacán.

The proletarian and feminist nature of the UP did not sit well with the rich Catholics. They believed, and rightly so, that the addition of a mass party to the resistance movement would intensify repression against Jalisco's Catholic population in general. In May of 1925 a group of *acomodados* unsuccessfully petitioned Archbishop Orozco y Jiménez to take the party under his jurisdiction with a view to defusing it.[15]

It may seem ironic that a man as wary of democracy as González Flores should head an organization as democratic as the UP. However, he approved of democracy for persons free of secularism, such as the faithful of the UP.

The Maestro, like many men of peace, was capable of flinty hardness when the occasion demanded. During the summer of 1926 the Catholics declared an economic boycott against the government. Every Sunday, in *Gladium*, there appeared a blacklist of Masonic-operated enterprises which Catholics were forbidden to patronize. One morning, in the hallway of the Archbishop's palace, González Flores ran into a priest of his acquaintance, Father Arnulfo Castro. The following conversation took place:

Father Castro: "Maestro, I've been looking for you."

González Flores: "At your orders, Father."

FC: "My business is very simple. The name of Alfonso Emparán has appeared on the blacklist of Masons in your paper. I promised him I'd have it removed because Alfonso Emparán is not a Mason."

GF: "Father, we have reliable information in the *Unión Popular* files. Alfonso Emparán is a Mason. We know what a serious responsibility we would incur if we published his name without proof."

FC: "But you're doing him an injustice. He may have been a Mason at one time but he's no longer one."

GF: "I'm willing to withdraw his name and run his ad gratis on condition that he makes a public retraction to our satisfaction."

FC: "I don't consider that necessary. Alfonso Emparán confessed to me."

GF: "Forgive my frankness, Father, but he is deceiving us. Alfonso Emparán, like all Masons, is not only given a dispensation to confess but can even take minor orders."[16]

Emparán continued on the blacklist. Shortly afterwards his business failed and he left Guadalajara. González Flores noted the development with fierce glee. "If we really knew how to act as Catholics," he told an assistant, "if we really knew how to do it, we could make our enemies die of hunger."[17]

But he still shrank at making them die violently. In this feeling he was joined by his ecclesiastical counterpart in the passive resistance camp, Archbishop Orozco y Jiménez. Due to increasing Federal pressure on the Church, the Archbishop had gone into hiding in October of 1926. From his place of refuge he wrote the Maestro, saying he had heard that an armed revolt was planned against the government. Under no circumstances did he wish the UP to be involved in the rebellion, since the party's functions were purely civic and social.[18]

Though Anacleto completely agreed with this view, events were moving too rapidly for him. In March of the previous year a nationwide organization of militant Catholics had been formed in Mexico City. Known as the Liga Nacional Defensora de la Libertad Religiosa (National League for the Defense of Religious Liberty), it was the largest and most important of the resistance groups. Other organizations acknowledged its leadership, and González Flores served as Jalisco delegate of the LNDLR as well as head of the UP. (Throughout most of 1925 the groups had maintained separate identities, but a merger of sorts was effected on 21 December of that year.)[19] The UP then reconstituted itself as the Unión Popular de Jalisco-LNDLR. Friction later developed, with the UP attempting to maintain as much local autonomy as possible.

On 25 November 1926 the Liga officially opted for armed rebellion at a Mexico City meeting. Sporadic fighting was already in progress and LNDLR leaders had concluded that the government could be overthrown by a concerted effort on the part of all resistance groups. Bartolomé Ontiveros, a Jalisco tequila manufacturer who served as head of the Liga's Special Committee (in charge of espionage and direct military action), was sent to Guadalajara to secure UP cooperation in a general uprising, scheduled for early January of 1927.

At first González Flores balked. "The Liga has dealt us a dirty deck of cards," he complained bitterly to an assistant.[20] He had dreamed of being the Gandhi and the Windthorst of Mexico, but now he was being asked to abet the violence he so deeply detested. In the end he acquiesced. He really had no choice. The bulk of the UP, including all his assistants, was hell-bent for rebellion. For Anacleto to withhold his prestigious support would be a dangerously divisive move.

Still, the Maestro made a final effort to keep the UP officially out of the rebellion. His plan was to name Heriberto Navarrete, the party secretary, as provisional UP chief. Navarrete was under strict orders to keep the UP completely out of the rebellion. At the same time, an engineer named Salvador Cuellar would take over as military chief, coordinating activity with local rebels as the Maestro's personal representative. As for González Flores, he would step down as UP leader and act as liaison between the party and the military insurrectionists.[21]

The plan didn't work for two reasons. First, Navarrete and his fellow *acejotameros* (popular acronym for ACJM member) were absolutely determined to take an active part in the rising; not even their devotion to the Maestro would deter them. Second, Anacleto's complicated orders were causing a great deal of confusion among the unlettered *campesino* chiefs who would lead the rebellion in the field. Their confusion becomes apparent in this exchange between Navarrete and Chema Huerta, leader of a band of Tepatitlán ranchers:

> *Navarrete:* "Didn't they explain it to you? The Unión Popular isn't going to have anything to do with the rebellion of certain Catholics, who are rightly indignant and want to fight the government."
>
> *Huerta:* "Yes, they explained it to us but I don't understand. Some are going to fight and some aren't. Is it that you're

afraid? Or is it that you have something to take care of? What is it you're taking care of?"[22]

Seeing the hopelessness of the situation, Navarrete went directly to González Flores. "Maestro," he said, "this can't be, it's not going to work. I want to go to the mountains with the rest. I won't carry out this little errand."[23]

Anacleto conceded defeat. Summoning six or seven of his most trusted followers, he took them up to the flat roof of the house that served as his temporary headquarters. Then he addressed them in the apocalyptic tone for which he was famous: "What is beginning for us now is a Calvary.... If any of you should ask me what sacrifice I ask of you, I will say it in two words: *your blood.*"[24] Despite his prophetic vision, the Maestro erred in the timing of this prediction of supreme sacrifice. Only one of his inner circle, Luis Padilla Gómez, preceded Anacleto in martyrdom—and only by a few minutes. Captured together, they were executed the same day.

THE MAESTRO'S FOLLOWERS

Who were some of these disciples, the men who carried on Anacleto's work after his capture and execution? The best-known was Miguel Gómez Loza. Known as "El Chinaco (The Stallion)," he was the only one of the Maestro's intimate following who was his own age. The two were lifelong friends and Gómez Loza, like González Flores, was a teacher, lawyer, and native of Tepatitlán. Their only difference was physiognomic. The Maestro was of mestizo origin, while Gómez Loza, blond, ruddy-cheeked, and blue-eyed, was more representatively *alteño* in appearance. In 1921 a band of leftist youths had invaded the Guadalajara Cathedral and planted a red flag in the steeple; Gómez Loza led the ACJM counterattack that expelled the intruders and removed the offensive object.[25] Gómez Loza served as Treasurer of the UP and later as *cristero* civil governor of Jalisco.[26]

Another of the Maestro's promising young men was Heriberto Navarrete, mentioned earlier as secretary of the UP. A twenty-three-year-old engineering student when the rebellion broke out, Navarrete was arrested in a roundup of Catholic activists following capture of the Maestro. After serving a four-month term in the Islas Marías penal colony, he was released and promptly found his way to the sierra, where he joined the *cristero* fighting forces. Rising to the rank of major, he came under attack in later years for his part in the downfall of the *alteño* folk hero Victoriano Ramírez (El Catorce).

Lauro Rocha, born in 1908, was only eighteen years old when the rebellion broke out. A student of veterinary medicine in Guadalajara, he belonged to both the UP and ACJM. Rocha was one of the most combative of the Maestro's young men and was imprisoned in the summer of 1926 for street fighting.[27] His pugnacity served him well when the *cristero* war began and by the age of twenty he was a twice-wounded veteran commanding a regiment in Los Altos. One of the minority who rose again during *la segunda* (the second *cristero* rebellion of the 1930s), he was killed by Federal police agents on the last day of 1936.

The name of Carlos Blanco is mentioned mainly as an illustration of the Peter Principle operating in the *cristero* rebellion: of a man in an organization being promoted to his level of incompetence. As an urban ACJM militant, the handsome, self-assured Blanco demonstrated great skill and resourcefulness. On one occasion, in a complicated maneuever Blanco managed to obtain information of a vital nature by impersonating a broken-accented Italian immigrant laborer.[28] It was perhaps Blanco's glibness that induced the Liga to award him a general's commission when the rebellion broke out. Of all the LNDLR's injudicious appointments, this was probably the worst, as Blanco's ineptitude caused incalculable damage.

Others included Luis Padilla Gómez, who shared the Maestro's martyrdom; Manuel Ontiveros, son of Bartolomé; and the three Chávez Hayhoe brothers, Luis, Salvador, and Arturo, who served as couriers and underground agents during the rebellion. With the exception of Blanco (who, to do him justice, would probably have functioned competently in another capacity), all the Maestro's pupils served well in the cause for which he died.

Without Anacleto González Flores there might never have been a *cristiada*. He was philosopher, propagandist, organizer, and strategist of the movement. In discussing this man and his influence, our narrative has carried us to the outbreak of the rebellion. We must now go back to the presidential accession of Plutarco Elías Calles, a key factor in transforming Los Altos from a sleepy backwater to a region savaged by a holy war of indescribable ferocity.

Callista Challenge, Catholic Response

THE SEEDS OF THE *CRISTERO* REBELLION are contained in five articles of the 1917 Constitution which practicing Catholics found intolerable. Article 3 mandated secular education in elementary schools, public and private, and barred members of the clergy from founding or directing such schools. Article 5 prohibited monastic vows and outlawed monastic orders. Article 24 forbade public worship outside the confines of churches. Article 27 placed stringent restrictions on the right of religious organizations to hold property or real estate.

But the bête noire was Article 130. Dictatorial and discriminatory, it effectively reduced the clergy to second-class status and was one of the most openly restrictive laws against a single group of citizens enacted in modern times. Clergy members were denied such basic liberties as the right to vote, to hold office, to criticize public officials, or to comment on public affairs in religious periodicals. The Church was denied a juridical personality, state legislatures were empowered to regulate the number of clergy allowed to practice in their states, and jury trial was denied in cases relating to violations of the articles. The 1857 Constitution and Reform Laws (which were made part of that constitution in 1873) had established separation of church and state, but the 1917 Constitution was a clear case of subordination of church to state.

These laws were passed mainly through the efforts of a strong radical wing at the constitutional convention. This faction included such figures as Franciso Múgica, later Communications Minister under Cárdenas; Adalberto Tejeda, Minister of the Interior *(gobernación)* under Calles; and Antonio Villareal, revolutionary general and early associate of the anarchist leader Ricardo Flores Magón.

In view of such openly hostile legislation one may wonder why the Catholics waited nine years before rising in revolt. The answer is simple. Venustiano Carranza was president when the 1917 Constitution was adopted and Alvaro Obregón held office from 1920 to 1924. Though neither man was a friend of the Church, both were flexible enough to avoid measures designed to provoke the Catholics into open rebellion. Enforcement of the laws was highly selective. In Tabasco, a fever swamp of anti-clericalism, the statutes were applied with the utmost rigor. The state governor, a fanatic named Tomás Garrido Canabal, pushed a decree through the legislature permitting only one priest per 100,000 population—and he had to be over forty and married. (The same Garrido Canabal named his sons Lenin and Lucifer and gave saints' names to domestic animals on his experimental farm.)[1]

In the more Catholic regions—including Los Altos—the statutes were barely applied at all. When efforts were made to enforce them, they were resoundingly defeated. In July of 1918 the state of Jalisco attempted to limit the number of priests and require clergymen to register with the civil authorities. The decree triggered a massive campaign of passive resistance, including cessation of public worship and an economic boycott. By February of 1919 the government was forced to back down and Archbishop Orozco y Jiménez, who had been expelled from Mexico at the time of the decree, returned to Guadalajara in triumph.[2] This test of strength occurred during Carranza's administration.

Obregón followed basically the same policy as Carranza: keeping the harsh laws on the books to placate the anti-clerical *enragés* but enforcing them selectively. Of the actions he did take against the Church, some were justified. His 1923 expulsion of Ernesto Filippi, the Apostolic Delegate, was on firm legal ground. Filippi had clearly violated the decree against outdoor public worship by attending the dedication of the

Cristo Rey monument on Mount Cubilete. Even the Vatican conceded later that Filippi had acted improperly by participating in the ceremony.[3]

The Obregón administration and the Holy See were, in fact, cautious collaborators in détente. The government allowed an apostolic delegate to be stationed in Mexico while the Vatican let it be known that it would attempt, as much as possible, to fill Mexican ecclesiastical vacancies with non-political churchmen.[4] The deterioration of church-state relations, unleashed by the Revolution, had been temporarily arrested and a shaky truce prevailed. It was the calm before the storm.

On 1 December 1924 Obregón stepped down from the presidency in favor of his hand-picked successor, Plutarco Elías Calles. If the anti-Catholicism of Carranza and Obregón represented a bark, that of Calles was a bite. Calles, like Obregón, was from Sonora but completely lacked the wit and spontaneity that characterized the descendant of Michael O'Brien, bodyguard of the last Spanish Viceroy of Mexico.[5] (Obregón is a Hispanicized version of the name.) A somber, stubborn, taciturn man, Calles was known to enemies as "El Turco (The Turk)", because of his part-Levantine origin. His earlier days had been marked by business failure and, according to some, by personal misconduct. (He had been fired from a municipal job because of shortages discovered in his department.)[6] The burden of a checkered past seems to have increased his natural moroseness which, in turn, added to his heavy-handedness in dealing with political problems.

PRESSURE FROM THE PRESIDENT

That quality was immediately apparent in Calles's relations with the Church. Though he didn't differ too much from Obregón philosophically, he lacked his predecessor's flexibility and realism. Carranza and Obregón were evolutionary in their anti-clericalism but Calles was not. The interests of the Revolution demanded that he solve the church-state controversy during his administration, and the fact that five important articles of the constitution were being flaunted in large parts of the country was an intolerable affront. There would be no more selective application of the laws; what was sauce for the Tabasco goose would be sauce for the Los Altos gander.

To ensure universal enforcement of the laws, he began to put pressure on state and municipal authorities. On 8 February 1924 a directive was sent to officials of the state of México relating to the coming Holy Week celebration. They were reminded that Article 24 of the constitution forbade outdoor religious observances and ordered to clamp down on any public processions, pageants, and parades.[7]

On 14 February Calles issued a general reminder to all state governments, urging them to exercise strict vigilance over the clergy and to make sure the constitutional provisions were enforced.[8] This move was only the beginning. One week later a band of armed men took over the church of La Soledad in Mexico City, evicted the pastor, and installed a schismatic priest in his place. He was Joaquín Pérez, self-styled "Patriarch of the Mexican Catholic Church," a sect which had declared its independence from Rome.

To regular Catholics, this action was a grave provocation. Rightly suspecting that the "Mexican Catholic Church" was a tool of the government, parishioners attempted to recapture La Soledad by force. A riot ensued in which the Catholics were finally dispersed by police and firemen using high pressure hoses. There were many injuries and one death was reported.[9]

Not wanting to appear too openly on the side of the schismatics, the secretary of *gobernación* (the powerful Interior Ministry) professed neutrality and piously enjoined the Pérez clique not to "resort to censurable methods to obtain what the authorities are prepared to grant them provided they seek it peacefully and comply with the requirements of the law."[10] The controversy was solved by closing La Soledad and giving Pérez control of the more centrally located Corpus Christi Church.

The schismatics never accomplished their mission of displacing, or even seriously challenging, their Roman rival and soon faded into obscurity. Not only were Mexican Catholics orthodox in observance but "Patriarch" Pérez was considered something of a joke. A onetime dropout from the priesthood, he had been a Freemason and officer in Carranza's army before resuming his clerical career.[11]

It was later learned that the "Mexican Catholic Church" was a creature of CROM, the national labor organization. The head of CROM, a rabid anti-clerical named Luis Morones, was only too happy to use Pérez as an agent provocateur and the plan for seizure of La Soledad had been worked out at a meeting between Pérez and Morones.[12]

CATHOLIC RESISTANCE ORGANIZATIONS

Although unsuccessful, the attempt to set up a rival church sent a wave of fear throughout the Catholic community. What would the government do next? Clearly, far-reaching measures were called for; massive provocation called for massive response. That response was the Liga Nacional Defensora de la Libertad Religiosa (National League for the Defense of Religious Liberty), the organization that helped force the Maestro's hand toward the violence he abhorred. The Liga came into being in the wake of meetings held in March 1924 and attended by leading members of Catholic lay groups. These representatives acted as delegates and formed a provisional general convention.

The opening session was chaired by Guadalajara-born Miguel Palomar y Vizcarra, one of Mexico's most conspicuous Catholic activists. Palomar, an energetic forty-five-year-old lawyer, had a reputation as a "white radical"—hostile to revolution, but a supporter of reform within a social Christian context. Through the years he had championed such causes as rural credit cooperatives, primary education for the working class, and fighting alcoholism among Indians. Palomar combined a mystic attraction to Mexico's Hispanic heritage with furious antagonism against Protestantism, Freemasonry, and yanqui cultural penetration into Mexican life.[13]

Another prime mover behind the Liga was sixty-five-year-old Rafael Ceniceros y Villareal. Ceniceros, a former governor of Zacatecas, had also been party chairman of the defunct Catholic-dominated National Republican Party. If Ceniceros was the grand old man of the convention, the up-and-coming young one was twenty-seven-year-old René Capistrán Garza. Capistrán, who headed the ACJM, was easily the most charismatic figure among young Catholics who opposed the revolutionary establishment. He was volatile, dynamic, a magnificent orator and debater; he was also contemptuous of bureaucratic infighting and ill suited to its ways, and it was this failing that would cause his downfall.

On 17 March the convention elected a three-man executive committee composed of Ceniceros, Capistrán Garza, and Luis G. Bustos. It also produced a document called the "Program-Manifesto of the National League for Religious Defense." The Liga, according to the manifesto, was "a legal association, civic in character, whose aim is to win religious freedom and all the freedoms that derive from it in the social and economic order."[14] Though the manifesto denied that its program was "a call to arms," a door to possible direct action was left open by the declaration that the League would pursue its goals both by constitutional means and "those required for the common good."[15]

The Liga was the most important of four major resistance organizations. Of the other three, one was a nationwide body; the remaining two operated solely in west-central Mexico, the sector that would become the war zone. The national group was the ACJM, while the regional ones were the Unión Popular and an enigmatic aggregation known simply as the "U." Another formation, the Feminine Brigades of St. Joan of Arc, was not founded until the rebellion was well under way.

The ACJM was founded by a French Jesuit named Bernard Bergöend. He came to Mexico in 1907 to teach philosophy in Guadalajara's Jesuit-run Institute of San José. From his work with young people he became convinced that Mexico needed a youth-oriented Catholic Action group to combat revolutionary and secular influences. With the approval of his superiors and Archbishop José Mora y del Río, Primate of Mexico, he planned an organization patterned after—and virtually identical in name—to the Association Catholique de la Jeunesse Française. Officially inaugurated on 12 August 1913, the ACJM was made up of a number of chapters, each supervised by an ecclesiastical adviser appointed by the local bishop. Every chapter was named after a distinguished Catholic—figures such as Windthorst, Ketteler, Daniel O'Connell, and Albert de Mun. Though the ACJM denied that it was political in nature, its charter obligated members to defend religious and political freedom. Its slogan, devised by Father Bergöend, was "piety, study, action."[16]

Among the resistance organizations that functioned in west-central Mexico, the "U" was a clandestine group, founded before the rebellion, that included every important resistance leader in that sector. Among its members were

Anacleto González Flores and Jesús Degollado Guízar, *cristero* commander in southern Jalisco and Colima. The "U" became involved in a bitter divisive controversy with the LNDLR, the latter claiming that the former was undercutting its authority. The Liga complained to the Mexican hierarchy and to Rome, charging the "U" with existing in violation of the Catholic ban against secret societies. The Holy See bowed to Liga pressure and, through Archbishop Orozco y Jiménez, ordered the "U" to suspend operations in 1928.[17]

Minor resistance organizations, playing a negligible part in the rebellion, included the Nocturnal Adoration, the Damas Católicas, and the Knights of Columbus. This last group eventually incurred the disfavor of Liga hardliners, and Palomar, that inveterate gringophobe, denounced the Knights as "an instrument of peaceful [American] conquest."[18]

Though the Liga was the youngest of Mexico's Catholic action organizations, it was also the fastest growing. Such growth was only natural because it was not regional in character, like the UP, nor was it geared to a particular segment of the population, as the Damas Católicas was to women or the ACJM to youth. By June of 1925 the LNDLR claimed a membership of thirty-six thousand, with almost every state in Mexico represented.[19] Catholic opposition to the government mounted as Liga chapters all over the country counseled militant resistance to the constitutional articles.

THE CALLES LAW

President Calles, however, would not be deterred. On 14 June 1926 he signed a decree which could be described as the "Intolerable Acts" of the Mexican church-state controversy. Though known officially as "The Law Reforming the Penal Code," it soon became referred to simply as "the Calles Law." The decree, which took effect on 31 July, consisted of thirty-three articles relating to the application of the constitutional provisions governing religion. Its purpose was to put teeth into the constitution and secure its universal enforcement. The Calles Law was very specific, with penalties spelled out in explicit terms. Clergymen were sentenced to fifteen days imprisonment or a 500-peso fine (the peso was then worth 50 cents) for such offenses as wearing clerical garb (Article 18), teaching religion in public schools (Article 3, applicable also to

laymen), or exercising priestly functions if they were not na-
tive-born Mexicans (Article 1). Priests were sentenced to five
years imprisonment for criticizing the laws or government
(Article 10) and to six years for advocating disobedience to the
laws (Article 8). Any person inducing a minor to enter a
monastic order was sentenced to five years, the penalty being
reduced to fifteen days or a 500-peso fine if the enrolee was of
age (Article 7). Particularly menacing was Article 19, requiring
priests in charge of churches to register with the government.
Since one of the penalties was closure of churches, this provision gave the government unlimited power over the clergy.[20]

The Calles Law was also supplemented by a number of
state and local statutes that infuriated Catholics as much for
their insulting terminology as for their severity. In Chiapas the
"Social Prevention Law" stipulated that the list of "harmful
elements subject to security measures" should include such
persons as "the insane, degenerates, drug users, alco-
holics...professional beggars, prostitutes, priests...[and]
homosexuals."[21]

The Calles Law was the ultimate challenge. While lay
Catholics girded for further battle, the hierarchy was not only
agonized but torn by dissension as well. A dove-hawk split
developed, with some bishops favoring suspension of public
worship throughout Mexico and others resisting such an extreme course. Moderates included the bishops of Veracruz,
Morelia, Cuernavaca, and Zamora while those of Guadalajara, Durango, Tacámbaro, and Huejutla favored a hard line.[22]
Caught in the middle was José Mora y del Río, the seventy-
two-year-old Archbishop of Mexico. In declining health and
with only two more years to live, his influence was rapidly
being supplanted by that of younger and more vigorous
prelates.

Among the bishops who opposed conciliation was Francisco Orozco y Jiménez of Guadalajara. Though against armed
rebellion, he was an uncompromising foe of any accommodation with the government. When war broke out and the other
bishops were exiled he and Amador Velasco of Colima were
the only ones to go underground and remain in Mexico.

Three other leading hawks were Bishops José González y
Valencia (Durango), Leopoldo Lara y Torres (Tacámbaro), and
José de Jesús Manríquez y Zarate (Huejutla). None shared
Orozco's reservations about armed resistance; Manríquez, a

fiery orator and master of impassioned rhetoric, even consid-
ered joining the *cristeros* in the field. He was restrained from
doing so, he said, only by fear of incurring papal disap-
proval.[23] The most prominent dove was Archbishop Leopoldo
Ruiz y Flores of Morelia. Other notable conciliators were
Bishops Nicolás Corona (Papantla), Pedro Vera y Zuria
(Puebla), Manuel Fulcheri (Zamora), and Francisco Bánegas
Galván of Querétaro.

Then there were two cases which must be regarded as
special—those of Bishops Pascual Díaz of Tabasco and Rafael
Guízar Valencia of Veracruz. Díaz, a Jesuit, embodied all the
qualities of that order ascribed to it by its unfriendliest critics.
Crafty, persuasive, and quick-thinking, he was the Talleyrand
of the Mexican Church, with that statesman's chameleon ability to adapt to changing circumstances. Now a hawk, now a
dove, he finally came down hard on the side of the conciliators
and emerged as the *cristeros'* most implacable enemy. The
church-state controversy was the making of Díaz, who rose in
less than three years from bishop of an unimportant see to
Primate of Mexico.

Unlike other détente-minded prelates, who took their
stand for loftier motives, there is a strong possibility that
Guízar Valencia of Veracruz may have been blackmailed into
his consistently dovish position. In an interview with a French
diplomat, Calles claimed to have a dossier showing that
Guízar "had been expelled from the diocese of Zamora for
embezzlement of funds" and later, in Mexico City, "had been
an intimate friend of all the procuresses [and] a most assidu-
ous client of the brothels and, thereafter, of the venereal spe-
cialists."[24] Dissenting from this unflattering view is Guízar's
biographer, Eduardo J. Correa, author of *Monseñor Rafael
Guízar Valencia: The Holy Bishop, 1878-1938.*

While the prelates were deliberating the challenge posed
by the Calles Law, the LNDLR's Executive Committee decided
on a nationwide economic boycott against the government.
Seeking Church support, League leaders requested an audience with Archbishop Mora y del Río. This was granted on 7
July. At the meeting, attended by Díaz, the *ligueros* made
known their plan and their desire for episcopal backing. Mora
y del Río asked the laymen to put their petition in writing and
promised a decision in the near future.[25]

Before deciding on the boycott, the bishops had another important matter to settle: the question of suspending worship and closing the churches. Díaz, who had been among the moderates, switched sides and on 11 July 1926 the bishops voted to stop all public worship in Mexico. The order would go into effect on 1 August. Now committed to a hardline position, the Episcopal Committee informed the Liga on 14 July that it endorsed the boycott.[26]

The boycott was officially announced by the League two days later. Catholics were enjoined to buy nothing except basic necessities, to use public and private transportation as sparingly as possible, to cut down on electricity, and to give up such entertainment as attending the theater, films, or sporting events.

Not surprisingly, success of the boycott was in direct proportion to the intensity of Catholic feeling in a given region. Beyond the areas controlled by the UP it was only a pinprick, but in the UP sector (Jalisco, western Michoacán, western Guanajuato) its effects were devastating.

Catholic militants in Guadalajara (the UP, the "U," and the ACJM) divided boycott action into four areas: recreation, commerce, transportation, and schools. Movie houses, severely feeling the pinch, cut admission prices and employee salaries by thirty percent.[27] Guadalajara became a city of pedestrians, and eight hundred primary school teachers resigned rather than serve in secular schools.[28] Between twenty-two thousand and twenty-five thousand children dropped out of the educational system, while the UP assumed responsibility for lodging and feeding defecting teachers.[29] Pressure from the UP and its allies caused an editorial change at *El Informador,* the city's leading daily; attacks on the Church disappeared from its pages.[30]

But even Guadalajara's fervor seems lukewarm when compared with the boycott's application in Los Altos. In Tototlán an ice cream vendor was hawking his wares on a hot August day, when a seven-year-old boy came running out of his house. "Give me a five-centavo ice cream," he said.

"Lemon?"

"Yes."

The vendor was scooping it out when the boy interrupted him. "Wait. First show me your Unión Popular card."

The man made a gesture of exasperation. "That again! I left it at home. But I belong to the UP like everybody else in town."

"Look...you better go on. I'm going to buy from another vendor. I'll buy from you tomorrow if you bring your card."[31]

In Arandas the mayor was a butcher who sold meat on a contract basis to the local Army garrison. But the UP had decreed a ban on meat eating; Catholics would be vegetarians for the duration of the boycott. In only two places was meat consumed—the mayor's house and the Federal barracks.[32]

Pénjamo, a medium-sized town in southern Guanajuato, had a fiercely Catholic mayor named Luis Navarro Origel. The party was as dominant here as in any community in Los Altos, and the mayor was also head of the local UP chapter. At Navarro's instigation all houses began lighting candles at night. The economic effect was so devastating that the electric plant was forced to suspend operations. The slaughterhouse, which had been killing an average of twelve head of cattle daily, reduced this figure to two every three days, since meat was reserved exclusively for the sick. A blockade imposed on incoming goods resulted in such a financial pinch that there were no funds to pay the two-man police force. They resigned and were replaced by a tailor and a shoemaker, paid by popular donation.[33]

By October (1926) the boycott began to lose steam, mainly because of the attitude of the rich Catholics. In the beginning they supported the boycott grudgingly, but as weeks passed and profits declined they began to oppose it actively. Silvano Barba González, then serving as interim governor of Jalisco, reported that the *acomodados* were requesting police and Army intervention against the boycotters. "I'm a businessman and I have obligations," said one well-heeled Catholic. "I'm losing money because of this damn boycott."[34] "I don't give them [the boycotters] one centavo," said another. "I want the Sonora regime to stay in power."[35] The boycotters had deployed pickets outside prescribed establishments; following pressure from the *acomodados*, picket lines were broken up by police.[36]

OPEN REBELLION

As the boycott waned, controversy shifted to another arena. No issue was more emotion-charged than the suspension of public worship. The first day of August (1926), official closing day for the churches, happened to be a Sunday. In the last days of July there had been a frantic rush of baptisms and weddings but on Sunday, for the first time since the Conquest, not a single church bell tolled in Mexico.

The law prescribed that churches should be closed a few days for inventory and then reopened under the control of neighborhood committees *(juntas vecinales)* appointed by the municipal authorities.[37] It was this decree that sparked the first of a series of violent clashes that would escalate to open rebellion before the end of the year.

The scene of the fighting was downtown Guadalajara's Santuario de Guadalupe (Guadalupe Sanctuary). On 1 August, the day public worship was suspended, a band of Catholic youths formed a protective cordon encircling the church. Round and round they paraded, carrying religious banners and shouting such slogans as "Viva Cristo Rey!" and "Viva la Virgen de Guadalupe!" This was a continuous demonstration. The young men replaced each other from time to time, but the slogan-chanting ring around the Santuario was never withdrawn.[38]

By the evening of 3 August the militants were stopping passersby, forcing men to remove their hats and shout "Viva Cristo Rey!" Shortly after nine they halted a man in an automobile. Though he was dressed as a campesino, his bearing exuded authority and people noticed that the car was driven by a chauffeur. When called on to shout "Viva Cristo Rey!" he responded with a stream of obscenities and ordered his chauffeur to drive into the crowd. The Catholics scattered and then began pelting the car with rocks. Drawing a pistol, the man fired a few shots at random. Though no one was hit, militants inside the Sanctuary returned the fire. The intruder snapped an order to his driver and the car took off at high speed.[39] The "campesino" was General Aguirre Colorado, commander of the city garrison. Moments later truckloads of troops were rumbling toward the Sanctuary. Streets were cordoned off as the soldiers descended from their trucks and formed a skirmish line outside the church entrance.

Fighting began when a young Catholic worker fired on an officer who had entered the Sanctuary garden. Another soldier, on firing shots into the church at the Virgin's statue, was stabbed in the back and killed by a girl of good family. There were several women inside the church; they sang, prayed, and shouted encouragement to the defenders.

Sniping continued all night and by dawn the Catholics were running out of ammunition. Surrender negotiations began and the Federals threatened to bring up machine guns if the defenders refused to give themselves up. General Ferreira, operations chief for Jalisco, finally authorized an arrangement whereby the men would accept arrest provided the women were allowed to leave freely. The Federals took 390 men into custody and imprisoned them within the military barracks.[40] Two days later they were released. Though the official death toll was 7, consular reports placed the number of dead at 18 and wounded at 40.[41]

The Santuario bloodletting was followed by two other urban clashes. On 4 August the parish church in Sahuayo, Michoacán, was stormed by a force of 240 soldiers. Among the casualties were the parish priest and his vicar.[42] Ten days later in Chalchihuites, Zacatecas, a purge was conducted against the local ACJM chapter, allegedly involved in an anti-government conspiracy. Father Luis Bátiz, the group's ecclesiastical adviser, and three *acejotameros* were imprisoned on 14 August, the next day they were taken outside the city limits and shot.[43]

It was the Chalchihuites massacre that caused the rebellion to spread to the countryside. When Father Bátiz and his associates were executed, a party of campesinos had been riding to their rescue. Leading the band was sixty-six-year-old Pedro Quintanar, a former army colonel and the region's most prominent rancher and businessman. Infuriated by the killings, he seized the Chalchihuites municipal treasury and declared himself in rebellion against the government.[44]

The sector Quintanar led into revolt will be known here as the "Three Finger" zone. It is an area of fifteen thousand square miles in southwestern Zacatecas and northern Jalisco, bounded on the west by the Sierra de Huicholes and on the east by the main road between Guadalajara and Zacatecas City. The Jalisco part of this area stabs into Zacatecas in geographical configurations resembling a giant thumb and two enormous fingers. The "Three Finger" zone is rolling, hilly cattle country, like Los Altos, and its inhabitants resemble the *alteños* in being ranchers, campesinos, and fervent Catholics. Principal communities are Valparaíso, Monte Escobedo, and

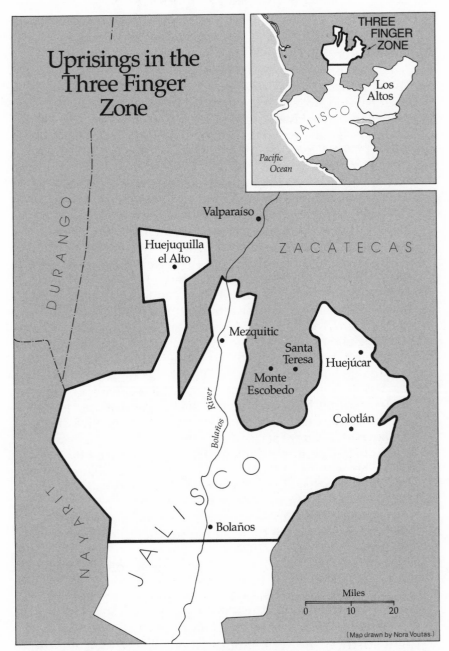

Uprisings in the
Three Finger
Zone

THREE
FINGER
ZONE

Los
Altos

JALISCO

Pacific
Ocean

DURANGO

Valparaíso

Huejuquilla
el Alto

ZACATECAS

Mezquitic

Santa
Teresa

Huejúcar

Monte
Escobedo

Colotlán

Bolaños River

JALISCO

NAYARIT

Bolaños

Miles

0   10   20

(Map drawn by Nora Voutas.)

Several uprisings in the *cristero* rebellion took place northwest of Los Altos, in an area of Jalisco which stabs into Zacatecas in geographical configurations resembling the first three fingers of a giant hand. Inset shows the location of the Three Finger zone relative to Los Altos and to the rest of the state of Jalisco.

Santa Teresa in Zacatecas and Huejuquilla el Alto, Mezquitic, and Huejúcar in Jalisco.

The uprising led by Quintanar took place on 29 August (1926) and originated in his home town of Valparaíso. Together with Aurelio Acevedo, the local ACJM chief, he led a thirty-man band into Huejuquilla at eleven in the morning. His unopposed entry was met with the ringing of church bells and cries of "Viva Cristo Rey!"[45] Another rebel band, led by Basilio Pinedo, rode in at noon.[46]

An hour later a third group of men entered Huejuquilla. They were Federals, sent to round up dissidents and unaware that they would be met by an armed enemy.[47] Caught unawares, the *callistas* were driven out of town by the Quintanar-Pinedo forces. But the rebels' triumph was temporary. On 4 September Huejuquilla was retaken by a combined Army-*agrarista* force personally led by General Eulogio Ortiz, Federal commander in Zacatecas. Quintanar was so badly mauled that he accepted amnesty and went back to his ranch.[48] On 4 January 1927 he rose again, remaining active until the end of the war. The five-regiment brigade that bore his name compiled a combat record second only to that of the Brigada de Los Altos.

Another major rising took place on 28 September 1926. Its leader was Luis Navarro Origel, mayor of Pénjamo and author of the "candle campaign" that had proved so effective during the boycott. Navarro seized Pénjamo but was unsuccessful in attempts to extend his domain. His plans betrayed by informers, he was roundly defeated by Federal General José Amarillas. He then decided to abandon the open *bajío* country (a fertile agricultural region in Querétaro and southern Guanajuato) and transfer operations to the rugged sierra of Michoacán. He fought there and in southern Jalisco until his battle death in August, 1928.[49]

Navarro was the most rigid ideologue among the *cristero* leaders. "I will kill for Christ those who are killing Christ," he said on taking arms, "and if nobody follows me in this enterprise I will die for Christ."[50] Puritanical to the point of priggishness (while mayor of Pénjamo he closed down the red-light district), he was almost killed by his own men in Michoacán. Angered because they were not behaving like "Christian soldiers," Navarro displayed a reckless excess of zeal in attempting to check such practices as looting and rape.

Saved from death by the intervention of a priest, he was forced to transfer to another unit.[51]

A day after the Pénjamo rising a local Liga leader named Trinidad Mora rose in Santiago Bayacora, Durango. A Federal detachment had been sent there to enforce an unpopular state ordinance prohibiting the wearing of religious medals or keeping holy pictures in homes. Mora successfully ambushed the detachment but took to the sierra on hearing that more troops were on the way.[52]

On 4 October (1926) an ex-Federal general named Rodolfo Gallegos rose in southern Guanajuato. A former Chief of Operations in that state, he had resigned his commission to protest against Calle's religious policies and put himself at the Liga's disposal. Gallegos waged a successful guerrilla campaign in Guanajuato and Querétaro that lasted seven months to the day. On 4 May 1927, he was ambushed and killed near the Guanajuato town of San Luis de la Paz.[53]

All this time Los Altos was strangely quiescent. There were only two actions in 1926—one in October and one in November. The first was a half-hearted attack on Tepatitlán that was easily turned back.[54] Perhaps it was meant to fail. One of the leaders of the raiding party, Mónico Velázquez, was a double agent in secret communication with Governor Barba González. The second incident took place on 7 November in San Juan de Los Lagos. A Federal lieutenant named Marcos Coello gave his platoon orders to remove ribbons bearing the legend Viva Cristo Rey from the headgear of some campesinos. In the riot that ensued the lieutenant and three ranchers were killed.[55] There was no immediate mass rising, even though a state of siege was declared and several shops looted by soldiers. In the morning, however, it was noticed that forty able-bodied men had disappeared.[56] There was no doubt that their destination was the sierra. The apparent submissiveness of Mexico's most Catholic region filled government partisans with dangerous overconfidence—just how dangerous, they would soon learn.

The failure of these premature risings can only partially be attributed to bad timing and inexperience. A substantial portion of the blame rests squarely on the shoulders of the Liga, whose ineptitude and heavy-handed meddling would prove a major liability throughout the rebellion. Unlike the UP chiefs, who were well acquainted with local problems and enjoyed the complete trust of their followers, many *ligueros* were cosmopolitan, comfortably situated men better acquainted with the United States and Europe than with vast sections of their own country.

This ignorance had disastrous consequences. General Gallegos, whose rising was ordered in the middle of the harvest season, rallied a limited number of men on declaring himself in rebellion.[57] Manuel Frias, a *cabecilla* in Querétaro, was ordered to attack the railroad junction at Empalme. Empalme, in Sonora, is over a thousand miles away.[58] *Cristeros* in the state of Colima were directed to cut the line of the South Pacific railroad—which passes nowhere near Colima.[59]

The LNDLR compounded military bungling with a rule-or-ruin policy toward smaller resistance organizations. Prime targets were the "U," forced to suspend activity due to Liga pressure on Rome, and the Feminine Brigades. In addition, many of the Liga's military appointments subordinated expertise to ideology. A case in point is that of Carlos Blanco, the glib Guadalajara *acejotamero* who talked himself into a general's commission.

Another of these ideological selections turned out surprisingly well. In May 1927 the Liga appointed a thirty-five-year-old druggist named Jesús Degollado Guízar to general's rank and gave him command of all rebel forces in southern Jalisco, Colima, and western Michoacán.[60] Apart from a record of Catholic activism, there was nothing in Degollado's background to qualify him for such an appontment. A modest man, he at first refused the commission. But the Liga insisted and Degollado reluctantly took the field.

In the beginning, it was costly, on-the-job training. Degollado lost his first three battles and in one engagement suffered the humiliation of seeing his troops break and run.[61] But the mild-mannered druggist persevered. He stiffened discipline and proved to be a natural military leader. Degollado did so well as commander of the *cristero* División del Sur that he ended the war as leader of all rebel forces.

Degollado was the most humane and chivalrous of the *cristero* chiefs. With the exception of a brutal *agrarista* leader, he refrained from shooting prisoners. In his memoirs he devotes an entire chapter to lauding the daring of an enemy, "the valiant *callista* captain Arnulfo Díaz."[62]

As violence mounted and the Liga floundered, the government and the hierarchy continued on a collision course. On 21 August 1926 Calles received Archbishop Ruiz y Flores and Bishop Díaz and told them bluntly that they had two choices: to appeal to Congress or take arms.[63] On 7 September the bishops petitioned Congress for reform of the offending constitutional articles. The petition was reinforced, a few days later, by a memorial carrying over two million signatures. The bishops' petition was rejected by the chamber of deputies by a vote of 171 to 1; the memorial was ignored.[64]

By the end of September the Liga had definitely decided on armed rebellion. A special War Committee was created under the leadership of Bartolomé Ontiveros.[65] Its task was to get information on risings against the government and, if possible, coordinate them. At the same series of meetings (the exact date is unknown) René Capistrán Garza was unanimously elected supreme leader of the movement. Capistrán, who was then in the United States on a fund-raising mission, had been proposed by Rafael Ceniceros y Villareal.[66]

The Liga's next goal was to secure clerical backing for the rebellion. On 26 November LNDLR leaders were received by the Episcopal Committee, Ruiz y Flores presiding in lieu of the ailing Mora y del Río. Ceniceros read the churchmen a manifesto stating that the League had decided to assume direction of spontaneous popular movements because all legal and peaceful means to solve the church-state controversy had been exhausted. In addition to a general endorsement of the rebellion, the bishops were asked to furnish field chaplains and—in a pointed dig at an old enemy—to solicit donations from rich Catholics so that "at least once in their lives they will understand the obligation to contribute."[67]

The prelates, requesting a copy of the manifesto, asked for a few days to consider the matter. The answer (whose true meaning was still being debated in the early 1980s) came on 30 November. At no time did the bishops give any commitment in writing. What the Liga received was an oral statement that the memorandum had been approved and that there was nothing in Church doctrine prohibiting rebellion against tyranny if peaceful means have failed and the rising has a chance of success. But the requests for field chaplains and for an appeal to rich Catholics were rejected. The bishops claimed that they did not have the canonical authority to assign chaplains; as for dunning the rich Catholics, they realistically pointed out that such a step would be "very difficult and almost impossible."[68]

As the war progressed and the *cristeros* became increasingly estranged from the hierarchy, a number of bishops began to hedge on their November commitment. The statement, they insisted, was not so much an endorsement of the rebellion as a definition of traditional Catholic policy on rebellion in general. But some of the hard-liners disagreed with this interpretation. Lara y Torres of Tacámbaro wrote that the rebellion "was approved by the Episcopal Committee, without our having committed ourselves to take a direct part in that action."[69] Curiously, the last part of Lara's statement was seen by a prominent peace Catholic as a sign that the Church was not connected with the rebellion.[70]

Whatever the final truth, there is no doubt that the Liga interpreted the Episcopate's message as a mandate for war. In the closing days of 1926 an official call to arms was sent to every League chapter in the country.[71] Drafted by René Capistrán Garza, it appeared over his name. In what should have been the greatest moment of his career, René was far removed from the events he had done so much to bring about. Since 14 August he had been in the United States, attempting to raise money and support for the Catholic cause in Mexico.

The story of Capistrán Garza's mission, and the role of Bishop Pascual Díaz in frustrating it, lies outside the scope of this work. Probably the most comprehensive and even-handed account can be found in Chapter 5 of David C. Bailey's *Viva Cristo Rey!* (Austin: University of Texas Press, 1974). But this much can be said: though he returned to Mexico and made his peace with the foes of Catholicism, Capistrán Garza retained to the end a deep and undying rancor against Díaz. In October 1973, eleven months before his death, he expressed the opinion that the prelate had been in collusion with Calles all along and that his "explusion" from Mexico was a maneuver designed to split and weaken the resistance movement in the United States.[72] The circumstances of Díaz's departure from Mexico were, in fact, strange. While the other bishops were expelled in April via the northern route to the United States, Díaz was sequestered from his colleagues and put across the Guatemalan border as early as 19 January 1927.[73] He then sailed for New York by way of Havana. Debarking on 1 February he promptly went into action as an opponent of the rebellion, a role he repeated in Rome later in the year.[74] Díaz's duplicity, according to Capistrán Garza, went to the extent of denying he had received an important message delivered to the Mother Superior of the Benedictine Academy near Elizabeth, New Jersey, where he was then residing. Díaz, states René, later explained lamely that the Mother Superior thought the message was intended for the Academy's chaplain, though it was clearly addressed to "the Bishop of Tabasco, Don Pascual Díaz."[75]

Capistrán Garza at least had the satisfaction of seeing his fiery proclamation unleash the rebellion for which he had worked so hard. Entitled "A La Nación," the manifesto declared war on "the present regime...of a group of men without conscience or honor." Denying that the movement was a rebellion, the document charged that the "true rebels" are those "who are exercising power in defiance of the popular will.... The hour of battle has sounded," concluded the *pronunciamiento*; "the hour of victory belongs to God."[76]

This unequivocal challenge banished the last hopes for peace. The rebellion was now official.

Los Altos
in Flames

THAT LOS ALTOS WAS NOT THE FIRST REGION to rise against the government can in no way be ascribed to any lack of ardor. On the contrary, nothing, not even their reverence for the Maestro (and awareness of his views on violence) had prevented UP leaders in Los Altos from preparing for rebellion. However, their policy was to propagandize, arm, organize, select the right leaders and choose the right moment; the mindless romanticism of premature rebellion was not for them. If the isolated, abortive risings in Pénjamo, Santiago Bayacora, and the "Three Finger" zone were scattered bombs going off in haphazard fashion, the explosion of violence that rocked Los Altos in the opening days of 1927 was concentrated, minutely planned, and calculated to inflict maximum damage at the most appropriate time.

On several occasions restraint had to be exercised—never an easy task when dealing with *alteños*. In November (1926) soldiers killed a youth in San Francisco de Asís. The response was not rebellion but intensification of organizational activity: daily meetings of the local UP cell, stockpiling of arms, and

selection of Nicho Hernández, an old *porfirista*, to lead the
rising when the time was ripe.[1] The Los Altos explosion took
place in the first ten days of January 1927, in line with the plan
of a massive blow at the right time. The fact that it occurred
after Capistrán Garza's proclamation gave it an official character, unlike the premature and abortive uprisings of 1926.

The first rising took place in San Julián on 1 January. It was
led by a veteran campaigner named Miguel Hernández who
had obtained the rank of general under Carranza and Villa.
Because of his revolutionary antecedents some of the townspeople at first mistrusted him, but he won them over with a
ringing, emotion-charged harangue in the main plaza. "I see
you fear my presence among you," he cried. "Don't you believe that I can help you in some way? If God gave me the
strength to cry 'Viva Villa!' and 'Viva Carranza!', don't you
think at this time he would give me the strength to cry 'Viva
Cristo Rey!' and 'my blessed mother, Santa María de
Guadalupe!'?" Hernández then burst into tears—accompanied by a sizable number of his audience.[2] After occupying
the town without resistance, Hernández joined his forces with
those of Victoriano Ramírez, who had initiated a successful
rising in Santa María del Valle. The following day Hernández
and Ramírez attacked San Miguel el Alto, garrisoned by local
self-defense forces. These were led by José María López, the
collaborationist mayor, uncle and bitter enemy of Victoriano.
Fighting lasted almost a day and a half, ending with the garrison's surrender on the afternoon of 3 January. The cease-fire
was arranged by Father Felipe González, a priest attached to
the San Miguel parish. Under terms of the agreement the
defenders would evacuate the town on condition that the
rebels allow them to leave in peace.[3] The *cristeros* themselves
left that night but, in what seems an afterthought, they returned briefly the following morning for the express purpose
of expelling Consuelo Altamirano, director of the girls' school,
from the city. A former nun, she had foresaken her vows to
enter the Federal school system.[4] The Hernández-Ramírez
group next marched on Arandas, where it linked up with the
local rebel leader Espiridión Ascensio. On the way they were
joined by ranchers, some armed with ancient firearms and
others only with axes and clubs. This scene was repeated in
communities all over Los Altos—Cuquío, Yahualica, San Juan
de los Lagos, Lagos de Moreno, and Unión de San Antonio.[5]

The attack on the last of these localities was carried out by a force from Jalpa de Cánovas, on the Guanajuato side of the Guanajuato-Jalisco line. (Since the Jalpa contingent was later incorporated into the Brigada de Los Altos, the geographical technicality can be ignored and the Jalpa-San Francisco del Rincón area can be considered part of the Los Altos operational sphere.)

That Jalpa should be so strongly committed to rebellion was not coincidence. Since 1918 its parish priest had been an energetic young *alteño* from Cuquío named Pedro González. Father González organized an ACJM cell which, by the end of 1926, numbered some thirty dedicated young men. Of these, the two most promising were Agustin Gutiérrez and Víctor López. Each led a small band when the rising began in Los Altos, Gutiérrez commanding thirty-seven men and López twenty-eight.[6] On 5 January the two Jalpa contingents rode across the Jalisco border to San Diego de Alejandría, there linking up with local rebels who had seized the town. The combined force then moved on Unión de San Antonio, fifteen miles north. To gain the advantage of surprise, the rebels decided on a night attack, to take place at 2100 on 6 January. This precaution proved unnecessary. The local defense force consisted of a handful of police who gave up without firing a shot.[7]

The only community in Los Altos that failed to join the rising was Cañadas (later renamed Villa Obregón). The inhabitants of this Jacobin island in a Catholic sea have always been deeply disliked by their fellow *alteños*. Throughout the red-clay country it was customary to refer to Cañadas as "the fly in the milk" and "the wart on Los Altos."[8]

PEDROZA AND VEGA:
THE SAINT AND THE EVIL GENIUS

It was during these early days that two remarkable men elected to donate their considerable talents to the rebellion. History has seldom witnessed a case of two individuals in the service of a common cause who were superficially so alike and intrinsically so different. Aristeo Pedroza and José Reyes Vega were both from the south of Jalisco, both mestizos, both priests (and fellow seminarians), and both military geniuses; here the resemblance ended.

Father Pedroza, a native of the tropic, predominantly Indian village of Túxpan, attended the seminary in Guadalajara and was ordained on 5 August 1923. He was such a brilliant student that the Holy See permitted him to take his ordination vows a full eighteen months before the statutory age of twenty-four. Among fellow seminarians he was known for a cheerful, outgoing disposition, combined with an independent spirit and coldly analytical intelligence. His sermons were held up as models of lucid prose, and one admiring colleague compared his pure, strong style to that of Cervantes.[9]

For a country priest, Pedroza's interests were surprisingly wide-ranging. He was well versed in mathematics, literature, geography, and—harbinger of the future—had a special affinity for military studies. While teaching at a Catholic boys' school in Ayo el Chico, Pedroza noted with distaste that an orchard had been planted on the grounds. Scornfully commenting that "this is not a school of agriculture," he ordered the trees uprooted and the area converted into a training ground for "military exercises that form character."[10]

Pedroza's independent spirit at times got him into trouble. Having conceived a dislike for Canon José Esparza, rector of the seminary, he broke a number of rules and then deliberately stood outside the canon's door and said, "I can't stand that man from Paso del Soto." (Paso del Soto was the rector's home town; it was later renamed Villa Hidalgo.) The words, delivered to a friend in a loud stage whisper, were intended to be heard. For this breach of discipline Pedroza was sent away for a year—ostensibly as a teacher—to a remote rural seminary in the mountain village of Totatiche.[11]

But Pedroza's waywardness never extended to the sphere of private morals. Unlike many clerics of his day, he rigidly observed his vows of celibacy, remaining as chaste in the field as he had been in his parish. Though fearless in combat, Pedroza always retained a distaste for violence. In two and one-half years of constant campaigning he is known to have used his weapon only once: in the last engagement, when he was wounded and captured. On other occasions he adopted a purely supervisory role, deploying his forces as he scanned the field with high-powered binoculars.[12]

Pedroza was venerated by his men. "If he wasn't a saint, I don't know who could be one," said Jerónimo Gutiérrez, a veteran of the Brigada. Even more astounding was the case of José Ponce, an Atotonilco *cristero* who deserted and then returned to Pedroza in tears: "I ask you to readmit me to the ranks," he said, "because I want to die for Cristo Rey. And if you refuse to admit me I want you to confess me and shoot me because I don't want to die with this sin on my soul." Ponce was readmitted. [13]

If the *cristero* movement produced an evil genius, he appeared in the diminutive person of José Reyes Vega. Five years older than Pedroza, he was born into a large turbulent family in Ciudad Guzmán, about fifteen miles northwest of Pedroza's home city of Tuxpán. Unlike Pedroza, Vega never felt destined for a religious career and entered the seminary only under pressure from his family. According to *cristero* archivist Father Salvador Casas, who was in the seminary with both Pedroza and Vega, Vega remained chaste as a seminarian and right up to the outbreak of the rebellion, when he was serving as vicar in the parish of Arandas. "But he was corrupted when he took the field with his troops." [14]

This corruption took place at two levels. Within the scope of self-indulgent sins, Vega completely abandoned the puritan lifestyle he had maintained up to now and eagerly began to share in the rough pleasures of his ranchero soldiers. Having acquired a taste for fiery tequila and beautiful *alteñas,* he gratified it often.

Unhappily, Vega's spiritual contamination was not limited to strong waters and pretty women. Not only was he a *mujeriego* (woman chaser) but, according to Cardinal Davila, a "black-hearted assassin" as well. [15] War had the effect of liberating a genie of ferocity and cruelty that had until then been bottled up by the conventions of priestly life. While Pedroza shrank from violence, Vega reveled in it. Prisoners who were shot could consider themselves lucky; the less fortunate included wounded Federal prisoners who were stabbed to death after the battle of San Julián and civilians burned alive in gasoline-drenched wooden cars during an attack on the Guadalajara—Mexico City train in April of 1927. [16]

Enrique Gorostieta, the anti-clerical *cristero* generalissimo, justified his rejection of Catholicism by pointing to Vega as a horrible example. "Whom would you have me confess to?" he asked scornfully. "Father Vega?" He went on to explain that he wasn't even talking about Vega's "great sins" but simply the "habitual state of his unrestrained passions."[17] (Gorostieta, devoted family man and father of three, lived chastely in the field and spurned the advances of a lovestruck *alteña* named Josefina Carmona. Josefina later became the mistress of a Federal captain, causing ostracism for her entire family.)[18]

Like Pedroza, Vega was highly intelligent. Though he lacked his colleague's icy intellect, no *cristero* leader—not even Pedroza—could match his talents as a tactician and improviser. Gorostieta esteemed Vega the soldier as much as he despised Vega the priest, generously praising his "military genius" and comparing it favorably with that of history's greatest commanders.[19]

Pedroza's attitude toward Vega was curiously ambivalent. While he can have scarcely approved of his colleague's drinking, wenching, and murderous cruelty, he seems to have borne him no personal animus. The two priests spent a lot of time together, and their favorite form of relaxation—when Vega could tear himself away from the cantinas and bordellos—was playing chess.

THE SOLDIER PRIESTS AND REBELLION

When the rebellion broke out Pedroza was serving as parish priest in Ayo el Chico and Vega as vicar in Arandas. The latter community had risen on 5 January, in accordance with a plan formulated in Guadalajara at a series of meetings between Guadalajara UP leaders and a delegation from Arandas that included Rafael Martínez Camarena. The meetings took place from 9 to 11 December, 1926. The visitors were told to return to Arandas and await a telegram that would be addressed to Martínez. The content of the telegram, signed by "Juan," would announce the date of his imminent wedding to "señorita Matilde."[20] That date would signal the rising. The telegram arrived early the next month; the "wedding" was scheduled for 5 January.

No sooner had Arandas risen than Vega, at the head of a small band, rode to Ayo El Chico to try to induce Pedroza to join the rebellion. Vega, with his bandit instincts, had joined the fight more to free himself from the tedium of priestly life than from any ideological motive. But with Pedroza it was a different story. He wrestled with his conscience, discussed the matter with another priest, consulted canon law and Thomistic texts (how Vega must have chafed!), and finally came to the conclusion that this was a case where armed rebellion was justified.[21] Due to the presence of a fifty-man Federal detachment Pedroza was unable to initiate a rising in Ayo, so he attached himself to Vega's group and the party rode off to San Francisco de Asís, arriving there sometime between 6 and 8 January 1927. (It had to be in that time span, due to a four-day gap between the Arandas and San Francisco risings.)

There Vega again faced the problem of motivating a fellow cleric. Father José Angulo, the parish priest, attempted to counter Vega's efforts to rouse the population to rebellion. Among other arguments he tried, rather naively, to dissuade Vega by telling him he was too young to die.[22] Since many of the rebels were youths in their teens, this reasoning must have sounded strange to the thirty-one-year-old Vega. In attempting to avert the rising, Angulo was swimming against the tide. His parishioners were entirely with Vega, Pedroza, and Nicho Hernández, the ex-*porfirista* chosen by the UP as local leader. Accepting defeat, Father Angulo held a mass and gave the rebellion his reluctant blessing.

On 9 January the rebels secured San Francisco without opposition. Flushed with success, Hernández immediately rode on neighboring Atotonilco. This attack coincided with a local movement led by a sewing machine company employee named Toribio Valadés; Atotonilco also fell without resistance.

Other leaders who delivered their communities to the rebellion were Genaro Gómez in Capilla de Guadalupe, Refugio Miranda in Jesús García, and Justo Galindo in San José de Gracia. Success then emboldened Galindo to attack Tepatitlán. He might have duplicated his triumph had not the pro-government mayor, Quirino Navarro, sent an urgent message to Guadalajara requesting help. The 30th Infantry Battalion was sent to the beleaguered city and, after a three-day siege, the attackers withdrew. Galindo was so discouraged by this defeat that he withdrew from the movement completely.[23]

The siege of Tepatitlán included a poignant bit of personal drama. Accompanying the relief force was Silvano Barba González, interim governor of Jalisco. A group of attackers had penetrated the city and barricaded themselves in the

Templo de San Antonio, a church at the northeastern end of town. Since Federal troops had cut off exit routes, the rebels—fourteen in number—surrendered. It had been reported that among the defenders was Miguel Gómez Loza, the Maestro's right-hand man. When the prisoners filed out Barba González received an unpleasant shock. Their leader was not Gómez Loza but a friend of his youth named Sergio Gutiérrez.

Barba immediately approached Gutiérrez and asked him why he joined in the attack on the city. Gutiérrez allegedly replied that he had been egged on by the parish priest of his home town, Pegueros, about fifteen miles northeast of Tepatitlán. He then asked Barba what was going to happen to him. Barba replied that if the matter was in his hands he would release Gutiérrez on condition that he go home and spread the word that the Church, not the government, was at fault in the religious conflict. At this point two generals, Ferreira and Izaguirre, came on the scene. As an armed rebel, Gutiérrez was subject to military authority. The generals exchanged a few words, an order was given, and five minutes later Gutiérrez was dead. While Barba is the most self-serving of chroniclers, his grief over an old friend's death appears genuine.[24]

Though the UP achieved its aim of a mass rising in Los Altos, the government was not excessively worried at first. True, the *alteño* civilian population overwhelmingly backed the rebellion, but popular support was offset by the *cristeros'* lack of military experience and inadequate armament. The feeling that they were fighting a ragtag enemy made the Federals complacent. "It will be less a campaign than a hunt," wired General Ferreira to Army headquarters in Mexico City.[25]

Ferreira's optimism was shared by Calles. Following the Tepatitlán engagement, he summoned Barba González to Mexico City and asked him for a situation report. Since Jalisco had played a relatively inactive part in the Revolution, Calles had a poor opinion of Jaliscans as soldiers, referring to that state as "the chicken coop of the Republic."[26] Barba, apprehensive of growing *cristero* strength, did his utmost to dampen the President's airy overconfidence. Producing three cartridges captured from the Gutiérrez group, he pointed out that they had been manufactured that year while the Federals were using ammunition two years old. Not only was Jalisco solidly behind the rebellion but the rebels, through underground contacts and corruption, had access to factory-fresh ammunition.

Though polite, Calles refused to take Barba's warning seriously. Thanking him for his information and loyal support, he assured Barba that "in two or three months, at the most, your state will be pacified." But Barba was an *alteño;* he knew his people. "I hope it won't be more than two or three years, Mr. President," he replied.

"You're very pessimistic," said Calles.

"How much I would like to be mistaken! If your prophecy comes true it will be good for all of us."[27]

It was Barba, not Calles, who proved the accurate prophet. Indicative of the rebels' growing strength was their ability, by the end of February, to hold their own against regular Army units. Their initial successes, in January, had been scored against police and local self-defense forces. When soldiers had come on the scene, as in Tepatitlán, the rebels had invariably been bested.

EARLY *CRISTERO* VICTORIES

In February the picture began to change. During the first six weeks of the rebellion the *cristero* units had been nothing more than hastily formed groups of marauding bands. Ranchers would attach themselves to some charismatic leader, like El Catorce or Miguel Hernández, and wander aimlessly to and fro, seizing one community, moving on to another and, more likely than not, returning to find the first one back in Federal hands. Typical was the case of an Arandas detachment led by a local militant named Pérez García. Having heard that the Army garrison had evacuated Ayo el Chico, he and his band rode south and seized the town. Then they returned to Arandas—only to find the city occupied by the Federal General Ubaldo Garza.[28] There were no defined operational zones, and communications were in a chaotic state. There was a desperate need for organization.

The first step was taken on 20 February (1927). At the behest of Miguel Hernández and Father Pedro González, activist parish priest of Jalpa de Cánovas, all rebel chiefs in eastern Los Altos were convoked for a conference. Site of the reunion was Rancho de la Mesita, just outside San Julián. Two important decisions were reached at the meeting. The first was to incorporate the Jalpa contingents of Agustín Gutiérrez and Víctor López with the San Julián effectives. The combined forces, headed by Miguel Hernández, formed the nucleus of what would later become the San Julián regiment of the Brigada de Los Altos. The second decision was to attack San Francisco del Rincón, just across the Guanajuato line, where local self-defense units were stiffened by a force of Federals from General Ubaldo Garza's command.[29] Should the attack succeed, the legend of Federal invincibility would be shattered. Joining in the operation was a contingent from San Miguel el Alto, led by El Catorce and two rancher brothers named Librado and Gerardo Mójica.

The attack was scheduled for 0400 on 23 February. That night the *cristeros* assembled on the slopes of El Romeral, a high hill overlooking San Francisco, while a twenty-five-man detachment rode ahead to cut off communications between San Francisco and León, Guanajuato's largest city, where the Federals were assembled in force.[30]

When the rebels attacked, they encountered three centers of resistance: the parish church, the town hall and the house of Federal deputy Aurelio Plascencia, an old enemy of Hernández.[31] To reduce these strongholds the *cristeros* split into three forces. The church was assigned to the San Miguel ranchers, led by Hernández, and El Catorce stormed the block containing Deputy Plascencia's house. The assault on the town hall, led by Víctor López, produced the hardest fighting. Braving heavy fire, the rebels closed in on the building and forced the front door with crowbars and pickaxes. Bursting in, they engaged the defenders in hand-to-hand combat on the ground floor, up the stairs, and in second-floor offices of this two-story building; the struggle was marked by brutal close-quarters fighting.[32] By mid-morning it was all over. Except for a few soldiers who had escaped over the building's flat roof, the Federals were all dead and the *cristeros* in complete command.

López's aggressiveness proved a boon to the Mojica brothers, whose force had been detailed by Hernández to capture the parish church. Seeing the nearby town hall in rebel hands, the Federals in the bell tower filed out and capitulated.[33] Now only one center of resistance remained: Deputy

Plascencia's house. Hernández and El Catorce first attempted a frontal attack, concentrating on the main entrance, but they were beaten back by heavy fire. Moving down the street, the attackers entered an empty house which afforded a good field of fire against the deputy's residence. Outgunned and out-flanked, Plascencia ran up a white flag.[34]

Surrender did not bring salvation, however. When Hernández ordered Plascencia and his men out into the street, the deputy balked. Possibly he feared a lynching at the hands of the pro-*cristero* townspeople. Angered by this defiance, Hernández ordered Plascencia shot.[35] Thus ended the fight for San Francisco del Rincón. Following their usual procedure, the *cristeros* immediately abandoned the town and set off in the direction of San Diego and San Julián.

Though minor in scope, the San Francisco action marked a major turning point in the rebellion. For the first time, this army of peasant revolutionaries succeeded not only in defeating a Federal force but in wresting—if only temporarily—a sizable population center from Federal control. (Earlier successes were accomplished against what amounted to quisling forces: unpopular and poorly motivated self-defense units in solidly *cristero* communities.) The "chicken coop" was turning into a viper's nest.

The next government defeat came the following day. On the morning of 24 February Father Vega arrived at the Rancho de la Gloria in the Cerro Blanco region, near Arandas, and sent messages to nearby ranchers requesting that they attend a mass he was celebrating. The object of Father Vega's mass was more recruitment than religion. Cleverly playing on *alteño* machismo, he addressed a fiery sermon to the ranchers. They would be less than men, he thundered, if they did not ride forth to defend the holy cause of Christ. While the sermon was still in progress a lone rider came into view from the direction of Arandas. Reluctant to interrupt the service, the horseman dismounted and whispered briefly into the ear of Luis Anaya, Vega's aide. Shaken by the courier's words, Anaya stopped Vega in mid-sermon and told him that a Federal detachment was riding into the Cerro Blanco that very moment.

Vega was equal to the occasion. He pronounced a quick blessing and formed the ranchers into three columns, placing himself in command of the center one. No sooner had the *cristeros* deployed than the Federals were upon them. In the engagement that followed the rebels made maximum use of their superior cavalry and terrain knowledge. At the end of three hours the Federals were thoroughly beaten. Breaking contact, they began a pell-mell retreat toward Arandas.

According to *cristero* sources, Federal losses were one hundred killed and three prisoners taken, while the rebels suffered only one dead and one wounded.[36] This doubtless exaggerated tally does not alter the fact that the government sustained a humiliating defeat—the second in two days.

These victories gave the *alteños* a much needed psychological boost. From the beginning they had considered themselves superior to the *"changos."* They were bigger men, tougher physically, better riders with superior mounts, they moved on familiar soil amid a friendly populace, and they were fighting for Cristo Rey against a contemptible rabble of drifters who had joined Calles's army to keep from starving. While they never felt an iota of respect for the Federals on a man-to-man basis, they were, in the early days, moved to caution by the enemy's material superiority and their own inexperience. This caution vanished after February. Fighting as infantry, the *cristeros* had bloodied their enemy in the streets of San Francisco; as cavalry, in the hills of the Cerro Blanco. Given anywhere near equal odds, the rebels would attack the "apes" on sight.

THE BATTLE OF SAN JULIAN

It was with this spirit of growing confidence that two hundred *cristeros* boldly engaged a four-hundred-man Federal force at San Julián on 15 March 1927. The rebels, under El Catorce, Father Vega, and Lauro Rocha, were in possession of the town. Occupying San Juan de Los Lagos, some thirty miles northwest, was an elite cavalry regiment, the 78th, under General Espiridión Rodríguez. Up to now, the *cristeros* had always abandoned towns when a Federal attack seemed imminent. Aware of this practice, Rodríguez and his officers first attempted to bluff the rebels out of San Julián. Knowing that Federal threats would immediately be communicated through a network of friendly civilians, officers of the 78th began haranguing townspeople in the main plaza. The star of this propaganda show was one Colonel Rangel. Mockingly declaring himself to be the Pope, he bragged to a crowd of stony-faced *alteños* that he would bring El Catorce's head back in his saddle bags.[37]

On 14 March the 78th moved on San Julián. From Rodríguez's action it is clear that until the last moment he thought the rebels could be frightened out of their stronghold. Five kilometers from town Rodríguez halted the column. Peering through binoculars he saw the plaza swarming with armed men: the *cristeros* would not be budged with threats.

In a final attempt to dislodge the rebels without a fight, Rodríguez sent a campesino named Margarito Ramírez into town. Ostensibly his function was to gauge *cristero* strength and report back to Rodríguez. But he had another, and more important, mission—to intimidate the rebels into leaving San Julián. This goal was clear because at no time did Ramírez act clandestinely or as a spy. He came into town, spoke openly with several of the *cristero* leaders, and left as conspicuously as he had arrived.

One of the rebel chiefs with whom Ramírez spoke was his flamboyant namesake. "Tell this general," said Victoriano, "that El Catorce is here and has four hundred men."[38] The fact that Victoriano so greatly exaggerated the size of his force shows that the *cristeros* may have been equally inclined toward keeping the enemy at bay with a well-timed bluff. Margarito Ramírez also spoke with Father Vega. Scornfully rejecting any notion that his men flee, Vega replied that he was not a *correlón* (runner) and that he would happily await the *callistas*.[39]

The Federals camped outside San Julián that night. The following morning, dismounted, they began a slow advance on the town. At first things went as they had planned. As the soldiers pushed into the outskirts, groping their way toward the main plaza, not a shot was fired. The townspeople had locked themselves in their houses and Rodriguez's men approached the plaza in an atmosphere of ghostly silence. It was now 0600. When they reached the main square the *callistas* set up a machine gun. By now the emboldened men of the 78th had abandoned caution and were pouring into the plaza en masse. Had the *cristeros* slipped out during the night?

Then came the answer. As more Federals left the comparative safety of side streets and joined their comrades in the open square, a deafening volley of fire rained down on the unprotected soldiers from upper stories of buildings surrounding the plaza. Though the rebels had complete confidence in their ability to handle the enemy, they suffered from their usual scarcity of ammunition. They had received, the night before, strict orders from Father Vega and El Catorce: make every shot count. No man was to fire unless he had a soldier firmly in his sights.[40]

The fighting that followed saw neither side gaining a clear advantage. The rebels continued to pepper the plaza but did not have the numbers or ammunition to drive the *callistas* back into the side streets. At 1300 all firing ceased. Among those observing the battle from a distance, some believed that the soldiers had crushed rebel resistance and secured the town, but this was not the case. The impromptu cease-fire was dictated on both sides by military necessity. While the 78th, seeking cover and concealment, regrouped for another push the *cristeros* held their fire. Ammunition was perilously scarce and the rebels could not afford to waste a bullet on a now partly concealed enemy.

Hostilities resumed exactly an' hour later.[41] The Federals attacked with fury and, bit by bit, began gaining the upper hand. By 1500 the *cristeros* were on the brink of defeat. Though their marksmanship was as good as ever they didn't have enough bullets to compensate for Federal superiority in numbers and material. It was only a matter of minutes before their ammunition would be exhausted.

Suddenly a great cheer went up from the *callistas*. From the southeast a huge dust cloud was visible, signaling the approach of fresh troops. "Se vino el indio Amaro! (The Indian Amaro has come!)" cried the soldiers.[42] General Joaquín Amaro, Secretary of War and Marine, had taken personal command in Los Altos since 10 March and was believed to be nearby. The prospect of a Federal victory had dramatically shifted from probability to certainty.[43]

As the column approached, the San Julián combatants could see horsemen carrying red, white, and green Mexican flags. Suddenly a horrified hush came over the Federals—and loud cheering and choruses of "Viva Cristo Rey!" from the rebels. The relief column was now near enough so the flags could be distinguished clearly. Emblazoned on the white center stripe of each standard was the figure of a woman—the Virgin of Guadalupe! While both Federals and *cristeros* carried Mexican flags, *la guadalupana's* image was added to those used by the *cristeros*.

The couriers sent by Father Vega had reached the San Julilán regiment.[44] The relief force consisted of 200 men, personally led by Miguel Hernández. As they neared the town

Hernández split his troops into three columns. In hopes of surrounding the Federals, one detachment rode on San Julián from the southwest, one from the northeast, and the third from the southeast.

Up to this moment the 78th had fought hard and tenaciously. With a two to one numerical advantage and plentiful ammunition, their leaders were willing to take their losses in the certainty that they could wear the *cristeros* down. The advent of Hernández utterly broke their will to fight. Now outnumbered and facing fresh troops, the 78th gave way to panic. Packs, weapons, excess clothing, and everything that might impede a hasty retreat was discarded in terror-stricken flight. Of possible escape routes, the only exit was to the northwest, back toward San Juan de los Lagos. Had Hernández been able to deploy another column, the 78th would have been not routed but annihilated. The rebels had the further satisfaction of capturing General Rodríguez's saddle bags and finding, on the battlefield, the bullet-riddled body of the boastful Colonel Rangel.[45]

ESCALATING BARBARISM

Also in *cristero* hands was a batch of prisoners—twenty in number. Of this total, some were wounded. These men met with a particularly grim fate: they were stabbed to death by a crazed *cristero* soldier, himself a walking casualty. (A relative of El Catorce, by 1982 he was known only as "the husband of Romanita." It was believed in Los Altos that he survived rebellion and died a natural death in Pachuca.) The unwounded prisoners were then taken to the San Julián municipal cemetery and shot.[46] This was the first mass slaughter of military captives by the rebels.

The revulsion that accompanied this atrocity was not confined to the government side. "God help us! Those of the Unión [Popular] also murder!" was the anguished comment of one witness.[47] The criticism stung El Catorce. "Did you think this was a pilgrimage?" he retorted. "I haven't found a way to defeat my enemies other than to kill them—something they themselves taught me."[48] Yet Victoriano took no part in the executions and refused even to witness them. His policy was to shoot only officers and *agraristas;* soldiers, after being disarmed, would be set free.[49]

The rebellion was rapidly escalating in barbarity. On 1 April 1927 Anacleto González Flores was captured in Guadalajara. Following torture, he was put to death. A few weeks later an attack, led by Father Vega, on the Guadalajara-Mexico City train led to one of the worst atrocities of the rebellion. Compared to the train attack, in which innocent civilians perished under nightmarish circumstances, the San Julián executions were acts of clemency.

In planning the operation, Father Vega was not motivated solely, or even primarily, by a desire to avenge the Maestro's death. There were more practical considerations involved. From spies in Guadalajara he had learned that a shipment of 120,000 pesos from the Bank of Mexico would be sent to Mexico City on 19 April. Gathering a force of 500 men, Vega positioned his troops near a whistle stop called El Limón (about nine miles northwest of La Barca), where Catholic railroad workers had torn up a section of the track. At 2030 on the 19th the train left Guadalajara. Along with passengers, the train carried a 52-man military escort. The soldiers occupied an armored car where the money and a supply of ammunition were stored. First-class passengers rode comfortably in metal cars while second-class ticket holders were crammed into wooden ones.

It was shortly after midnight when the train jumped the track. In the no-quarter, three-hour battle that ensued, every member of the escort lost his life. Since the soldiers had dispersed through the other cars, using the passengers as shields, a number of civilians died in the cross fire. They could consider themselves lucky. Other passengers, including wounded of both sexes and all ages, died horribly when Vega ordered the wooden cars drenched with gasoline and burned.

Vega was driven to this extremity by the death of his brother Jesús. Hearing that Jesús had been wounded, Vega went to his brother's side and found him dead. Crazed with rage, he ordered the cars set on fire. Of the dead, fifty-one were verified as having died in the flames, while about twice that number had been killed by other means.[50]

Before leaving, the *cristeros* ransacked the armored car and seized the money and ammunition. Of the 120,000 pesos, a donation of 20 was awarded to each man in the attacking force. Another 5,000 was earmarked for the regimental treasury. This small amount was the only benefit that the rebels derived from the attack. The remainder of the sum, turned over to a rich Catholic for the purpose of buying arms, simply disappeared.[51]

Vega's barbarity furnished the government with a major propaganda victory. The outrage triggered by the train attack furnished Calles with a perfect pretext for two strong retaliatory measures: expulsion of the remaining Catholic bishops from Mexico and the *reconcentración* program, which removed the people from their land, confiscated their goods, and "relocated" them in designated urban areas.

Father Vega's dark brush succeeded in tainting a number of his cleaner colleagues. In fulminations against clerical barbarism, the government-controlled press declared that the attack was led by not one but three priests—Vega, Angulo of San Francisco de Asís, and Pedroza. Though this version circulated even in 1982, it is completely false. Angulo, later Bishop of Tabasco, was a noncombatant whose allegiance to the movement was at best lukewarm. (Earlier he had attempted to dissuade Vega from joining the rebellion.) As for Pedroza, he had flatly refused Vega's invitation to take part in the assault.[52] From beginning to end, in conception, planning, and execution, the butchery at El Limón was the work of José Reyes Vega.

The train attack was as self-defeating as it was savage. Tactically, it accomplished nothing greater than the death of fifty-two *callista* soldiers and the acquisition of some ammunition. Financially, it enriched the cristero war chest by $60,000—of which $50,000 was promptly entrusted to a thief. In addition, Vega's reckless sadism unleashed an avalanche of retaliation. Federal military action, already widespread, was cruelly intensified. Brutal measures would soon be applied against *alteño* civilians. The three and one-half month period between New Year's Day of 1927 and the train attack in mid-April had witnessed the emergence of Los Altos as the rebels' most successful theater of operations. By mid-summer resistance in this vital sector was virtually extinguished.

Repression
and
Reconcentración

BEFORE THE TRAIN ATTACK by Father Vega, Federal response to the *cristero* challenge had been one of gradual escalation; afterwards, the policy changed to massive retaliation. During the first period (the early months of 1927), as these excerpts demonstrate, Calles's military planners yielded to no one in discerning light at the end of the tunnel:

> 17 January: "The rebellion has been annihilated."
> 24 January: "It [the rebellion] is ending."
> 16 February: "The region [Los Altos] has been completely pacified."
> 4 March: "Jalisco will soon be at peace."
> 11 March: "General Amaro, from Ocotlán, will personally direct a campaign that will be decisive."[1]

San Julián came four days after the last prediction. This humiliating defeat, followed by the train assault, finally convinced the Federals that Jalisco—or the *alteño* sector, at any rate—could only be subdued with all-out offensive action. Prior to El

Limón, the *callistas* viewed pacification of Los Altos primarily as a military problem. The only civilians marked for death or imprisonment were those, like Anacleto González Flores or Miguel Gómez Loza, who were known to play leading roles in the rebellion.

This policy did not mean that the *alteño* civil population was treated with tenderness. Requisitions were frequent and capricious and the anti-religious laws strictly enforced. Still, for an unrealistically long time the government believed its own propaganda that the rebels were a minority of fanatics who lacked whole-hearted popular support. This attitude was especially prevalent in the earliest days, when the task of fighting the rebels was left largely to local self-defense forces. A Federal battalion was sent to Tepatitlán only after an urgent appeal from the mayor.

Unwise optimism prevailed even after it became clear that all Los Altos backed the movement and that local forces had no hope of holding their own against the rebels. What matter if these idiot ranchers were hopelessly infected with fanaticism? How could their ragtag bands stand up against well-armed, well-supplied regular troops? Then came the shocking events of late February and March. As if the defeats—San Francisco del Rincón, Cerro Blanco, San Julián—weren't bad enough, the Federals couldn't even derive solace from their "victories." These were engagements at Cuquío, Jalostotitlán, and Valle de Guadalupe in which the rebels, after bloodying and out-maneuvering a numerically superior foe, withdrew for lack of ammunition.[2]

The train attack shattered the Federals' last illusions. Not only were the *alteños* fanatical, but to such a degree that they were capable of burning innocent people alive. (It was not then known that the massacre was solely Father Vega's responsibility; widely believed were reports that Pedroza, Angulo, and others had also participated in the assault.)

As noted, Federal activity against civilians was at first selective and directed only against known Catholic activists. The two most wanted leaders were Gómez Loza and González Flores. Though the former remained at large for another year, the latter was captured on the first day of April 1927.

On 5 January of that year the two old friends had parted in Guadalajara with an emotional *abrazo*. Leaving his wife and children in the city, Gómez Loza vanished into the Cerro

Gordo. Two days later a printing press was smuggled to his hideout. Federal vigilance had made it too dangerous to publish *Gladium*, the UP journal, in Guadalajara. With his customary energy Gómez Loza took on the tasks of editing a clandestine publication and setting up a civil infrastructure for rebel-held Jalisco.[3]

At a final meeting of the UP chiefs, just before New Year's Day, it had been decided that "the Maestro will assume leadership of the movement in Jalisco...from his hiding place in Guadalajara."[4] This refuge was the house of a family named Vargas González, only a few blocks from the center of town. Despite the central location, there was little fear that the Maestro would be caught if he exercised the proper precautions. Popular feeling was solidly behind the rebels, and Jalisco was a hospitable sea for *cristero* fish to swim in.

THE YOUTH AND THE SPY

Had it not been for a remarkable feat of Federal counterespionage, González Flores might well have succeeded in evading capture. The trail that led to his hiding place began 150 miles away, in a dingy boardinghouse in León, Guanajuato. Occupying lodgings there was a youthful ACJM member, Salvador Alvarez Patrón. When the rebellion broke out Alvarez had been sent to serve as liaison between the Liga and clandestine rebels in that Federal-occupied city.

One day Alvarez heard a knock at his door. He opened it and a stranger addressed him by name, seeking a few minutes of his time. Though Alvarez had never seen the man before, he spotted him immediately as a typical *alteño* rancher. The visitor was fair skinned and blue-eyed and his partly unbuttoned shirt revealed a wooden crucifix resting on a hairy chest. His hands, work-worn and calloused, were caked with a residue of red clay so characteristic of the *alteño* region. His speech was rough, ungrammatical, and studded with the localisms of the red clay country.

Humbly addressing the young man half his age as "don Salvador," the rancher identified himself as a *cristero* sympathizer and friend of El Catorce. There was some business he had to attend to and he would be grateful for whatever assistance "don Salvador" could render. With awkward sincerity he assured the youth that he was "one of us."

At first Alvarez was suspicious. "Who is 'us'?" he inquired ironically. "What does all this have to do with me?"[5]

"Ay, don Salvador," said the rancher with a trace of exasperation. He was, he insisted, a friend of don Anacleto,
Navarrete, and all the UP chiefs. He came from Guajalarita, a
ranching community in Los Altos, and there had accumulated
a group of followers and a store of three dozen rifles and
carbines. Anxious to join the movement, he wanted to be
recognized as head of his band so he and his men could take
the field. But difficulties had arisen. He'd approached a number of local *cabecillas,* including Chon Ibarra and Jesús Macías,
but not one had been willing to grant him the autonomy he
sought. He was frankly afraid to go to Father Vega who, he
believed, would confiscate his arms and maybe even shoot
him. If he could only speak to someone in higher authority—
someone empowered to ratify his status and allow him to take
the field as *cabecilla* in his own right.

Though the rancher mentioned González Flores, at no
time did he press the point. If Alvarez was unwilling to disclose the Maestro's whereabouts, that was perfectly all right:
any other leader would do.

As the rough words tumbled out, Alvarez's suspicion
began to melt. The man's humility, his sincerity—even his
familiarity with Father Vega's murderous reputation—convinced the inexperienced youth that his visitor was a genuine
cristero. "Do you swear on your crucifix that you won't tell
anybody what I'm going to tell you?"[6]

The man complied and again disclaimed any particular
desire to know the Maestro's whereabouts. "If you think I can
settle my business with another *jefe,* I have no wish to see don
Anacleto. You guide me."[7]

Now thoroughly convinced of the rancher's sincerity,
Alvarez became as loquacious as he had been tight-lipped a
few minutes before. Not only did he disclose González Flores's hideout but also blew the cover on Navarrete and Luis
Padilla Gómez, president of the Guadalajara ACJM's Arch-
diocesan Committee.

No sooner had the rancher left than Alvarez felt a pre-
monition of disaster. Had he unwittingly betrayed his friends?
What should he do now? For some reason he rejected the idea
of escape. The rancher had certainly seemed genuine; if so,

what could be more senseless than panicky flight? Yet apprehension continued to gnaw. Alvarez paced the floor of his second-story room and then, as if seeking psychological assurance, he closed his window shutters, barred them, and pushed the bed up against the front door. Then he heard footsteps. From the sound, there were at least five men climbing the stairs. "Son ellos (it's them)," he said to himself.[8]

It was. Accompanying the "rancher" were six agents of the Secret Police. Alvarez was held for a week in the León military barracks, then transferred to the Inspección de Policía prison in Mexico City. During that week all three men he had named were rounded up—González Flores and Padilla Gómez in Guadalajara and Navarrete in Mexico City.

The spurious rancher was Nicolás Vela, a detective whose twenty-five-year career dated back to the days of Porfirio Díaz. A shrewd, apolitical specialist in political counterintelligence, Vela served revolutionary governments as ably as he had served the old regime.

While in prison, Navarrete had a long and revealing talk with Vela. Now that González Flores had been apprehended, the agent spoke with complete frankness. He had infiltrated the UP and successfully managed to obtain credentials as a delegate to one of the party's conventions. From this vantage point he was able to compile complete dossiers on Catholic activists, particularly the youthful militants of the ACJM. Why had he keyed in on Alvarez Patrón? Vela's answer was an eloquent testimonial to his shrewdness. Alvarez was chosen because Vela had come to consider him "the thread that would unwind the entire spool."[9] Of all the young men in the movement, Alvarez was "the most ingenuous, the most impetuous, and the most imprudent."[10] After intercepting injudicious letters Alvarez had written his mother, Vela began tailing him. So discreet was his surveillance that, as the León encounter demonstrated, Alvarez never learned the identity of the spy until the very end. Vela's expertise becomes even more impressive when we learn that one time he accompanied his young prey on a round trip by train from Guadalajara to El Paso, Texas.

Thanks to Vela's astute sleuthing, González Flores was arrested in the early morning of 1 April 1927. Also taken into custody were his protectors, the Vargas González brothers, and Luis Padilla. Like Padilla, the brothers were dedicated *acejotameros*. Jorge, twenty-seven, was employed by the city electric company and Ramón, twenty-two, was a medical student. Their father was a doctor who had treated wounded Catholics free of charge after the Santuario de Guadalupe riot.

THE MARTYRDOM OF GONZALEZ FLORES

The prisoners were taken to Cuartel Colorado, the military barracks, and tortured in the presence of General Ferreira. Particularly savage was the treatment reserved for González Flores. He was beaten, hung up by his thumbs, had the soles of his feet lacerated by a razor blade, and his shoulder broken by a rifle butt. Though the Maestro freely admitted his own participation in the movement, he steadfastly refused to implicate others. (His questioners were particularly anxious to learn the whereabouts of Archbishop Orozco y Jiménez.) The other prisoners, while not treated as brutally as Anacleto, followed his lead in declining to give information.

At length Ferreira wearied of the game. Seeing he was dealing with unreasoning "fanatics," he convoked a drumhead court-martial that promptly sentenced the four men to death for "being in connivance with the rebels."[11] On hearing the sentence, González Flores begged Ferreira to spare his friends, offering to take responsibility for all charges against them. When this request was denied, the Maestro asked that he be shot last so he could administer spiritual solace to his comrades at the moment of death. That plea was granted.

Padilla wanted to confess before he died, but Anacleto realized this would be impossible. Ferreira would never delay the execution long enough for a priest to be summoned. "No, brother, there is not time to confess," he said. "A Father, not a Judge, waits for you. Your own blood will purify you."[12] Aloud, the four condemned men recited the Act of Contrition. Then the brothers were taken before the firing squad. It was then Padilla's turn. Granted permission to recite a brief prayer he had composed, he received the fatal fusillade on his knees.

Now only Anacleto was left. He first addressed General Ferreira. "I forgive you, General, with all my heart. Very soon we will see each other before the heavenly tribunal. The same God who will judge me will also be your judge. At that time you will have, in me, an intercessor before God."[13]

Hearing these words, some of the men in the firing squad lowered their rifles. Infuriated by this show of weakness Ferreira signaled to a captain standing near the condemned man. The officer jabbed a bayonet into the Maestro's side. Then the soldiers, wanting to end Anacleto's agony, brought up their rifles and squeezed off the death volley. "I die but God does not!" he shouted. "Viva Cristo Rey!"[14]

In other circumstances such terminal heroics might smack of an extract from some hagiographic work. But the words were completely in keeping with the man. Given his courage, selflessness, love of high-flown rhetoric, and blindly exalted sense of mission, it would have been out of character for Anacleto González Flores to exit in any other way.

If the Federals imagined that disposing of the Maestro would bring an end to the rebellion, they were grievously in error. The revolt has been described as "leaderless," that is, failing to produce an indispensable man whose death would automatically cause it to destruct. The movements they headed died with such diverse men as Boulanger, Huey Long, Gandhi, and Hitler, but Mexico's Catholic resistance did not die with Anacleto González Flores. While the *cristero* movement's hydra-headed quality may have had its drawbacks, it had one impressive feature: the capacity to survive the death, defection, or removal of any of its leaders.

Yet, in an indirect way, the death of González Flores led to the virtual extinction of the rebellion in the late spring and summer of 1927. The slaying of the Maestro was one of the reasons for the train attack; from shock over the train attack came *reconcentración*—a word symbolizing the tactics of annihilation that would be applied in Los Altos.

THE EFFECTS OF *RECONCENTRACION*

The principle of *reconcentración* was as follows: the civilian population of a prescribed area was given a fixed amount of time to evacuate that area and move to any of a number of designated population centers. The abandoned rural sector was then declared a free-fire zone (though that term was not used) and anyone found there would be shot on sight or subjected to aerial bombardment. *Reconcentración* had an economic as well as a military aspect. To deny the rebels access to food supplies, soldiers moved into the cleared zone and seized harvests and domestic animals. Fields were burned and all animals that could not be transported by train or truck were machine-gunned. Throughout the rebellion Colonel Alexander J. MacNab, the U.S. Military Attaché, consulted with Mexican civil and military officials on such counterinsurgency techniques.[15]

Reconcentración was officially initiated on 22 April 1927, two days after the train attack. It was first announced in the form of a telegram from Governor Barba González to the municipal presidents of thirty-six Jalisco communities. As an indication of the rebellion's geographic nature, it is interesting to note that twenty-six of these townships were in Los Altos and seven in the "Three Finger" zone. The text read as follows: "Recommend you make known to neighbors by any means at your disposal 4 May aerial bombardment will begin in all areas harboring rebels.... [Make sure to]...insist on necessity of their concentrating themselves in places designated by chief operations."[16]

On the same day General Espiridión Rodríguez, the loser at San Julián, ordered the evacuation of all smaller villages in the San Juan de los Lagos sector, giving the inhabitants twelve days to crowd into San Miguel el Alto. The next day, to make sure nothing had been overlooked, General Amaro decreed that *reconcentración* would apply to all of Los Altos, not just the twenty-six communities mentioned in Barba's telegram. While the Barba and Rodríguez directives had only mentioned air bombardment, Amaro capped the bottle by announcing that troops would blanket the evacuated areas and kill everything that moved "without notification."[17]

For the "reconcentrated," *reconcentración* was a hell that not even these hardship-conditioned people could have imagined. Following confiscation of their goods, they were crammed into already crowded urban areas during the hottest time of the year, the months of April and May immediately preceding the rainy season. Tepatitlán, with a normal population of 10,000, swelled to 50,000.[18]

For others, *reconcentración* was the key to El Dorado. Obvious beneficiaries were corrupt Federal officers, plus the legion of profiteers and speculators who bought the refugees' domestic animals at scandalously low prices. "On May 12, 1927, in San Pedro Tlaquepaque, chickens sold for five cents each...[and] a pig was worth a dollar."[19] This passage was written by Carleton Beals, a man of the political Left, whose sympathies were unshakably pro-grovernment and anti-Church. Yet he was objective enough to see that the Los Altos rebels were the rural poor who suffered so horribly under *reconcentración*. And what of the rich Catholic *hacendados*, eternally depicted by government propaganda as instigators of the rebellion? Again, Beals proves a useful chronicler:

> Los Altos in Jalisco is declared a combat zone. All the inhabitants are ordered to migrate into concentration centers under penalty of being considered rebels. "Let me leave ten men on my hacienda to harvest the crop," pleads the owner of Hacienda Estrella to General F. [obviously Ferreira], an officer who has risen with the ideals of the Revolution but now owns an entire block of the most fashionable residences in Guadalajara.
> "If a man is there after May 1st, he'll be shot," announces General F., "unless, of course..."
> "What would be the consideration?" demands the owner.
> "You might contribute 15,000 pesos to the Social Defense Fund," announces General F., "in cash, delivered to me personally."
> "I have no ready cash."
> "Too bad," declares General F. As the owner leaves the office, he dictates: "Colonel M., 6th Regiment: Send captain and twenty-five men to harvest crop Hacienda Estrella, same to be delivered as promptly as possible ready for shipment Station Ocotlán. [signed] General F."[20]

Beals summarized his views in an article that appeared two months after *reconcentración* was decreed. The sorry state of affairs in Mexico "cannot be attributed to the Catholics but to military chiefs and irresponsible bandits....In the entire country civil law has disappeared and life is not worth a straw; property belongs to those who have arms."[21]

Inevitably, epidemics broke out among the *reconcentrados:* smallpox and typhoid ravaged the unsanitary *barrios* where the refugees huddled. *Alteño* villages, once characterized by their austere cleanliness, began to resemble a series of miniature Calcuttas. Yet morale remained amazingly high. All hatred was directed toward the government—"el mal gobierno"—and *alteños* retained an intergroup solidarity comparable to Londoners during the Blitz. Far from resenting the inundation of humanity from the countryside, townspeople in Purísima and San Francisco de Asís formed reception committees at the outskirts of town and took the *reconcentrados* into their houses.[22]

But there was a limit to the hospitality that urban *alteños* could extend to their luckless compatriots. When, as in Tepatitlán, the population of a community quintupled overnight, provision had to be made to locate the *reconcentrados* elsewhere. Usual destinations were the three nearest large cities outside Los Altos—Guadalajara, Aguascalientes, and León. Whenever possible these transfers were made by train. Railway travel could be easily monitored and the government didn't want to take the chance of letting the *reconcentrados* slip into the rebel-infested sierra.

It was during these trips that the refugees suffered particularly at the hands of the Federals. At a railhead near Unión de San Antonio, a group of farm families was waiting for the León train. Soldiers guarding them began searching their belongings and "on finding religious books and rosaries, blessed candles or images, they threw them on the ground and trampled them after committing all kinds of sacrileges. Then they slapped their faces, saying 'Fanatics! Hypocrites! What good does all that stuff do?' "[23] Some of the refugees were dragged off the platform and thrown into Unión de San Antonio's plague-infested jail, where most of them died.

Death also came to those civilians who had either ignored the *reconcentración* order or failed to meet the government's deadline. On 6 May, two days after the time limit had expired, a band of refugees from the Cerro Gordo had still not reached Atotonilco, their designated concentration center. Bone-tired, they had taken refuge in a ravine called Rincón del Molino. While eating a simple meal of *gorditas* (corn tortillas), they heard a shot. Federals were approaching, shooting everything in this free-fire zone. The refugees ran to and fro, hiding as best they could, but the hunt continued all day and through the night. The next day a rebel band appeared and drove off the *callistas*. Of the survivors, every male joined the *cristeros* on the spot.[24]

Though frightful, *reconcentración* was mercifully brief. Officially it lasted a month, but *reconcentrados* were returning to their farms and ranches as early as 15 May, with the tacit permission of the government. In displaying such permissiveness, the Federals were not motivated by altruism. The above date had marked an exceptionally early beginning of the rainy season, and the government had never intended that *reconcentración* last beyond the dry spring. The rains usually begin in mid-June and the early May–early June *reconcentración* timetable would have been ideal in a normal year. The Federals had planned to smother the rebellion by the end of the dry season and then allow the *reconcentrados* to return for the seeding of new crops. They were not overly concerned by the early rains, however, since by mid-May the rebellion seemed virtually over.

The *callistas* had another reason for relaxing *reconcentración* with the beginning of the rainy season: they feared the plague might get out of hand. With the campaign going so well they wanted to break up the disease-ridden concentration centers before contagion spread to their own troops.

There is no doubt that *reconcentración* proved an effective short-term panacea against the rebellion. With their food supply endangered and civilian support abruptly withdrawn, the insurgents seemed on their last legs. Federal columns swept everything before them and on 25 May Amaro extolled the success of *reconcentración* in an interview with a Mexico City newspaper. Conceding that the rebels had "from the beginning enjoyed the general sympathy of the masses," the Secretary of War and Marine said that it was for exactly this reason that *reconcentración* and aerial bombardment were necessary. Amaro continued the interview by predicting final victory within two weeks.[25]

The Secretary's sanguine view was shared by American observers. A confidential message from the Guadalajara Consulate to the Secretary of State, dated 26 May 1927, reported that "the Federal government has been able to place a decided restraint upon the various rebel groups, particularly in the district known as Los Altos." The reports also observed that the Federal military campaign was drawing to a close.[26]

But there was one aspect of *reconcentración* that boomeranged. This all-out war against civilians united the *alteño* population against the government as never before. However sympathetic local campesinos may have been to the revolt, there were many who previously had drawn the line at taking arms. With *reconcentración*, that line was erased. Some joined the rebellion because they had nothing to go back to, others because their sullen resentment had been fanned to hatred, still others for both reasons. One month of *reconcentración* did more for rebel recruitment than all the preceding years of Catholic evangelism and anti-Catholic repression.

Summer
of Despair,
Autumn of Hope

THE EFFECTS OF RENEWED REBEL RECRUITMENT were not immediately felt. The period from late May, when General Amaro made his optimistic statement on the imminence of Federal victory to the press, until early fall saw *cristero* fortunes reach an all-time low. Of the leading *cabecillas* in Los Altos, only three remained in the field: El Catorce, Víctor López, and Toribio Valadés. Father Pedroza went into hiding, Lauro Rocha was incapacitated by a wound, while others, including Miguel Hernández and Father Vega, took refuge in the United States.[1]

That bleak summer was a time of extreme pessimism for the rebels. Gloom pervaded everywhere, infecting even the youthful militants of the ACJM. Some Catholics tried to disassociate themselves from the rebellion, referring to it half-scornfully as *"lo de la sierra* (that business in the mountains)." Antonio Gómez Robledo, future biographer of the Maestro, declared that the rebels had become nothing more than "little groups of bandits who, bit by bit, will be crushed by the Federal troops."[2] At a clandestine ACJM meeting in Mexico City, only two out of twelve voted against a resolution that armed resistance was now useless and that "it was necessary to await new events that would show more suitable ways of [defending] Catholic interests."³ Significantly, all attending the meeting were from Jalisco. The situation was so desperate that some opposition leaders decided there was no choice but to broaden the base of the movement and give it a less Catholic aspect. Such a solution, they believed, would attract wider support in Mexico and, they fervently hoped, eventual U.S. recognition.

THE UNION NACIONAL

Chief promoters of the plan to broaden the rebel base were three *ligueros:* Luis G. Bustos, a law professor named Alberto María Carreño, and José Ortiz Monasterio, a former *porfirista* general who served the Liga as military adviser. On 31 July the three men met in New York and Carreño drafted a manifesto calling for the creation of a new political party. It would be called the Unión Nacional. Ideologically eclectic, the Unión would combine three elements—old-line liberals who had supported Díaz, Catholics, and anti-Calles revolutionaries.

The manifesto was a curious mixture of nineteenth-century liberalism and Rerum Novarum Catholicism. The Constitution of 1857 was to be restored with certain amendments in line with the bishops' 1926 memorandum to Congress. Pleasing to the liberals were provisions mandating separation of Church and State and affirming the no-reelection principle. Pleasing to Catholic progressives was the manifesto's endorsement of such social legislation as support for trade unions, pensions for the elderly, industrial accident insurance, and recognition of women's rights. All Catholics applauded the stipulation that religious bodies could own and administer property while *acomodados* (both liberal and Catholic) derived comfort from a provision requiring just compensation for expropriated land.⁴

An early and fervent supporter of the Unión Nacional plan was Bishop Pascual Díaz. Bustos and his colleagues had informed him of their project five days after the New York meeting. Díaz was delighted and, with Pauline enthusiasm, began evangelizing the Unión Nacional idea among his colleagues in the episcopate.

Díaz's success in gaining their support was not entirely due to his own efforts, especially in his dealings with the hard-line faction. González Valencia of Durango was won over not by Díaz but by Bustos's making appropriately hawkish noises. Writing with the frankness of a co-conspirator, Bustos counseled González to make a show of going along with the plan but not to be taken in by is liberal façade. This, he assured the bishop, was purely window dressing designed to please the American: "Without silencing the cry of 'Viva Cristo Rey!'," he wrote, "we throw dust in the eyes of Washington and of the American public."[5]

All factions were united in a desire to win American support. Díaz, with that end in mind, began overtures to the State Department through the offices of Monsignor Pietro Fumasoni Biondi, apostolic delegate in Washington. What happened next is somewhat vague. Fumasoni Biondi, through mysterious (and never identified) intermediaries whom he referred to only as "certain persons," submitted the Unión Nacional plan to the State Department in July 1927. The response, as transmitted to Díaz by Fumasoni, was highly encouraging. The bishop was given to understand that Washington approved the project and praised it as the best of all the plans regarding Mexico that had been reviewed.[6]

On 11 November, four months later, the new party was officially launched at a secret meeting in Mexico City. This conclave, chaired by Bustos, proclaimed itself the National Assembly of the Unión Nacional. Though the assembly nominated a triumvirate—one liberal, one revolutionary, and one Catholic—to head a provisional government, the occasion was more a wake than a christening.

What had happened in the meantime to dim the bright hopes of midsummer? For one thing, a dramatic improvement in rebel military fortunes had removed much of the new party's raison d'être. Of the three provisional leaders selected, only the liberal (ex-General José Ortiz Monasterio) had agreed to serve. No such commitment was ever obtained from the Catholic nominee, Bartolomé Ontiveros, or the revolutionary, Emilio Madero, younger brother of Francisco. The only reason the meeting was held at all is that Bustos and his colleagues were still pursuing the elusive wraith of American recognition. Bustos returned to the United States after the meeting and forlornly waited out the winter in hopes of a favorable sign from Washington. It was not forthcoming.

By early spring of 1928 it was clear that Bustos's attempt to "throw dust into the eyes of Washington" had aborted. But his disillusionment was nothing compared to the fury displayed by more militant Catholics. Having failed, with revolutionary and liberal cosmetics, to make their cause attractive to Washington they reacted with the outrage of a scorned lover. On 29 March 1928 a San Antonio–based group of *acejotameros* sent a furious memorandum to the Liga's Directive Committee and to Bustos. The letter, overflowing with pent-up resentment, fiercely attacked the Unión Nacional plan and those who would "raise as a banner...the decrepit Constitution of 1857." Anacleto González Flores, Miguel Gómez Loza (who had been killed earlier that month), and "other illustrious martyrs would not have fought or died for the rag of '57. To raise it now as a banner would be an unforgivable desecration of the blood of our heroes, a horrendous sacrilege against the blood of our martyrs."[7]

The death blow to the Unión Nacional plan came a week later. On 4 April three men met in the San Juan de Ulua fortress in Veracruz harbor for the first of a series of vitally important meetings. The conferees were President Calles, American Ambassador Dwight W. Morrow, and Father John J. Burke, Executive Secretary of the National Catholic Welfare Conference. Father Burke attended the meeting as a representative of the apostolic delegate. It was now official: all ties with dissident Mexican groups would be severed and henceforth the State Department would deal directly with Calles in efforts to solve the religious question.

THE LEGEND OF EL CATORCE

While the Unión Nacional morning glory was enjoying its brief bloom during 1927, resistance in Los Altos was kept alive mainly through the efforts of two men. One, who led the fighting arm, was Victoriano Ramírez, El Catorce; the other, who maintained the civil infrastructure, was Miguel Gómez Loza.

Encouraged by the temporary defection of Miguel Hernández and Fathers Pedroza and Vega, General Ubaldo Garza decided to try to neutralize the only dangerous armed rebel left in Los Altos. For all their military predominance, the Federals had been unable to put El Catorce out of action. Unlike Pedroza and Vega, Victoriano was an *alteño* and roamed his *patria chica* with complete impunity.

Taking a leaf from Obregón's book, General Garza decided on a strategy of "canonazos de cincuenta mil pesos (cannonballs of 50,000 pesos)." Only his offer—10,000 pesos—was decidedly more modest. The overture made to El Catorce also included a guarantee of safe conduct to the United States. It was rejected on the spot. Dictating his message to Rafael Martínez Camarena, Victoriano spurned Garza with contempt: "Don't give me anything," he said, "just settle the business of the *padrecitos* (little fathers) and the churches and I'll be at peace. But as long as you don't settle it, don't think you're going to buy me with money."[8]

Victoriano backed up his defiant words with equally defiant actions. El Catorce was by now a legend. But what is truly astounding is the brief time in which the legend developed. In January 1927 he was little more than a colorful local figure—an *alteño* rancher endowed with an extra measure of prowess in brawling, marksmanship, and amatory exploits. By March, after San Julián, he had become an adversary of mythic proportions. Believed to possess a charmed life, his presence alone proved the equalizer in more than one encounter when the rebels found themselves outnumbered. Two engagements that took place during the *cristero* nadir demonstrate the psychological whip hand he held over his enemies.

In June, the month when most of the rebel leaders were scattered or in hiding, Victoriano had returned to the terrain he knew best—the sierra around San Miguel el Alto. During most of that month he confined himself to a primitive but effective brand of morale boosting. He defied and tantalized the San Miguel garrison, he showed himself to friend and foe alike, and he engaged in as many acts of harassment as his limited resources would permit.

In the first days of July a local traitor informed the Federals that El Catorce was holed up in a house near the village of Rincón de Chávez, about ten miles north of San Miguel. A party of eighty soldiers was dispatched to the scene. On approaching the house, the *callistas* were seized by a spasm of panic. Abruptly changing course, they began the return trek to San Miguel. Then, overcome with rage and shame, they rode into Rincón de Chávez and shot three civilians. The victims, all surnamed Ramírez, were believed to be relatives of El Catorce.[9] While one may be skeptical of rebel claims that Victoriano had only "six or eight companions" with him, it's a reasonable assumption that the house where he was holed up could not have accommodated more than a score of men.[10]

The next event that added luster to El Catorce's legend took place almost a month later. On 17 July there had been a change of garrison in San Miguel: after their return to Mexico City, the Presidential Guards had been replaced by General Ignacio Leal's 3rd Cavalry Regiment.[11] Eleven days later a detachment of undetermined size was patrolling the rolling slope of the Cerro de Camaleón, a few miles south of San Miguel. Sighting a corral, they immediately surrounded it. Any large, man-made structure in that unfriendly countryside was immediately suspected of being a fortified site. Sure enough, a volley rang out from within. In the ensuing fire fight the *callistas* suffered heavy casualties. Then five men, with Victoriano in the lead, came galloping out of the corral and right through the circle of besiegers. Taken completely by surprise, the Federals could do no better than wound one of Victoriano's men, Macario Llamas.[12]

Through June and July El Catorce confined his activities to the immediate environs of San Miguel. In the two events described above it is doubtful that he commanded a combined total of more than fifty men, but the psychological advantage he derived from these minor actions completely dwarfed the scope of the actions themselves. The fact that he had frightened and humiliated a numerically superior foe added immeasurably to his legend. It was at this point that the "recruiting" by-product of *reconcentración* began to make itself felt. If Victoriano could work such miracles with just a few men, how much more could be accomplished if his ranks were swelled by tens and then hundreds of revenge-hungry *reconcentrados*?

As July gave way to August in 1927 a new peasant army gathered in the sierra around San Miguel. With a handful of men El Catorce had kept resistance alive in Los Altos. Now he had hundreds, and pin-prick harassment was no longer enough. The time had come to really bloody the *callistas*.

In selecting a target, El Catorce displayed all his finely honed instinct for the jugular. Fifty miles south of San Miguel is the town of Tototlán. Though geographically part of Los Altos, Tototlán, like the neighboring community of Atotonilco, lies in the rich, black-loam agricultural country that begins where the *alteño* plateau ends. Tototlán also skirts the main highway between Guadalajara and Mexico City. In planning the attack, these factors must have figured in Victoriano's calculations. What better way for the *cristeros* to demonstrate their rebirth than to boldly attack a community outside the *alteño* heartland?

There was another element that lent zest to the adventure: Tototlán was garrisoned mainly by *agraristas,* with only a small Federal detachment in support. Since San Julián, El Catorce had refrained from killing *callista* soldiers; their officers and the *agraristas* enjoyed no such immunity. Consciously or not, the choice of a town occupied mainly by the hated rural militia was a clever stroke. Victoriano's followers, after the ordeal of *reconcentración*, were out to wreak as savage a vengeance as possible. What more perfect target than *agraristas* who, especially in Los Altos, were considered the most contemptible of traitors?

The Tototlán raid took place on 24 August 1927. As El Catorce had anticipated, surprise was complete. His men rode in at 1400 and the action was less a military engagement than one of those annihilative strikes so typical of irregular warfare. All 200 *agraristas* were slaughtered at the cost, according to rebel sources, of only one *cristero* life. As for the soldiers, they fled their barracks and took up positions on the outskirts of town. The rebels occupied Tototlán overnight and left at 1100 the next day. A strong relief force, they heard, was advancing from Ocotlán.[13]

With this victory, the rebels in Los Altos were back in business. Before Tototlán, Victoriano's men had borne the brunt of the action. Now other *cabecillas* began to return to the fighting. Among them was Lauro Rocha, recovered from his wounds, and Father Pedroza, who had been hiding with a family named Gutierrez in a village near Ayo el Chico. Rocha began recruiting in the Sierra de Picachos and Pedroza among his parishioners in the Ayo area.[14]

El Catorce continued to remain at center stage. Another of his exploits, still a legend in Los Altos in the early 1980s, is one that may confound the historian as much as it did Victoriano's enemies. Though there is agreement on the sequence of events, two reliable chroniclers differ sharply on the date of the action. Víctor López states that it took place at "the end of July" (1927) while Rafael Martínez Camarena fixes the date at 27 September. [15] Thoughtful examination of available evidence supports the Martínez version. In order to reach this conclusion, certain facts have been taken into account. López was a combat officer and such tasks as remembering dates and keeping records were not part of his function. Though his *Memorias* is an invaluable document, the absence of specific dates is maddening, but only natural. López wrote these reminiscences more than a quarter century after the rebellion and his information derives from memory rather than written records. While the raids and skirmishes in which he participated were clearly remembered, dates were not. One can read as many as three installments without encountering a single date; actions, on the other hand, are described in vivid detail.

Martínez, by contrast, functioned in a purely civilian capacity. As assistant, and then successor, to Gómez Loza it was his job to keep records, help edit *Gladium*, and attend to any number of details related to civil administration. Also militating in favor of the Martínez version is the fact that he names an exact date: 27 September. He was able to do so because he and Gómez Loza had planned to meet El Catorce that day. Victoriano failed to attend the meeting for reasons that become clear in the following account: "The forces of Victoriano could not attend this meeting because, while camped in a place called La Cacayaca [about ten miles north of Arandas], they were attacked by General Leal's forces." [16] The narrative is then taken over by Victoriano himself:

> When they forced us from our positions in La Cacayaca, I sent my people over a dam [in a nearby stream]....I came to a gateway that was choked with *sardos;* I took out my pistol and irrigated them, hear, and they fell....I came upon one of my boys who was dismounted, [so] I hoisted him up into my saddle, and when I reached the middle of the dam I took off my hat, made a bow [to the soldiers] and said "So long, you stupid bastards." [17]

La Cacayaca was a minor engagement (though the *cristeros* claimed over 150 enemy casualties), but of interest as an example of El Catorce's style.

THE PALMITOS SUMMIT

By 30 October—in 1927 the feast day of Cristo Rey—the rebels in Los Altos were powerful enough to hold what amounted to a summit meeting. This reunion, organized by Gómez Loza, took place in the Cerro de Palmitos, a high hill several miles south of San Julián. After being driven from one hiding place to another, he and his staff selected this remote mountain location as their new headquarters. Palmitos served as a combined military command post and seat of civil government. It also functioned as a publication site for *Gladium*.

Twelve hundred *cristeros* attended the Palmitos summit.[18] Though their ostensible purpose was to celebrate the fiesta of Cristo Rey, planning and strategy were not neglected. For the first time the rebel bands in Los Altos were formed into organized units with official designations. This formal organization was a decision of the Liga, which had sent Carlos Blanco to Los Altos with sealed dispatches authorizing ranks, commissions, and establishment of regular military formations. Three regiments were created, formed from a nucleus of the bands that had been operating on a regional basis.

The first regiment, known as San Miguel (or Dragones del Catorce), was drawn from that community and from a sector that reached as far west as Capilla de Guadalupe and as far east as the northern outskirts of Arandas. Commanding the regiment, with the rank of full colonel, was Victoriano.[19]

The second regiment, designated Leales de San Julián, covered the portion of Los Altos that spilled over into Guanajuato. Within the area were San Julián, San Diego de Alejandría, Jalpa de Cánovas, and all the Jalisco-Guanajuato border country west of San Julián and Arandas. Serving as caretaker commander was Toribio Valadés, with the rank of lieutenant colonel. Second in command was Víctor López, a newly created major. Since the regiment was largely composed of Miguel Hernández's followers, it was understood that he would take charge on his return from the United States. Hernández, in absentia, was commissioned with the rank of brigadier general in recognition of his services with Villa and Carranza.[20]

The third new unit—Tiradores del Cerro de Ayo—was headed by Father Pedroza. Its operational sphere included all of Los Altos that lay south of Arandas and east of Atotonilco.

This zone included such *cristero* strongholds as Jesús María, Degollado, and, of course, Ayo el Chico. Since Pedroza continued to administer his parish during the rebellion, it is probable that he requested a command in this area. He received the rank of colonel.[21]

Blanco, accompanied by Luis Anaya, then traveled southwest to distribute more commissions and activate two fresh regiments. One—Carabineros de Los Altos—was commanded by Colonel Rodolfo Loza Márquez and controlled a sector completely outside the *alteño* heartland: the rich agricultural country around Tototlán, Poncitlán, Ocotlán, and La Barca. The other, under Colonel Gabino Flores, was centered in the Cerro de Picachos and roamed the triangle delineated by Tepatitlán, Atotonilco, and Zapotlanejo. Its designation was Tepatitlán.[22]

MIGUEL GOMEZ LOZA: REBEL GOVERNOR

In addition to the military decisions reached at the Palmitos meeting, civil matters, under Miguel Gómez Loza, were also attended to. From 5 January 1927, when he bade an emotional farewell to the Maestro, until late October of that year, when he arrived at Palmitos, Gómez Loza lived the life of a hunted fugitive. His first headquarters was in the Cerro de Picachos, near Tepatitlán. There he remained until the end of February. At that time, following a skirmish in nearby Troneras, the Federals made an intensive sweep of the Picachos area and Gómez Loza took up new quarters in the more inaccessible Cerro Gordo. In mid-April, just before the train attack, Gómez Loza sent his aide, Rafael Martínez Camarena, to Mexico City to report on conditions to the Liga. Martínez returned with the news that, effective 26 April, the LNDLR Directive Committee had appointed Gómez Loza provisional governor of Jalisco.[23] In June, following *reconcentración*, Gómez Loza was again forced from his place of refuge. Leaving the Cerro Gordo, he trekked to the Sierra de Culebra, between Arandas and San Miguel el Alto. Early October witnessed Gómez Loza's final move—to Palmitos in the Sierra San Judas.[24]

Though conditions were hard—in the Cerro Gordo Gómez and Martínez lived almost entirely on toasted corn—the leaders of this mini-government never made a move without transporting their precious printing press.[25] This instrument was needed not only for continued publication of *Gladium* but also for the printing of propaganda to be distributed to the civil chiefs Gómez Loza had designated in Los Altos. The area under his direct control, which included Guadalajara, had been divided into ten sectors. All were in Jalisco except one in western Guanajuato that contained Jalpa de Cánovas. The sectors were broken down into subsectors, municipalities, small rural settlements *(caseríos)*, and ranches. (In Guadalajara, which contained three subsectors, the smallest units were city blocks and houses rather than *caseríos* and ranches.) In September of 1927 the Guadalajara sector was designated a special zone because it served as a communications line between Gómez Loza and General Degollado.[26] Since it was considered too risky for Gómez Loza to leave Los Altos, he gave—through Guadalajara contacts—Degollado the names of civil appointees for the south and west of Jalisco.

The infrastructure created by Gómez Loza was divided into six sections: finance, war, publicity, welfare, intelligence (espionage and courier services), and justice. That the new governor understood the importance of organizing at the village level is shown by the fact that in 1927 alone he created fifty-seven *cristero* municipalities in Jalisco. Of these, twenty-five were in Los Altos.[27] Gómez Loza's administrative ability becomes even more apparent when it is considered that this work was accomplished during the rebels' most difficult period. Though an improvement in the rebel military situation occurred between 1928 and 1929, the quality of civil government declined sharply after Gómez Loza's death (in March 1928). The fifty-seven municipalities he created in 1927 had grown to only ninety-two when the rebellion ended in 1929.[28]

To finance the war effort, Gómez Loza announced in September of 1927 the imposition of a 2 percent capital tax, to be levied semi-annually. Committees in each municipality would assess capital goods, and only that in excess of 250 pesos would be taxed. The property of *cristero* soldiers was exempt from the levy, and those who had suffered from Federal expropriation were entitled to discounts equal to their losses.

The municipal committees had also been instructed by Gómez Loza to prepare a survey to estimate how much tax money could be collected. The estimate was completed in November 1927; the figure submitted for the region under

Gómez Loza's control was 300,000 pesos.[29] Through no fault of the committees, their estimate proved wildly optimistic. Neither their members nor Gómez Loza could possibly know that a new *reconcentración* would be decreed in December. That, combined with continuing parsimony on the part of the rich Catholics, resulted in a collection far below expectations: Gómez Loza had expected 300,000 pesos from twenty-five communities, but he received 25,000 from six.[30] To ease the ravages of the new *reconcentración*, Gómez Loza reduced the tax to 1 percent and raised the exemption to 2,000 pesos.[31]

Gómez Loza and his staff suffered still another disappointment, involving disposition of the 25,000 pesos. The money was entrusted to a Liga representative in San Antonio, Texas, for the purpose of buying arms and supplies, but not a rifle or round of ammunition ever reached Los Altos. Angry and bewildered, Gómez Loza wrote two letters to Father González Pérez, an LNDLR representative in San Antonio, asking what had happened. As far as is known, he never received a reply. From that day on, the rebels in Jalisco attended to their own provisioning, bypassing the Liga in all matters of procurement.[32]

Though Gómez Loza was a civil official, he played an important role in keeping military resistance alive during the *cristeros'* summer of despair. Shortly after the first *reconcentración*, while on a mission to appoint civil chiefs and distribute propaganda, Gómez Loza and Martínez Camarena had a meeting with Victoriano Ramírez in the Cerro del Carretero overlooking San Miguel el Alto. To continue the struggle, El Catorce wanted some sort of official sanction. This he received from Gómez Loza, in his capacity as newly appointed governor. Though the exact date of the meeting is not known, it probably took place around the middle of June. This time would have been at a point between the end of *reconcentración* and the beginning of Victoriano's campaign of harassment against the Federals in San Miguel. It was this meeting that triggered the renewal of rebel activity in Los Altos.[33]

RENEWED REBEL ACTIVITY

Gómez and Martínez next traveled southwest to the environs of Federal-held Zapotlanejo. There they met with Lauro Rocha, who was training recruits in the Cerro de Picachos. Again, the exact date for the encounter is unknown, but it can safely be assumed that it took place not more than a week or two after the session with El Catorce. Rocha remained out of combat another month, drilling his men. Then the group moved east to a ranch outside Arandas called Los Robles. There they clashed with troops under General Leal and inflicted, according to rebel sources, over a hundred casualties.[34]

The next *cristero* commander to be activated was Víctor López. His Jalpa detachment had served—and would serve again—with the San Julián group, but that unit had been so demoralized by Miguel Hernández's departure for the United States that for the time being it ceased to exist. López temporarily joined El Catorce and served with him until the San Julián force was reestablished at the Palmitos summit.[35]

That crucial summit meeting also produced a significant psychological triumph for the *cristeros*. Since almost every armed rebel in Los Altos was attending the gathering, it would have been inconceivable for the Federals to be unaware of it, and they weren't. A *callista* detachment under General Ubaldo Garza set forth from Arandas on 27 October. Climbing into the sierra they arrived, shortly after noon, at Presa de López, a high dam site that afforded an excellent view of the Cerro de Palmitos. For months Garza and his colleagues had been stalking *cristeros* like hunters after elusive game. Now here were twelve hundred of them crowded on the slopes of a single elevation. Men on both sides reached for binoculars and for a tense moment these enemies gazed at each other across a ravine that separated Presa de López from Palmitos. Then Garza gave a signal and his soldiers prudently began the return trek to Arandas. No incident symbolized the revival of the *cristiada* in Los Altos more than so public a challenge and so public a refusal to accept it.[36]

Collaboration and Resistance

The Meaning of Treason in Los Altos

THE *CRISTERO* RESURGENCE OF LATE 1927 was preceded by cata-strophic early defeats, a seemingly lost cause, a refusal to give up hope, and a dramatic reversal in the tide. Such a reversal—especially in a guerrilla war—could never have taken place without the existence of a dedicated and effective resistance movement. There also existed, however, a pattern of collab-oration in Los Altos. (Though not all resisters resisted for the same reasons, their motives are infinitely less complex than those who willingly accepted a role that made their peers, lifelong friends, and even their families regard them as trai-tors.) A group of French writers, pooling their views, have identified three main avenues of collaboration: tactical collab-oration, collaboration through conviction, and collaboration through greed.[1]

Tactical collaborators are usually persons who have at-tained, and then lost, positions of prominence. Later, certain that they are riding a wave of the future, they risk temporary unpopularity to repair their careers. Since their primary con-cern is power, not ideology, they can be found anywhere in the political spectrum. Collaborators through conviction are those whom Rebecca West describes as "sincere traitors."[2] True believers in the dogmas of the enemy, they pass him secrets, disseminate his propaganda, and serve him as police and military auxiliaries in the firm conviction that they are fulfilling a noble end. These collaborators are never summer soldiers; their constancy is unwavering. On the bottom rung of the ladder are collaborators through greed or opportunism, the sordid collection of profiteers and stool pigeons for whom collaboration is an instrument of enrichment or settling personal scores.

ALTEÑO COLLABORATORS

Though *alteño* collaborators were few in number, all three patterns of collaboration emerged during the *cristiada*. Best known of the tactical collaborators was Silvano Barba González, nicknamed "El Semáforo (The Traffic Light)" because his eyes were of different colors.[3] A native, like the Maestro, of Tepatitlán, he had been the latter's disciple in the ACJM.[4] There are sharply differing versions about Barba's political past. One is his own, and the other of ex-friends who worked closely with him in the ranks of Catholic activism. Commenting on his association with the ACJM, Barba writes that "I do not precisely recall the year...in which they [the ACJM] began their labors in the state of Jalisco, but I have a sure recollection that my brother Federico and I were invited to attend their meetings in Guadalajara at the beginning of 1919.... Although I was not in sympathy with that invitation, I agreed to go so I could know the ideas and political position of the meeting's organizers."[5] Barba goes on to say that he only attended three sessions and then stopped going altogether because of his shock over a denunciation of the 1917 Constitution by Luis Beltrán y Mendoza. Particularly offensive to Barba, as he recounts it, was Beltrán's attack on those clauses of the constitution designed to regulate the Church. Then, by his own account, he joined the Liberal Party in 1919.[6]

It is a matter of record that at a meeting in early 1920 Barba González was elected subsecretary of the Jalisco ACJM's Regional Committee. Also significant is the fact that the main decision reached at that meeting was to launch a "Campaign of Liberty" for the purpose of stripping the 1917 Constitution of all anti-Catholic provisions.[7] An explanation of Barba's disingenuousness has been ventured by a Catholic writer, one of his contemporaries, who analyzed Barba's actions during his brief term as governor:

> In Jalisco the duties of governor had been assumed on July 28, 1926, by a former member of the Regional Committee of the Asociación [ACJM], Silvano Barba González. Contrary to optimistic predictions, given his...antecedents in the ranks of Catholicism, Barba González scorned the friendship of his former comrades and tried to erase every trace of his past, repudiating his beliefs and initiating a policy of narrow antireligious intolerance.[8]

The writer continues with the comment that the mood of Catholics during the boycott was lightened by wisecracks and lampoons aimed at Barba González.

While some of these verses were humorous, others were breathtaking in their rancor. An example of the latter is this parody of the sad love song "En Noche Lóbrega (In Dismal Night)":

> And the poor turncoat,
> Who yesterday was a mystic
> And today is a leper governor,
> They gave you orders
> To affix your rubber stamp,
> And you, vile one, obeyed without question.

> Silvano, hear me!
> Don't be the whip of Masonry.
> Vile impiety!
> Kill yourself first!
> If a mad dog dies
> Everyone is happy.

> If you were a viper,
> A centipede, or a bat,
> People would regard you with less horror;
> But you are a vassal of perfidious Judas,
> Who for silver
> Sold out his Lord.[9]

There are nine other verses, none yielding to the above in strident hostility.

Once he crossed the street Barba González's rise was meteoric. In 1920 Barba was a high-ranking officer in the ACJM; six years later he was appointed by Calles to fill out the unexpired term of Governor José Guadalupe Zuno, who had been forced from office for unconstitutionally removing five members of the Jalisco state legislature. Barba proved his new allegiance so successfully that Calles selected him over three other potential nominees, all political veterans and staunch anti-clericals.

At first Barba turned down the appointment. This action was not due to lack of ambition but to the special insight he possessed into the revolutionary potential of his former allies. He alone was convinced that the Catholics in Jalisco would rise; the opinion was not shared by Calles or by Generals Amaro and Ferreira. Warning the President against false optimism, Barba summarized the situation in Jalisco, reiterating his belief that the Catholics would rebel and that pro-government elements would be overwhelmed without the presence of a strong Federal force. "Under these disastrous conditions," he told Calles, "I don't think I should accept the enormous responsibility of such a weak government.... I sincerely believe that my sacrifice would serve no purpose."[10] Stripped of euphemism, Barba drew the line at being a puppet governor only if he thought he wasn't getting enough protection.

Calles, if not entirely convinced, was at least responsive to Barba's strongly felt convictions. Again he urged him to take the post. "I assure you," he said, "that you can count on the support of the Federal Army."[11] That was all Barba needed to hear; his fondest ambition would now be realized.

Though Barba's enemies would have loved to arrange his destiny along lines of a medieval morality play, there is no evidence that the "Judas" of *alteño* Catholicism ever suffered greatly for his defection. In 1929, right after the rebellion, he helped incorporate the Jalisco Liberal Party into the National Revolutionary Party (PNR), that perpetually dominant political aggregation later known as the PRI (Institutional Revolutionary Party). He also served two terms in the state legislature as deputy from Tepatitlán and, later, as Minister of Labor under President Cárdenas. When he died in 1967, he lacked for nothing in wealth and honors. A high school in Tepatitlán was named after him.

The other prominent tactical collaborators were Quirino Navarro and Mónico Velázquez. Both were from Tepatitlán and from strongly Catholic families. Navarro, who served as municipal president of the city during the rebellion, was firmly on the Federal side as early as October 1926. During that month he defended Tepatitlán against a raid led by Velázquez and El Catorce.

Velázquez, a big, fair man (therefore known as "El Güero Mónico"), had been chief of police in Tepatitlán from 1922 to 1924. Ten years earlier he had organized a cavalry regiment in Jalisco and placed it under the orders of the *obregonista* General Enrique Estrada. Under his bluff *alteño* exterior, Velázquez was a skilled, devious intriguer who for a time operated as a double agent. Even while helping El Catorce harass Navarro, he was working in close underground contact with the Federals. In July of 1926 Velázquez wrote a long letter to Barba González giving detailed information on the Catholic resistance movement in Jalisco, such as the number of men involved, identity of their leaders, and focal points of incipient rebellion. Barba had the letter with him during his interview with Calles and read it to the President verbatim.[12] This document played a large part in influencing Calles to send massive troop reinforcements to Jalisco.

Obviously neither Navarro nor Velázquez was an ideologue. True condottieri, they served such diverse causes as liberal reform, Catholic activism, and radical anti-clericalism with fine impartiality. Though born (as was Barba) in the most Catholic part of Mexico, they were shrewd and politically experienced enough to realize that the unpopular central government was too strong not to win. Yet even a man of El Güero Mónico's icy temperament must have been moved by the fact that his sons fought with the *cristeros*.[13]

A far different type of collaborator was Víctor Contreras, a twenty-five-year-old native of San Miguel el Alto. Of comfortable petit bourgeois background, he was the son of a merchant and small landowner. Both parents, as well as Víctor's siblings, were pious Catholics.[14] Though *alteños* have always been notoriously clannish, Víctor, from early age, showed himself to be free from such parochial instincts. He made friends easily—not only with other *alteños*, but also with members of a group that was viewed with suspicion and shunned by the townspeople. These were government employees from Mexico City and Guadalajara and soldiers attached to the Federal garrison.

Víctor's friendship with the outsiders troubled his family. Their apprehension increased as he began to express opinions that shocked them profoundly. Born with a bright and inquiring mind, Víctor had long chafed under the rigid Catholicism of his *patria chica*. Association with these new companions, all skeptics and freethinkers, widened the breach between Víctor's ideas and those of his family. When the church-state crisis broke, Víctor found himself at a crossroads. Unhesitatingly he sided with his new friends. It was a crucial decision. Up to now he had been viewed as a smart-aleck nonconformist; he would henceforth be considered a traitor.

As is often the case, ostracism intensified defiance. He announced to his shamed and silent family that he was on the side of the government. Cut off from Catholic social life, Víctor began attending dances and fiestas given by his Federal cronies. Many of these functions were military and he was able to cultivate friendships with high-ranking officers, including colonels and generals. They were attracted by Víctor's intelligence and, even more so, by his dedication. Here was a young man so drawn to liberal and anti-clerical doctrines that he was willing to live on in his home town as a virtual pariah. Anyone that motivated could obviously be put to use.

Víctor became an active Federal partisan in early August of 1926. The churches had just closed down and the Ley Calles was being applied with increasing severity. Unlike Mónico Velázquez, Víctor was too well known a government sympathizer to be used in an undercover capacity. His job was to act as the eyes, ears, and nose of the occupying forces. He would gather information from agents, furnish the names of actual or potential rebels to the authorities, and help ferret out centers of clandestine religious activity.

Víctor was an excellent bloodhound. It was customary, after the rebellion broke out, for *cristeros* to take periodic leaves from their units. These furloughs were used to supplement family income by doing a little farming or day labor. With his native-son background, Víctor had an unerring ability to spot the seemingly innocuous farm worker or casual laborer who might that very night be heading back to his unit in the sierra. These men were discreetly placed under surveillance. Then, on their way out of town, they were apprehended and shot.

Víctor was also responsible for detecting the whereabouts of a secret community of nuns. Soldiers invaded their hiding place and placed them all under arrest. According to *cristero* sources, some of the younger sisters were raped.[15]

Knowing how bitterly he was hated, Víctor stuck close to his protectors and never ventured far from the center of town. But one day he grew careless and went unescorted to a small ranch just beyond the city limits. His exit was noted by a rebel lookout and, by methods ironically similar to Víctor's own, word quickly got out to the sierra. At the ranch he was seized by a raiding party from El Catorce's regiment.

When he reached the *cristero* camp, in the Cerro del Carretero, Víctor found himself looking into the faces of men whom he had known from infancy. In not one of these faces did he detect a glimmer of pity. His execution was delayed only by the fact that so many of his boyhood friends vied for the privilege of being assigned to his firing squad.

The intensity of Víctor Contreras's conviction is as remarkable as the magnitude of his betrayal. No opportunist, no tactical collaborator, could have continued living among a people who so fiercely detested him. True, Quirino Navarro served as puppet mayor of Tepatitlán throughout the rebellion, but the situations were different. Tepatitlán, the capital of Los Altos, was only forty-three miles from Guadalajara. It was protected by a large Federal garrison, supplemented by an *agrarista* force that served as Navarro's personal bodyguard. Then there were the swarms of civil officials and bureaucrats, constantly shuttling in from Guadalajara and Mexico City. San Miguel, by contrast, was a frontier outpost. Barba, in Guadalajara, and Navarro and Velázquez, in Tepatitlán, can never have known the loneliness of Víctor Contreras, who walked like a leper among those who had once loved him.

There were two types of collaborators through greed—the profiteers and the thugs. An example of the former is reflected in the speculators who descended on starving refugees, buying their chickens for five cents and their pigs for a dollar, during the *reconcentración*. The latter were young hooligans and delinquents who flourished under Federal occupation. Unlike Víctor Contreras, who was educated enough to embrace anti-clericalism intellectually, these toughs became local quislings for reasons that had nothing to do with ideology. Some were simply bored, others wanted to tweak the noses of authority figures, still others used their new-found power as a means of seducing hitherto unattainable girls.

Of this aggregate, one of the best remembered was a disagreeable young man named Salvador Martín. Known as "El Bombín" because of his fondness for derby hats, he was a native of San Miguel el Alto. In May of 1927 San Miguel was occupied by General Limón's regiment of Presidential Guards. Father Fermín Padilla, the town's parish priest, was being hidden within the city limits, and Martín had smoked out his hiding place. On reporting this discovery to General Limón, he received an unpleasant surprise. Limón, unlike such clerophobes as Generals Vargas and Ortiz (who had a soldier shot for wearing a religious medal), was a nonpolitical professional soldier. Coldly informing El Bombín that he was pursuing rebels, not priests, he ordered him out of his office.[16]

On 27 June 1928, Martín had an experience similar to the one that caused the downfall of Víctor Contreras: he was seized by a band of *cristeros* and taken to their camp. But he fared better than Víctor. The rebels who apprehended him were members of the San Gaspar regiment, which operated in a zone west of San Miguel. While Víctor's captors had all known him from infancy, El Bombín was a stranger to these men. Thinking they had picked up a harmless civilian, they let him go after a brief interrogation.[17] This act was not calculated to inspire gratitude among the people of San Miguel.

Once back in his home town, Martín resumed his jackal career. On 3 March 1929, he capriciously shot a rebel sympathizer who had been caught by soldiers cutting a telephone line. The soldiers had apprehended the man on their way from Lagos to San Miguel and were planning to take him to the latter destination for questioning.[18] This incident took place on the eve of a military rising against Calles. During this new rebellion, which was suppressed in a few weeks, Los Altos was evacuated by the Federals and such main population centers as Tepatitlán, Arandas, and San Miguel el Alto temporarily reverted to *cristero* control. It is safe to assume that El Bombín either fled town or went into hiding during this interim.

The Federals re-occupied San Miguel on 12 April and Martín lost no time in again making his presence felt. The next incident took place on 20 April. Susano Ortega, a puritanical Catholic, was exercised over the fact that some San Miguel girls were bobbing their hair and wearing short skirts. Imprudently, he took it upon himself to upbraid a girl in public for her moral laxity. These fulminations were overheard by El Bombín and a friend named Hermenegildo. Interrupting Ortega in mid-tirade, they brutally beat him up and threw him in the city jail.[19]

Three days later Martín had the opportunity to work an even greater mischief. J. Jesús Delgado, a suspected *cristero* civil official, was captured on the slopes of the Cerro de la Llave by a Federal patrol. Taken to San Miguel, he was accused by El Bombín of being Father Vega's secretary. Put to torture, he admitted to being a *cristero* but denied Martín's accusation. Then his ordeal suddenly ceased. The Army was adopting a more humane policy in these final days of the rebellion and Delgado suffered no worse fate than to be exiled to San Luis Potosí.[20]

Just before the rebellion ended El Bombín became an *agrarista* officer. He figured in two clashes with the rebels, one on 7 June and one on 5 July. In the latter engagement he is said to have turned tail and run.[21] After that, nothing is heard of him except that he left San Miguel forever. One unverified report states that he changed his name and went to Mexico City; another, simply that he "went north," presumably to the United States. Neither version has been authenticated.

THE RESISTANCE MOVEMENT

The *alteño* resistance movement compels attention for the fact that it operated under conditions that were as adverse psychologically as they were materially. The resisters in Los Altos did not have the comfort of outside allies. The only foreign power involved, the United States, was arming and supplying their enemy. Yet, in the face of supreme adversity, the ranchers and farmers of Los Altos produced an exemplary resistance movement, one whose dedication was matched by its effectiveness. According to *cristero* civil government directives, those who voluntarily paid taxes to the "*callista* faction" and "tax collectors of the criminal usurper regime" would be considered "collaborators and accomplices of tyranny."[22] Having sternly defined the limits of treason, the rebel military and civil chiefs set out to organize resistance. They were working fertile soil. All the potential was there—it was simply a case of using it in the most efficient manner.

A continuing problem confronting the rebels was the attitude of rich Catholics. It is perhaps harsh to call them collaborators. If one did, it would be necessary to classify a fourth category—that of collaborators through fear. Unlike the profiteers and speculators who collaborated through greed, few of the *acomodados* were out to enrich themselves at the expense of their poorer co-religionists. They were simply interested in holding on to what they had. Luis Rivero del Val is the author of a realistic novel based on the diary of Manuel Bonilla, *cristero* leader in the Sierra de Ajusco. The feelings of the *cristeros* concerning the rich are captured in the words of his protagonist: "Catholics?" asks a Colima *cristero*. "Who knows? They're the ones who years ago complained about the Revolution and now ally themselves with the revolutionaries to maintain their privileges. They deny all assistance to our cause, they won't even help our orphans or wounded."[23]

Non-cooperation was only one part of the picture. The self-protective zeal of the *acomodados* led them frequently into acts of commission as well as those of omission. In Jalostotitlán the hacendado José Dolores called in troops after he learned that his foreman had been aiding the *cristeros*. The man was shot and Dolores, fearing reprisals, arranged for a bodyguard of soldiers to be lodged on his property.[24]

Actions like these did much to intensify *cristero* animus against rich Catholics. Of all the rural *cristero* leaders, only sixteen were *acomodados* and, of this total, only three were hacendados.[25] So—mutual Catholicism notwithstanding—it wasn't difficult for resistance leaders to persuade the embattled poor of Los Altos to make life miserable for the disloyal and self-protective rich. One of the first victims was Padilla Cruz, a wealthy Tepatitlán merchant. Kidnaped and held for ransom, he was shot on 25 February 1927, when payment was not forthcoming.[26]

Another method used by the rebels to collect taxes from rich Catholics was blockade. The *cristeros*, masters of the countryside, were able to obstruct trade by preventing entry and exit of all goods but the most essential foodstuffs into Federal-held towns. In making these exactions, the rebels made sure never to do anything that might alienate the poor. They followed this policy so faithfully that at times they allowed the *acomodados* to escape rather than cause suffering to the innocent. An example is the case of the enormously rich Braniff family, who owned land near Jalpa de Cánovas. Enjoying Federal protection, the Braniffs refused to pay taxes to the *cristeros* civil government. General Gorostieta, the new rebel commander, wanted to blow up a dam on the Braniff property. But he was dissuaded by Víctor López and Gómez Loza. Such a move, they argued, would flood the fields of neighboring campesinos and aggravate their already intense suffering.[27] (The second *reconcentración* was then in progress.)

The rebels also cracked down hard on *cristero* soldiers found guilty of fleecing the poor. El Catorce had a man shot for stealing corn from campesinos. Father Pedroza court-martialed some of his men who had been stopping mule drivers on the road between Arandas and Atotonilco and charging tolls.[28]

This enlightened policy paid off handsomely. Los Altos civilians outdid themselves to cooperate with the rebels. Especially appreciative of this support were area combat commanders. Luis Luna (his nom de guerre was Manuel Ramírez de Olivas) who led the San Gaspar regiment, warmly praised the attitude of civilians in Encarnación de Díaz, the largest community in his sector: "Encarnación de Díaz," he wrote, "was a town very drawn to our movement;...the underground organization was [one] of the best."[29]

Another military leader who benefited from friendly civilian support was Father Pedroza. His network of operatives included several telegraphers. He frequently received messages destined for Generals Figueroa, Cedillo, and Avila Camacho before they did themselves. In his archives are a number of key telegrams sent out at the height of the rebellion.[30]

The BBs

No coverage of the resistance movement in Los Altos—and other *cristero*-held areas—would be complete without mention of a group called the Brigadas Femeninas de Santa Juana de Arco (Feminine Brigades of St. Joan of Arc). This was the *cristero* women's auxiliary, known familiarly and fondly as the

BBs. It was composed of young Catholic women, most of them between fifteen and twenty-five, who acted as nurses, spies, couriers, propagandists, and as an informal but highly effective service of supply. Women were less likely to be searched than men and many a seeming *campesina* on her way from Guadalajara to the countryside was a BB member with fresh cartridges sewed into the lining of her voluminous dress.

Initially the BBs were an offshoot from a Guadalajara women's syndicate called the Union de Empleadas Católicas (Union of Catholic Employees). The parent group, an affiliate of the UP, was founded by a lawyer named Luis Flores González and María Goyaz, daughter of the editor of *El Cruzado*, a Catholic publication. The UEC's membership was predominantly urban lower-middle and working class, and it was concentrated mainly among office and clerical workers, salesgirls, and dress shop employees.[31] The BBs were officially founded on 21 June 1927, in the outlying town of Zapópan. The Zapópan Cathedral houses one of the most famous Virgins in Mexico, and it was before her image that a founding group of seventeen constituted themselves into the First Brigade.[32]

The guiding spirit behind the BBs was Anacleto González Flores. Though he died before their formal inauguration, the Maestro had always been a believer in the political efficacy of women. Impressed by the service they rendered during the boycott, Anacleto, shortly before his death, selected some girls from the UEC and suggested that they organize a special unit to aid the rebels in the field.[33]

From the modest beginning at Zapópan, BB membership grew to 25,000.[34] This total was apportioned among twenty-six brigades, eighteen in west-central Mexico and eight in and around Mexico City. Organization was along military lines and the BBs counted five generals, including founder María Goyaz. So successful were the BBs at operating clandestinely that not one member was arrested until the last days of March 1929. As late as the twenty-sixth of that month the American military attaché could report to Washington that "as yet no definite organization supplying arms to the rebels has been discovered."[35] Another impressive testimonial to the BBs' discretion is the fact that one of their generals, Luz María Laraza de Uribe, was married to a traveling salesman who was unaware of her activities from beginning to end.[36]

The BBs were particularly active in Los Altos. Of eighteen brigades dispersed through the seven-state area comprising west-central Mexico, seven operated out of towns in or adjacent to the *alteño* region: Zapotlán, Atotonilco, Tepatitlán, Tonalá, Ocotlán, and two in Arandas. Moreover, all of the five generals were natives of Jalisco.[37]

Along with the ammunition they sewed into their dresses, the BBs also handled arms and explosives. These implements of war were concealed in carts, hidden in bundles of hay, and at times transmitted to the rebels through bribery of an ever-corruptible foe. As a result of these activities, some BBs died violently. The best-known incident, in Colima, claimed the life of General Sara Flores Arias. On 11 November 1927, she and two comrades were manufacturing grenades at the *cristeros* camp on the Colima Volcano. A sudden explosion killed all three BBs and Dionisio Ochoa, rebel commander in that state.[38]

Every sizable *cristero* field unit had a BB officer who attended to matters of supply. In Los Altos, Elodia Delgado served as Lauro Rocha's quartermaster; in the south, Degollado was provisioned by Lola Castillo.[39] The Los Altos BBs functioned as nurses as well as quartermasters. Lightly wounded men were treated in the field; the more seriously injured (like Lauro Rocha after the Battle of San Julián) were smuggled into Guadalajara or smaller communities and secretly nursed to health in private houses. (They could not be sent to city hospitals without arousing suspicion.) The BBs performed nursing services at primitive field hospitals in Los Altos, southern Jalisco, and Colima.[40] Best-known of these facilities in Los Altos was the "Hotel Palmitos," subject of an entire chapter in Heriberto Navarrete's technically fictional but almost entirely historical *El Voto de Chema Rodríguez*.

Regrettably the BBs became involved, through no fault of their own, in a controversy with other elements in the Catholic camp. The Liga, based in the Federal District, was unhappy because only eight of the twenty-six BB brigades were operating there. The BBs also offended a section of the clergy, one who believed they were violating the Vatican's injunction against secret societies. Father Leobardo Fernández, a Jesuit, meddled so heavy-handedly in BB affairs that Archbishop Orozco y Jiménez secured his removal from the Guadalajara archdiocese.[41]

Liga and clerical harassment hampered BB activities in the field and the effects of this bickering were particularly felt in Los Altos. General Gorostieta, the new rebel commander, spent much of his time in that key sector and was greatly angered by the controversy. When Carmen Macías came under attack, Gorostieta strongly defended her. He coldly informed the LNDLR that "if it had not been for the service of supply that I organized for each regiment...during the last quarrel between you and the BBs, we would all have succumbed."[42]

Though the BBs' role was essentially noncombatant, the dedication of these women at times resulted in direct action of the most violent kind. One such incident involved a former nursemaid in the Obregón household, known as "La Yaca." La Yaca stabbed to death a schismatic priest, Felipe Pérez, who was believed to be a government spy.[43]

The BBs were dissolved at the end of the rebellion. Much vital information about their activities has been lost to history because their archives were deliberately burned. This act was performed by Father Miguel Darío Miranda, later cardinal and Primate of Mexico, on the order of Bishop Pascual Díaz.[44] (The destruction of the archives may be interpreted as a gesture of appeasement on the part of Díaz or as an attempt to destroy evidence that might link BB activities to members of the hierarchy.)

The Role of Federal Corruption

The role played by Federal corruption in keeping resistance alive in Los Altos and elsewhere should not be underestimated. Carleton Beals has described the shakedowns of wealthy *alteño* ranchers during *reconcentración*, disguised as "voluntary contributions" to the Federal Social Defense Fund. Corruption didn't stop there. Some transactions were clearly treasonable, involving disclosure of vital information and even outright sale of arms and ammunition to the rebels:

A man in an embroidered leather jacket, tall gray-braided sombrero, and skin-tight trousers and an officer sit in a Guadalajara cantina over tequila. Says the officer with a leer, "Next Tuesday, 2,000 rounds of cartridges, five machine guns, and 200 rifles will arrive in [the *alteño* village of] Actopán. The Federal garrison will then be reduced to fifteen men."

"In that case, the Viva Cristo Rey rebels will very likely attack the town," chuckles the other. "They can well use such supplies."
Twenty-five thousand [pesos] in bills change hands. The officer visits the nearest jewelry store, buys his newest sweetheart a 2,000-peso ring, and telegraphs 200 pesos to his wife and five children in Mexico City."[45]

While some of these arrangements were made through middlemen (or through the auspices of the BBs), others were actually transacted between combatants in the field. For example, Lauro Rocha was in secret contact with the commanding officer of the 74th Cavalry Regiment, stationed in Atotonilco. He or one of his men would make regular trips to town to procure ammunition; the go-between was a sacristan.[46] For the Federal commander, this was a highly profitable business. He would sell, say, 15,000 rifle cartridges to the *cristeros* and then immediately order his troops into action. Another 5,000 would be expended in an inconclusive skirmish and the commander would requisition 20,000 more rounds at a unit cost of 15 centavos.[47] There was, of course, a considerable markup on resale price to the rebels.

The scarcity of collaborators—combined with the multiplicity and devotion of resisters—prevented the rebellion in Los Altos from being extinguished during the time following the first *reconcentración* in the spring of 1927. But the *alteño* resistance movement was more than just a mechanism of survival. With the coming of 1928 it began to furnish its beneficiaries, the armed *cristeros*, with a clear hope of victory.

Gorostieta

The Caudillo *As* Liberal

THE LEADERLESSNESS OF THE *CRISTERO* REBELLION was a factor that had both positive and negative aspects. This absence of an indispensable *caudillo* existed on both civil and military levels. On the positive side, removal of a single person did not cause the end of the movement. René Capistrán Garza was exiled, and Anacleto González Flores, in hiding, became the most dangerous rebel. After his death the infrastructure he began stayed alive through the efforts of Miguel Gómez Loza. General Gallegos, a regular soldier, was ambushed in Guanajuato, but Colonel Victoriano Ramírez reignited resistance in Los Altos. On the negative side, various branches of the *cristeros* often worked against each other. For example, the Liga, trying to exercise overall leadership, worked at cross purposes with the nominally subordinate (but far better organized) UP. Confusion thus bred both strength and weakness.

It was finally decided that such a chaotic situation could no longer be tolerated. Perhaps never in history had a national insurrection been so slow in producing a leader. The decision to seek one was made by the LNDLR in 1927. The time element

[105]

is important because it had the most profound influence on the Liga's eventual choice. Mid-summer of that year, with the rebellion on the brink of extinction, was a time when most (though not all) of the *ligueros* were stressing pragmatism at the expense of ideology. It was the heyday of the Unión Nacional flirtation, of soft-pedaling the Catholic aspect of the rebellion, of widening its base to include liberals and anti-*callista* revolutionaries. Most *ligueros* had had their fill of well-intentioned Catholic zealots; what they wanted now was a competent *técnico* (expert) to put their flagging movement on a sound professional basis. The name of Enrique Gorostieta Velarde was proposed to the LNDLR by Bartolomé Ontiveros, a Guadalajara *liguero*. The two had known each other a long time and Ontiveros was convinced that Gorostieta was the man to bring the moribund rebellion back to life.[1]

Born in 1890, Gorostieta was a native of Monterrey and descended from one of the heroes of the Spanish Independence War against Napoleon. After attending the Colegio Hidalgo in his home state, he graduated with high honors from the Colegio Militar de Chapultepec (Mexico's West Point). His specialty was artillery and he also demonstrated a keen aptitude for the physical sciences.

Of *porfirista* inclination, Gorostieta lent his services to Victoriano Huerta after Madero's overthrow. Rising to the rank of general, he served the dictator against both Pascual Orozco and Emiliano Zapata. He also helped resist American intervention at Veracruz. After Huerta's defeat he went into exile, having no use for either Carranza or Obregón. His first destination was Cuba, followed by the United States. Granted amnesty, he returned to Mexico and used his knowledge of chemistry to secure employment as an engineer with a soap company. Bored with this uninspiring work and missing the challenge of military life, Gorostieta was ripe for the Liga's offer when it came.

His decision to accept the offer had nothing to do with Catholicism. Gorostieta was a man of the Enlightenment, a skeptical, anti-clerical liberal. He was certainly a Mason though he may not, as some detractors claim, have reached the exalted thirty-third degree.[2] Though he had little love for the Church—a distaste that would increase as the rebellion progressed—his special rancor was reserved for the 1917 Revolution. The chaos, the discord, the ravaging bands of campesinos, the puffed-up illiterates who called themselves generals—all of these things had resulted from the Revolution and were repugnant to the orderly mind of a man who combined soldierly professionalism with gradualist political doctrines.

Admiring chroniclers, most of them Catholic, have found it convenient to claim that Gorostieta came to the *cristero* rebellion an anti-clerical but later became a convinced religious believer. There is no evidence to support this contention. True, he took to wearing a large crucifix in the field but this was little more than window dressing for the benefit of his Catholic campesino soldiers—like the "sincere" tie worn by advertising men on Madison Avenue. If anything, Gorostieta's antipathy toward Catholicism increased during his participation in the *cristiada*. A number of examples come to mind—his venomous sarcasm toward the Liga and hierarchy, his contempt for Father Vega as a representative of the clergy, his repeated practice of ridiculing the religious observances of his unlettered troops.[3]

Inevitably, such behavior brought Gorostieta into disrepute with his more pious colleagues. Miguel Palomar y Vizcarra, Knight of St. Gregory and pillar of Jalisco Catholicism, was particularly offended by his irreverence. "Gorostieta is careless with his tongue in front of the people who make up his forces," wrote Palomar to Luis Bustos. "He attacks the prelates...[and] he shows contempt for religious practices."[4]

GOROSTIETA AND THE *CRISTEROS*

How could such an unlikely individual rise to the leadership of an armed Catholic rebellion? When Gorostieta decided to accept the Liga's offer, he tried to induce two fellow ex-officers, Colonel Ignacio Muñoz and General Luis Velasco, to join him. Though foes of the Revolution, Velasco and Muñoz were, like Gorostieta, liberal and anti-clerical. Both refused. "Neither of us is Catholic," said Muñoz to Gorostieta. "What are we going to do in this movement?"[5]

One reason for Gorostieta's adhesion to "this movement" was his hatred of the results of the Revolution. This reason was closely related to another. Like many educated Latin military men, Gorostieta was a man of vaulting ambition. This ambition was, in good part, based on a realistic appreciation of his considerable talents. Along with military and scientific

aptitudes, Gorostieta was well-grounded in history, philosophy, and political theory, and he never doubted that he could
govern better than Obregón, Calles, or any *obregonista* or
callista who might succeed to power. His dream was of a
reformed *porfiriato*, an efficient, technocratic authoritarian-
liberal state in which the worker, the businessman, the campesino, and the military labored harmoniously in the national
interest. Civil liberties would be preserved (as long as they
didn't tend toward a new revolution); revolution itself would
be harshly suppressed. As for the Catholics, on whose backs
he planned to ride into Mexico City, they would enjoy religious freedom but within rigidly secular parameters. Political Catholicism, especially if it challenged separation of
church and state, would be viewed with the most jaundiced
eye. As the war progressed, and the rebels began to think
increasingly in political terms, these views of Gorostieta
clearly surfaced. Should the society he dreamed of be established, there is no doubt that Gorostieta saw himself at the
helm—as military dictator, as constitutional president, or,
more likely, in both roles, with the first preceding and paving
the way for the second.

There is a final reason why Gorostieta decided to join the
rebellion: he came to the war as a handsomely paid mercenary.
The Liga had authorized a monthly salary of 3,000 pesos in
gold, plus a 20,000 peso insurance policy to be paid to his wife
in the event of his death in action.[6] By contrast, a Federal
divisional general received only 1,620 pesos a month.

Though Gorostieta was designated to take command in
Los Altos, he didn't fight his first engagement there until early
1928. Between his appointment in July 1927 and the end of the
year, he was kept shuttling around in a baffling manner. Part
of the confusion was caused by Liga ineptitude and unfamiliarity with the geography of western Mexico. (An example was the LNDLR's farcical order to the Querétaro *cabecilla*
Manuel Frias, commanding him to attack a railhead a thousand miles away.) Even the wording in Gorostieta's orders was
confused. His command area read "Jalisco," while it should
have been "Los Altos." (The rest of the state was already
under control of General Degollado's División del Sur.)

Gorostieta was the victim of more than simple blunder-
ing. The controversial new chieftain caused prominent
ligueros to work furiously at cross purposes. While a majority

wanted to speed him into action immediately, a powerful minority was so displeased with his ideology that they actively obstructed him. One of the latter group was the *acejotamero* Mauricio Baz, who complained to the Liga that Gorostieta was trying to get rid of ACJM officers and replace them with ranchers. "Once victory is obtained," he worried, "he will return to the times of Porfirian liberalism."[7] While the accusation is undoubtedly true, it understandably glosses over another important reason why Gorostieta preferred battle-tested campesinos and, later, liberal-Masonic professional soldiers as comrades in arms. However pure their Catholicism, most of these young ideologues weren't much good in combat. (The only exceptions were *acejotameros* of campesino origin.) "Los catrines no sirven en el campo para nada (The swells are worthless in the field)," said Aurelio Acevedo.[8]

Caught between pragmatists and purists in the LNDLR, Gorostieta experienced maddening frustrations in his efforts to take the field. He was first sent to the city of Zacatecas, far north of his designated command area. There, in a hotel, he waited two weeks for a contact who never showed up. He went to Guadalajara, awaited further orders, and a Liga guide again conducted him to Zacatecas—not to the capital this time, but out to the extreme southern part of the state, a land of gorges and canyons that faces south toward Guadalajara and east toward Los Altos. This sector was controlled by the Libres de Jalpa, an independent regiment that operated between the "Three Finger" zone and Los Altos.

By this time Gorostieta was so impatient that he was willing to fight anywhere, whether or not the area was under his official jurisdiction. More than six weeks had passed since he had left Mexico City to assume his command and, apart from dodging Federal patrols, he had done no soldiering at all.

His baptism of fire, on 14 September 1927, took place at the Mesa del Coyote near government-held Jalpa. Gorostieta, in charge of 250 men, was holding this small plateau against 600 advancing Federals from Colonel José Ortiz's 75th Regiment. The *callista* assault on the mesa began at 1500 and continued until nightfall. For several hours the rebels held, denying Ortiz's troops access to the mesa. At dusk the *cristeros* withdrew in good order to a higher elevation, the Cerro Alto. The 75th renewed the attack the following morning but could make no headway against this loftier redoubt. This surprising show of rebel strength in what had not been considered an important theater caused the Army chief of operations in Zacatecas, General Anacleto López, to send an urgent telegram to Mexico City requesting help. The message was intercepted by Gorostieta.[9]

By 23 October Gorostieta felt strong enough to mount an attack on Jalpa. In initial control of the operation was Colonel Jose María Gutiérrez, whose commission had just been made official by Gorostieta. (Like Carlos Blanco, he was authorized by the LNDLR to award grades and commissions.)[10] Gutiérrez's task force, made up of about 100 men, began the attack at 1900. Defending Jalpa were elements of the 75th Regiment and a contingent of local collaborators.

Jalpa did not fall easily. The following day, at 1000, Gorostieta arrived with another 150 men and took charge of the battle. The Federals held out another twenty-six hours. By noon of 25 October it was all over and Jalpa was in rebel hands. All Federal prisoners, 48 in number, were released except for a captain who had ordered a *cristero* decapitated during a 16 August clash at the Mesa de Alagunas. The captain was shot.[11]

Gorostieta continued to operate in Zacatecas through the end of 1927. On 3 to 4 November, at the head of 250 men, he beat back a 1,000-man Federal-*agrarista* force in the Sierra de Morones, near Tlaltenango. On the 17th he led 800 men in a train raid near Palmira. The take, to his great disappointment, was only 17,000 pesos.[12] December (1927) and most of January (1928) saw him on an inspection tour of the "Three Finger" zone. There he awarded Quintanar the rank of general, ratified his authority over the five regiments he had been commanding, and appointed Vicente Viramontes civil chief for the sector. Gorostieta's final action with the Zacatecas *cristeros* took place on 31 January. Reunited with the Libres de Jalpa, he led a successful attack against El Teul.[13]

On 14 February, in Moyahua, Gorostieta bade farewell to the Zacatecas troops and picked up a 200-man *alteño* escort under Major Gabino Alvarez. The party moved south to Ixtlahuacán del Río and on the following day crossed the Santiago River into Los Altos. After more than six months of incredible—though by no means futile—delay Gorostieta finally arrived in his command sector. While the useful service he rendered in Zacatecas pleased some elements in the Liga, grumbling was still heard from the powerful ultra-clerical minority over the fact that these victories had been won by "an impious, blaspheming thirty-third degree Mason."[14]

In Zacatecas Gorostieta had shown himself both an organizer and a man of action. His organizational work in the "Three Finger" sector effectively complemented his combat role in other areas. This dual function was repeated on a far larger scale in Los Altos. By the end of February Gorostieta was convinced that the rebellion was going well enough for the *cristeros* to abandon guerrilla warfare and take on the Federals in set-piece battles. Even without Gorostieta the *alteños* had been performing so creditably that General Ferreira, Federal commander in Jalisco, was removed from his post and replaced by General Andrés Figueroa. This top-level shake-up took place on 24 January 1928. Once the transition to conventional warfare was completed, Gorostieta planned to deploy the Los Altos and Zacatecas forces in a grand offensive against the *bajío*, breadbasket of the Republic and key to Mexico City.

Two elements were needed to transform the *cristeros* into a force capable of seizing the *bajío*: ammunition and organization.[15] The cartridges would have to be supplied by the Liga. Gorostieta placed a request on 26 February, estimating his need at three million rounds.[16] In doing so, he must have had misgivings about the Liga's ability to deliver. It can be safely assumed that Gómez Loza told him about the missing 25,000 pesos in tax money.

In the meantime, Gorostieta planned to further the organizational work among the *alteño* troops that had been started at the Palmitos summit. Despite a promising beginning there was still a lot of work to do. The command structure was loose, and, though units were generally identified with a given sector, there was no well-defined operational zone system. Gorostieta's first move was to fix these limits. Scrapping the informal regionalism that had prevailed up to that time, he created a six-regiment force, to be known as the Brigada de Los Altos, plus an independent regiment that would act as liaison between the Brigada and the Zacatecas *cristeros*. Each regiment would remain in its own operational zone unless it received a request for aid from a neighboring unit and was ordered out of its sector by higher authority.[17]

The autonomous regiment, known as San Gaspar, patrolled the section of Los Altos nearest to Zacatecas. Its role was flexible and, depending on military exigency, San Gaspar worked with either the Brigada or the Zacatecas rebels. Commanding this unit, with the rank of colonel, was Manuel Ramírez de Olivas.[18]

Five of the Brigada's regiments have already been identified—Ayo under Father Pedroza, San Julián under Miguel Hernández (who had since returned from the United States), San Miguel under El Catorce, Carabineros de Los Altos (also known as Ocotlán) under Rodolfo Loza Márquez, and Tepatitlán under Gabino Flores. To these Gorostieta added a new regiment (known both as Atotonilco and Guadalupe), headed by Gabino Alvarez, Gorostieta's escort commander when he left Zacatecas for Los Altos. On taking over his new regiment, Alvarez was promoted to colonel. Within a month the Tepatitlán and Atotonilco regiments had received new names. Miguel Gómez Loza had just been killed and, in his honor, Tepatitlán became Gómez Loza I and Atotonilco became Gómez Loza II. Following his return from the United States in June 1928, Father Vega was placed in overall command of the two Gómez Loza regiments.[19]

Knowing the importance of Los Altos, Gorostieta made it his headquarters for the rest of the rebellion. Working in close harmony with the Brigada, he not only reorganized the *alteño* forces but had ample opportunity to expose them to this particular style of leadership.

To some, this style was not entirely a blessing. Like George S. Patton, Gorostieta was far more kindly remembered by civilian admirers than by subordinates in the field. Handsome, blue-eyed, and ruddy-complexioned, he was at once a dashing and terrifying figure. "He reminded me of d'Artagnan," said René Capistrán Garza.[20] To dash and daring, Gorostieta added a dictatorial manner and a savage temper. Commanding men whose beliefs he despised, this authoritarian liberal forever destroyed the easygoing camaraderie that had prevailed among *alteño* troops. Rafael Martínez Camarena, though a civil official, took part in an action between elements of the Brigada and a Federal detachment led by General Miguel Z. Martínez:

> In this action our people for the first time received orders given in a harsh and despotic tone, orders which he [Gorostieta] always gave with a pistol in his hand, threatening to kill

anybody who wouldn't carry them out. This was a thing to which our soldiers were not accustomed.... From that day on our people felt the change. The loving words of their chiefs had been suddenly exchanged for the rude and imperious shouting of a vulgar soldier who imposed his authority in this manner.[21]

More harmonious was Gorostieta's relationship with Fathers Pedroza and Vega. The former accommodated himself to the general's ideological failings as readily as he had to Vega's moral ones. Their relations were always cordial, with Gorostieta showing the greatest respect for Pedroza's cold intelligence and capacity for command. The priest was one of the few *jefes* in Los Altos who escaped the dreaded tongue-lashings for which Gorostieta was famous. On one occasion, displeased with how his orders had been executed, the general angrily convoked his staff. "All of you, except for Father Pedroza, are a breed of insubordinates," he thundered. "I am ready to end this state of affairs by reducing in rank or, if necessary, shooting any officer who does not submit to discipline. And you should know right now that, if I die before him, Father Pedroza will be my successor as commander in Los Altos."[22] Though that commitment was fulfilled, the cause was not Gorostieta's death (which came later) but his elevation to supreme command over all rebel forces.

As for Father Vega, Gorostieta initially had serious misgivings about that improbable cleric. In June Rafael Martínez Camarena, who had been named interim governor following Gómez Loza's death, received a letter from the Liga. According to the letter, Vega had arrived in Mexico City and was planning to rejoin the rebellion. The communication instructed Martínez to make sure Vega didn't return to the combat zone, stating that "we *order* [underlined in the original] you to impede this individual from again rejoining the movement."[23] Martínez took the matter up with Gorostieta who, for once, agreed with the LNDLR's views completely. "If I see that priest I'll kill him," he told the governor.[24] Gorostieta suspected that Vega had been a party to the embezzlement of the funds taken during the El Limón train attack.

Vega arrived in Los Altos the following month and immediately requested a meeting with Gorostieta. Though what took place during the interview is not known, it is a matter of record that Gorostieta completely changed his attitude toward Vega. They left the meeting—according to Martínez— "in perfect harmony" and from then on Vega became one of Gorostieta's most trusted aides. Vega was a perfect foil for Gorostieta. On the one hand, he served him as a skilled and courageous subordinate; on the other, by personal example, he reinforced all of Gorostieta's prejudices against the Church. In Gorostieta's mind he completely separated his admiration for Colonel Vega from his contempt for Father Vega.

Pedroza and Vega, for their part, prudently chose to overlook Gorostieta's periodic acts of irreverence, such as an incident that took place in Arandas's San José Church. The *cristeros* had temporarily recaptured the town, and Gorostieta led a group of soldiers in to hear Mass. The service began and Gorostieta, with calculated insolence, stretched out on a back pew and smoked a cigarette. The sacrilege was witnessed by a youth named Juan Pérez, who later became San José's parish priest.

The interaction between Gorostieta, Vega, and Martínez emphasizes the general's role in civil government. Gorostieta resented Gómez Loza's autonomy; he wanted civil officials who obeyed him as blindly as his military officers. But for a time his hands were tied. Gómez Loza, considered the spiritual heir of the Maestro, was too independent to become a puppet of his Masonic-liberal military counterpart.

For Gorostieta, that period of frustration was very brief. He arrived in Los Altos in mid-February (1928); five weeks later Gómez Loza was dead. The circumstances leading to his death stemmed from the quarrel between the Liga and the BBs. The work of the feminine auxiliary was so hampered by LNDLR interference that the flow of ammunition delivered by the BBs to troops in the field had dropped off to a trickle.[25] Alarmed by the situation, Gómez Loza had decided to go to Guadalajara in an effort to straighten things out. Accompanied by an assistant, Macario Hernández, Gómez Loza had reached the vicinity of a hamlet called El Lindero, where he had an appointment with the *cristero* civil chief for Atotonilco. Surprised by a Federal patrol while on his way to the meeting, he and Hernández had been captured and shot.[26]

Following Gómez Loza's death, the Liga named Martínez Camarena his successor on 10 April. Like Gómez Loza, Martínez Camarena was an *alteño*, a Catholic activist, and strongly opposed to Gorostieta's liberalism, anti-clericalism, and authoritarian ways. The uneasy truce between the two men ended with the return of Father Vega. Following his meeting with Vega, Gorostieta furiously turned on Martínez. Charging him with misappropriation of the train raid funds, he placed the interim governor under arrest.[27]

It is doubtful if Gorostieta actually believed this accusation. Had a man of his choleric temperament been convinced of Martínez's guilt in a matter involving such a large sum, he certainly would have had him executed. More likely the accusation was a ploy to rid himself of Martínez so Gorostieta could make over the *alteño* civil infrastructure to his own liking. Martínez was held prisoner only a few hours and then released. Ordered to relinquish office and leave the combat zone, he was threatened with instant execution if he ever returned to Los Altos. Martínez went to Mexico City and made a report to the Liga. When his complaint was ignored he severed all connection with the movement.[28] Martínez's successors as civil chiefs in Los Altos, Agustín Sanchez and José Montes, were docile puppets of Gorostieta.[29]

Gorostieta was equally firm in disposing of military rivals. Carlos Blanco, city-bred and without military experience, had talked the Liga into awarding him a general's commission and designation as commander in Los Altos. (Though Gorostieta actually commanded there, his technical title was general in charge of Jalisco.) To add to the confusion, Lauro Rocha challenged Blanco's leadership. Though Rocha, at twenty, was fifteen years younger than Blanco, the former far surpassed the latter in combat experience. Twice wounded, Rocha had distinguished himself in some of the hardest fighting in the rebellion and did not look kindly to submitting to a *catrín* like Blanco. "The solution is that Carlos must go," he told his friend Heriberto Navarrete.[30]

Blanco, deft at intrigue, fought tenaciously to maintain his position. Though both he and Gorostieta enjoyed the Liga's full authority in awarding grades and commissions, it wasn't long before Blanco began trying to undermine his nominal chief. In November 1927, when Gorostieta was still in Zacatecas, he circulated the report that the general had pocketed funds captured during a train attack.[31] To this charge he added that Gorostieta was an opportunist and enemy of the movement who had hoodwinked the Liga.

Blanco's next step, taken just before Gorostieta's arrival in Los Altos, revealed his detachment from reality as much as his flair for conspiracy. On his own authority he issued a circular disbanding rebel forces in Los Altos. All fighting was to cease, weapons and stores were to be hidden, and the armed movement was to be suspended until a cadre of young officers (to be trained in clandestine military schools) was ready to lead a new rebellion.[32]

By this time the *alteño* leaders realized they were dealing with a dangerous fool as well as an intriguer. Gómez Loza immediately issued letters repudiating Blanco to every civil and military *jefe* in Los Altos.[33] Then, to counteract his influence at higher levels, he decided to go to Guadalajara for a meeting with local UP and Liga leaders. Accompanying Gómez Loza were Rocha and Navarrete.

The trip, as it turned out, wasn't necessary. It was mid-February, and, when the trio reached the Cerro Gordo, it encountered Gorostieta and his party who had just left Zacatecas. Gorostieta's arrival solved everything. Except for Luis Anaya, Father Vega's former aide, every *jefe* in Los Altos sided with the general and upheld Gómez Loza's repudiation of Blanco. Completely discredited in Los Altos, Blanco and Anaya traveled west and tried to set up an independent command in western Jalisco and Nayarit.[34] The attempt was a failure. By the end of March, Blanco was in the United States. There, in San Antonio, he joined the emigré ACJM community and helped prepare a shrill memorandum attacking the Unión Nacional plan and "the rag of '57" while paying tribute to the movement's "illustrious martyrs."[35] Ironically, in view of his relations with Blanco, one of these fulsomely lauded martyrs was Gómez Loza.

If Gorostieta was anxious to get rid of a troublemaking noncombatant like Blanco, he was equally eager to retain the services of Lauro Rocha, the other *jefe supremo* aspirant for Los Altos. He encountered no problem in this matter. Respecting Gorostieta as much as he had despised Blanco, Rocha willingly accepted his authority. He was posted to the Ayo regiment, as second-in-command to Father Pedroza. Later, when Pedroza was placed in charge of the Brigada de Los Altos, Rocha succeeded him as Ayo commander. Both Pedroza and Rocha ended the war as generals.

These last promotions took place on 28 October 1928—the feast day of Cristo Rey. The 1927 celebration had produced the Palmitos summit, and this one was even more significant. On that day Gorostieta was given supreme command over all rebel forces and the name of the *cristero* military organization was officially changed from Ejército Nacional Libertador (National Liberation Army) to Guardia Nacional (National Guard).[36]

THE PLAN DE LOS ALTOS

Gorostieta marked the occasion by launching his long awaited Manifesto to the Nation. This document, also known as the Plan de Los Altos, was a fifteen-point declaration of rebel aims, or—to put it more accurately—Gorostieta's aims. (The original draft had been written by Miguel Palomar y Vizcarra, but it was extensively rewritten by Gorostieta.)[37] The Plan represented a complete victory for Gorostieta's views over those of the Liga and the expatriate ACJM intransigents. While the two groups contemptuously denounced the "rag of '57," Gorostieta's manifesto called for reestablishment of the 1857 Constitution—minus the Reform Laws.

The Plan de Los Altos had several features in common with the Unión Nacional program that had so greatly offended Catholic diehards. Both manifestos based themselves on the 1857 Constitution, both promised to better the lot of the industrial worker and campesino, and both supported traditional democratic liberties. The main difference between the two plans was one of emphasis. While the Unión Nacional proposed a triumvirate (consisting of one liberal, one revolutionary, and one Catholic), the Plan de Los Altos divided power between the Directive Committee of the LNDLR and the "military chief" of the Guardia Nacional, that is, Gorostieta.[38] This arrangement was a radical departure. The movement had previously been led by that many-headed hydra, the Liga. Now one man, the military chief, had equal power with the entire LNDLR.

Gorostieta made sure that his nominal co-equal, the Liga's Directive Committee, did not interfere with his conduct of the war. Though he agreed in principle (Article 10) to the right of the Liga to eventually appoint a civil chief for the movement, this article effectively gave the National Guard commander veto power by stating that nobody could be named to the post who was not satisfactory to both the Directive Committee and the military chief. Article 11 further strengthened the generalissimo's position by giving him control in matters of war and finance, while Article 12 assigned him further veto power by denying the Liga's right to modify the plan without his approval.[39]

The salient feature of the Plan de Los Altos was its secularism. Virtually free of religious orientation, its only sop to the Catholics was a brief statement in Article IV to the effect that the manifesto was in line with the two petitions of September 1926 (one by the hierarchy, one by two million laymen), requesting reform of Articles 3, 5, 24, 27, and 130 of the 1917 Constitution. Since the Plan de Los Altos recognized only the 1857 Constitution (minus the Reform Laws), this was a case of offering the Catholics what they already had. The rest of the manifesto was a combination of classic liberalism, feminism (Article 6), vague pro-labor and pro-campesino rhetoric, and extremely specific provisions for extending the power of an ambitious military leader.

Acceptance of such a document was a great concession on the part of the LNDLR. Though the hearts of the *ligueros* were undoubtedly with the ACJM emigrés in San Antonio, they were hardheaded enough to realize that it was the Gorostietas and not the Carlos Blancos who would win the war for them. The Plan de Los Altos marked a dramatic change in the nature of the opposition. What had been a Catholic rebellion became a coalition rebellion embracing both Catholics and military men of the Gorostieta stripe—liberal, Masonic, anti-revolutionary and anti-clerical.

Profound changes were also taking place on the other side. Alvaro Obregón, defying the principle of no-reelection, had been chosen as president-elect on 1 July 1928. He was scheduled to take office on 1 December. Two weeks after his election he was assassinated in Mexico City by a young Catholic fanatic named José de León Toral. At first it was feared that Calles would use Obregón's assassination as a pretext to perpetuate himself in office. (Some *obregonistas* even suspected him of complicity in the murder.) But these fears were groundless. Though Calles had every intention of continuing as strong man of Mexico, he planned to do so without presidential trappings. On 1 September, in his annual message to Congress, Calles called on that body to choose an interim president until national elections could be held. (Since the presidential term had been increased from four to six years, these were scheduled for November 1929.)

The man chosen was Emilio Portes Gil, former governor of Tamaulipas and secretary of *gobernación* (internal affairs) at the time of his selection. Since Portes Gil was considered more conciliatory toward the Church than Calles, the peacemakers, whose efforts had been dealt a serious blow by Obregón's assassination, began to regain hope. On 21 November (1928), less than a month after Gorostieta's manifesto, the Mexican hierarchy issued a collective letter in San Antonio which went so far as to praise part of Calles's message to Congress. What they wanted, the bishops insisted, was not a Catholic government but "a friendly separation of church and state."[40] The following day, just after leaving Rome, Archbishop Ruiz y Flores announced that the Pope was in favor of negotiations without insisting on reform of the restrictive laws as a precondition.[41] Portes Gil's inauguration was only nine days away and the peace Catholics were clearly viewing his accession with optimism.

Thus, there was a curious irony: as the hierarchy moved toward settlement and conciliation, a new breed of hard-liners was developing within the rebel movement. Led by Gorostieta, it included that small but growing nucleus of liberal-Masonic officers that he was enthusiastically recruiting into the Guardia Nacional. So there now existed not one, but two groups of last-ditch intransigents: the ACJM exiles and the Jacobin officers who began joining the rebellion after the Plan de Los Altos. For the former, this situation must have been a spiritual crucible. Here they were, paladins of the Church and foes of liberalism, anti-clericalism, and Masonry; here was the Church moving steadily toward accommodation with a hated revolutionary government; and—worst of all— here they were on the sidelines while a collection of liberals, anti-clericals, and Masons was increasingly taking direction of *their* war.

If the Catholic ideologues winced at the presence of these newcomers, the campesinos and rancheros made no such fine distinctions. The only objections they raised were practical ones, based on misgivings that the non-Catholic officers might be spies and infiltrators. On 29 March 1929 (Good Friday), four Federals who had gone over to the rebels were about to be inducted into the Brigada de Los Altos at Tepatitlán. The ceremony would be public and Gorostieta himself would officiate in awarding them commissions and assignments. But two veteran Brigada officers objected. How did Gorostieta know this wasn't a ruse? How could he be sure that the four apparent renegades weren't acting as bait for the same kind of trap Zapata fell into in Morelos? Gorostieta brushed aside the warnings: he had known all four men a long time and trusted them implicitly. He was correct in this estimate and the movement gained the services of Generals Urquizo and Barrios, Colonel José López, and Major Fernando Martínez.[42] Another able officer recruited by Gorostieta was General José Posada Ortiz, who led the rebellion in eastern Guanajuato and Querétaro during the last months of the war.[43]

However harsh his discipline and impure his ideology, there can be no doubt that Gorostieta's presence in Los Altos acted as a tonic. As early as 2 March 1928, two weeks after he had taken command, the American consul in Guadalajara reported that "conditions have grown steadily worse"; the same memorandum described Federal troop movements as "hysterical and ineffective."[44] This period between mid-February and mid-March saw Gorostieta progressing impressively toward his objective of getting the *Brigada* out of guerrilla operations and into conventional warfare. Larger numbers of troops were deployed in *cristero* actions and increasingly important objectives were assaulted. On 10 March Father Pedroza led 500 men in a bold attack against San Juan de los Lagos. After annihilating the local garrison, they followed their normal practice of abandoning the town.[45] Though the *cristeros* were still unable to hold larger population centers, they were strong enough to defend their Palmitos sanctuary against all comers. Two attacks on Palmitos were repelled during this period—one launched by the 35th Regiment from San Miguel el Alto and another by the 54th based in Arandas.[46]

Fighting died down in the latter part of April. A second *reconcentración*, decreed on 28 January 1928, had caused another smallpox epidemic, one that affected *callista* and *cristero* alike. Though some communities had been under quarantine since 12 February, General Figueroa, the new Federal commander, didn't move to alleviate the situation until the end of April. Even then the *reconcentración* was but partially remitted; only persons living in Federal-garrisoned areas were allowed to go home.[47]

May (1928) brought both good and bad news to the rebels. On 22 May a *cristero* raiding party wiped out the *callista* garrison in Tesistán, only ten kilometers from Guadalajara. But eight days later Gorostieta lost one of his most valued subordinates. Gabino Alvarez, commander of the second Gómez Loza regiment, was arrested while visiting his family's ranch near Atotonilco. Shot the same day, he was succeeded by his brother Cayetano as regimental chief.[48]

FEDERALS ON THE DEFENSIVE

Cristero pressure continued to mount in June as the Federals, for the first time, found themselves on the defensive. Virtually abandoning the *alteño* countryside, the Army confined itself to defending railroad lines, main roads, and principal population centers.[49]

In July 1928 Obregón was assassinated and Gorostieta, wanting to see which way the wind was blowing, wound down offensive activity throughout west-central Mexico.[50] During this lull the *cristeros* engaged in hit-and-run harassment by groups of 4 or 5, while larger bands (100 to 200) were deployed only on special call.[51]

It soon became apparent that no solution was in sight that the rebels could live with. The hierarchy, seemingly oblivious to *cristero* victories in the field, was determined to come to terms with the incoming Portes Gil administration. Additional impetus to the peace offensive was provided by American Ambassador Dwight W. Morrow and his colleague, Father John J. Burke. Though Obregón's murder had temporarily checked American diplomatic efforts, the Morrow-Burke forces were quick to recover. Morrow lost no time in establishing friendly relations with Portes Gil while Burke discreetly but firmly began nudging the Vatican in the direction of détente with the Mexican government. Burke's most important contact was Archbishop Pietro Fumasoni Biondi, apostolic delegate in the United States. (Burke acted as his agent in ecclesiastical matters pertaining to Mexico.)[52]

Convinced that Obregón's death would not pave the way to a settlement he could accept, Gorostieta began to organize for victory. The months of August through November (1928) were devoted to consolidation, with combat operations playing a relatively minor role. (It was during this period that the Plan de Los Altos was promulgated.) So intent were the rebels in building a solid internal organization that the hard-pressed Federals were able to regain the initiative in some sectors. But the Brigada suffered little damage. As the *callistas* resumed forays into the countryside the *cristeros* simply hit, ran, and melted away.[53]

In December the rebels returned to the offensive. Serving impressive notice that they were back in business, a *cristero* force under El Catorce deliberately attacked the most heavily defended stronghold in Los Altos on the 14th. This was San Juan de los Lagos, protected by four *callista* regiments.[54] Though technically a standoff (the *cristeros* failed to capture the town), the *callistas* were severely battered and subjected to an agonizing crisis of confidence. If the rebels dared attack the most powerful troop concentration in Los Altos, what limit was there to what they might try next? The Brigada also beat back another assault on Palmitos and triumphed in smaller actions at San Julián and San Isidro.[55]

The situation continued to deteriorate in January and February (1929). Over two hundred actions were fought in those months and the government acted with growing desperation. On Amaro's order six fresh regiments and two squadrons of war planes were sent to Los Altos.[56] In early January Figueroa ordered a new *reconcentración*. Far more sweeping than its predecessors, it covered fourteen states and ranged from Durango to Guerrero.[57] The pinch was also being felt financially. In mid-February the government announced that all Federal employees would have to take a thirty percent pay cut. The money was needed to finance the war effort.[58]

By the end of February it was clear that the initiative had passed to the Guardia Nacional. *Cristero* victories were not confined to Los Altos. In the "Three Finger" zone Quintanar was scoring impressively against General Vargas's 84th Regiment. That unit had become so depleted that the government was forced to scrape the bottom of the barrel for replacements. These included miners from Pachuca and vagrants from León. Though the miners were tough physically they had no stomach for a struggle of whose causes they knew nothing. The new recruits deserted on the first day of combat.[59]

In Michoacán, another crucial sector, the rebels benefited greatly from the leadership of Fernando González, a former Federal general and close friend of Gorostieta. González had entered the struggle on 29 July 1928, and *cristeros* under his command scored more successes in the next seven months than they had since the beginning of the rebellion. The changing ideological nature of the war was also reflected here. González, a man of Gorostieta's persuasion, directed the rebellion in the very diocese of Archbishop Ruiz y Flores, the staunchly anti-*cristero* prelate.[60]

Another area of rebel success was southern Jalisco and Colima. Pushing to within twenty-five miles of Guadalajara, the División del Sur posed almost as much of a threat from the south and west as did the Brigada de Los Altos from the north and east.[61] The government was further hampered by increasing tension between *callista* and *obregonista* elements in the capital. Fearing a putsch attempt by Obregón's disaffected followers, Portes Gil was forced to keep nineteen regiments in the Federal District and fifteen in Veracruz—troops desperately needed in the *cristero* combat zone.[62] The critical situation can also be measured in statistical terms. Military expenditure for 1929 was 37.3 percent of the budget, a proportion exceeded only during the 1917 to 1918 period of almost constant civil war.[63]

By the end of February highly placed revolutionaries in Mexico City began for the first time to consider the possibility of defeat. In a caustic address, Senator Caloca openly challenged government statistics as he asked why seven operational headquarters were needed to fight "I don't know whether one or three or four or seven thousand [rebels]." Caloca's query struck a sensitive nerve. Faced with a dilemma, the government continued to minimize rebel strength, but at the same time was unable to explain why it was so difficult to crush a rebellion that had supposedly attracted so few adherents.[64] Complementing Caloca's irony was the pessimism of Senator Juan de Díos Robledo. In tones of anguish he wanted to know whether it was necessary to "kill thirty thousand *jalisciences*...to convince them that the Revolution tries to bring material and moral betterment to the people."[65]

The nervousness of the Federals was shared by American observers. "It seems unlikely," wrote the U.S. Consul in Guadalajara, "that the state [Jalisco] can be successfully pacified in spite of every effort on the part of the President and the local military authorities until the settlement of the religious question."[66] With the government unable to defeat the *cristeros* in the field, the burden of ending the rebellion was increasingly shifting to the shoulders of Morrow and his allies in the hierarchy.

The situation that prevailed in 1929 as February gave way to March was as follows: the *cristeros* were successful in every sector of the combat zone, the Federals were completely unable to control the rebellion, and the American State Department and a majority of the Mexican hierarchy were in virtual alliance with the embattled central government. March—the most crucial month of the rebellion—brought severe internal shocks to both sides, but with significantly different results. While the Federals were able to surmount brilliantly their period of maximum internal dislocation, the crisis within the ranks of the *cristeros* dealt the rebels a blow from which they never recovered.

The
El Catorce
Affair

THE CRISIS that shattered unity and morale among the *cristeros* centered around the flamboyant figure of Victoriano Ramírez. During the very period that the rebels were wresting the initiative from a battered enemy, the *cristiada's* greatest popular hero was embroiled in a bitterly divisive controversy with five men who exercised a decisive influence in the movement generally and the *alteño* sector particularly. These five—not one an *alteño* —were General Gorostieta, Fathers Pedroza and Vega, Heriberto Navarrete, and Mario Guadalupe Valdés.

Valdés, who would replace Victoriano as commander of the San Miguel regiment, was a native of Chihuahua who had come to Los Altos as one of Gorostieta's aides, having been recommended by the Liga.[1] Though absolute proof is lacking, there is strong evidence that Valdés was an agent provocateur. That he was a spy is an article of faith in Los Altos, where in the early 1980s his name was still a symbol of treachery. *Alteño* passions about Valdés are so fierce that, in 1976, the ninety-year-old, bedridden Concepción Alcalá expressed a desire to "burn him alive with green firewood."*

*This statement and much data in this chapter are from a 1976 series in *IMPACTO*, a Mexico City weekly, and are supplemented by field work in San Miguel el Alto.

THE MAN AND THE LEGEND

Legendary figures have always presented a vexing problem to the historian, since they inevitably have fictitious accomplishments ascribed to them. The myth-making process is intensified if the person is a martyr, as Victoriano has been considered in Los Altos. It was myth that played an important part in bringing on El Catorce's martyrdom. His adversaries were so concerned with the legend that they vastly overrated the man. Had the truth been known they might not have found it necessary to kill him. This observation is not to imply that Victoriano was a fraud. His accomplishments were considerable, even remarkable. Yet he fell short of being the sort of miracle worker who would threaten the authority of men as able as Gorostieta, Pedroza, and Vega—an authority he never coveted.

Victoriano's martyrdom must be assessed in the light of his life and career. What follows is an attempt to set forth relevant data with complete accuracy, sifting myth from reality and critically examining premises that have too long been accepted as fact. The assessment can begin with his nickname: the popular version is that Victoriano broke out of jail after slaying a man in a cantina brawl and then killed all fourteen members of the posse sent to track him down; hence, "El Catorce (The Fourteen)."

It is interesting that this account first appeared in a book written by one of the five men who destroyed him: Heriberto Navarrete.[2] Since Navarrete's book has sold well, this version has become accepted not only by historians of the *cristiada* but by a younger generation of *alteños* thrilled by such a feat of machismo. Yet it has been accepted by none of his contemporaries. Vicente Ramírez, El Catorce's brother, pooh-poohed the story and provided an infinitely more prosaic tale.

Victoriano, born on 23 March 1892, was the son of Carlos and Bibiana Ramírez, tenants on a ranch belonging to Juan Lozano (brother of José María Lozano, one of the "Quadrumvirate" of rightist liberals who connived in the overthrow of Madero). One day don Juan went to the kitchen where Victoriano was eating and asked him to bring some animals in from the field. "When I finish my lunch," said Victoriano. Lozano returned to the kitchen later and found his employee still eating.

"Haven't you finished yet?" he asked.

"No," replied Victoriano, "I'm still filling myself and I won't be full until I've eaten fourteen tortillas."

"Fourteen tortillas!" said Lozano incredulously. Then he laughed. "Andale Catorce! (Go to it, Fourteen!)" he concluded with an ironic bow.[3]

There are two other versions of the nickname's origin; one derogatory, the other complimentary. José Casillas, a San Miguel-born Guadalajara merchant, has stated that Victoriano received the nickname because he could count only to fourteen. This explanation must be viewed with skepticism. Though unable to read or write, Victoriano was one of those intelligent illiterates who abound in regions where there is an oral, rather than written tradition of communication. Later, during the rebellion, he gained fame as a tactician who astutely deployed hundreds of men in actions against the Federals. Such feats could never have been accomplished by a man incapable of counting beyond fourteen.

The more flattering version is told by Dr. Salvador Ibarra, a native of San Miguel who later lived in San Juan de los Lagos. As a boy Dr. Ibarra was taken during vacations to Buenavista, a village near the Lozano ranch. He formed a friendship with Victoriano, who was a few years his senior. One day Victoriano proudly announced that he had lassoed fourteen head of cattle—a considerable accomplishment for a boy that young.

There is no reason to doubt this version, nor does it negate the "tortillas theory" advanced by Victoriano's brother. It is entirely conceivable that Victoriano, during his youth on the ranch, had both eaten fourteen tortillas at one sitting and lassoed fourteen head of cattle. There is even a grain of truth in the popularly accepted Navarrete version. Victoriano figured in an incident which bore a slight resemblance to the Navarrete account and, with exaggeration, may have formed the basis for it.

How did Victoriano become a *cristero?* Uncritical chroniclers favorable to him cite his fervent Catholicism; detractors, equally subjective, dismiss him as a bandit who took advantage of the rebellion to win glory and plunder. There may be some truth to these theories, but the prime mover behind Victoriano's decision to rebel was neither a religious ideal nor a dream of riches. It was a man. That man was his maternal uncle, José María López. When the *cristiada* broke out, López was mayor of San Miguel. He was also Victoriano's bitterest enemy. This animosity, its cause unknown, was sufficiently strong to stir López into an attempt on his nephew's life. Having heard that Victoriano was attending a horse race in nearby Santa María de la Paz, the mayor summoned a band of *pistoleros* and offered them money to kill him. Their leader was a man known as "El Pulga (The Flea)." At first the gunmen hesitated; Victoriano's marksmanship was even then a legend. López responded by plying them with tequila. The ploy worked and Pulga's men, filled with alcohol-induced courage, set off for Santa María.

When Victoriano saw them coming he knew immediately why they had come. But he made an attempt to avoid bloodshed. "Look, Pulga," he shouted, "don't come any closer or I'll kill you!"[4] Pulga and his men continued their advance. Again, Victoriano shouted a warning. It was ignored and the would-be assassins came ever closer. Then two shots rang out—both fired by the quick-drawing Victoriano. Pulga and the man behind him lay dead. Shocked into sobriety, the remaining *pistoleros* took to their heels— "a stampede," as one eyewitness described it.[5]

The next clash between Victoriano and his uncle took place just before the rebellion. It was a Sunday morning and Victoriano, accompanied by his brother Vicente, was drinking in a San Miguel cantina. Also on hand was the police *comandante*, a staunch ally of Victoriano's uncle. Emboldened by tequila, the brothers began taunting the police chief. "It seems to me he has the face of a thief," said Vicente. "That's true," replied Victoriano, "he has the face of a thief."[6] Victoriano then pulled out a knife and drew the blade menacingly across his throat. Paling visibly, the *comandante* left the cantina immediately. But he was back within minutes—accompanied by the entire police force. Pistols drawn, they herded Victoriano and Vicente off to jail.

That López didn't invoke the Ley Fuga and shoot his troublesome nephew for "trying to escape" was due solely to the intervention of Victoriano's father. The elder Ramírez, who seems to have been on good terms with his brother-in-law, secured his sons' release on condition that Victoriano surrender his pistol and never return to San Miguel. On leaving,

Victoriano couldn't resist a parting taunt. "It's good you're keeping the pistol," he said, "you're going to need it some day."[7]

The final episode of this bitter rivalry occurred at the rebellion's outbreak in Los Altos. During the fighting—before Father González arranged the truce that saved the defenders' lives—Victoriano had the satisfaction of shooting two fingers off the hand of his cousin Miguel, José's son.

It is not difficult, from the preceding, to deduce how the accepted version of Victoriano's nickname came into being. He *was* known as El Catorce, he *had* been in the San Miguel jail, and he *had* killed men sent to hunt him down. The myth makers did the rest.

It is interesting to speculate on what might have happened if the political roles of uncle and nephew had been reversed. Had José María López joined the *cristeros* it is not inconceivable that Victoriano might have turned up as a Federal partisan.

This is not to imply that Victoriano was devoid of religious feeling. He had all the clannish faith of his *patria chica* and there is no doubt that his anger over religious repression was genuine. Yet his doctrinal ignorance was abysmal. Heriberto Navarrete, before he quarreled with Victoriano, recalls a conversation with the man who was then his regimental commander. "Listen, Victoriano," asked Navarrete, "what's your wife's name?"

"Which one?"

"Your legitimate one."

"Hmmm. They're all legitimate."

"That can't be. You're a Catholic and now you're a soldier of Cristo Rey. You must know that the Church condemns irregular unions."

"Look, these are different things. I'm a Catholic and I go to church whenever I can; and I'm furious because the damned government runs out the padres and robs churches. And I know how to pray. But that has to do with being a Catholic. Relations with women have to do with being a man. What have the two got to do with each other?"[8]

Victoriano's remark introduces another part of the El Catorce legend: his prowess with women. This appears to be an area where the man was as big as the myth. Tall, powerfully built, ruddy-complexioned, and fiercely mustachioed, Victoriano was the epitome of an *alteño* macho. He maintained a chain of *casas chicas* (love nests) in the San Miguel area and in each was welcomed by a lonely woman as master of the house.

Among this total of informal alliances there was one legitimate liaison in Victoriano's life. The account that follows is, in fact, the first definite confirmation of Victoriano's marriage to be published. The first part of the story came from the parish records of San Miguel, where there is an entry dated 17 June 1916: "Victoriano Ramírez, bachelor, age twenty-three, has contracted matrimony with Crescencia Macías, maiden, age seventeen."⁹ The rest of the story came from María Macías, the sister of Crescencia. A son born to the couple died in infancy. The marriage then disintegrated, and Crescencia moved first to Durango and later to the United States, where she died. It seems logical to assume that Crescencia's disillusionment with Victoriano may have been related to his freewheeling sexuality.

Of Victoriano's other loves, probably the best known is the mother of his only acknowledged living child, a daughter named Natalia. Her name was Guadalupe and she appears to have been every bit as lusty as Victoriano. At the time of their union he was traveling extensively about the countryside, bartering goods. During these absences Guadalupe soon found ways of relieving her loneliness. One time Victoriano returned unexpectedly and found her in flagrante with a lover. The interloper, knowing Victoriano's reputation, was so frightened that he almost died of heart failure. But Victoriano calmed him. "It's not your fault," he said, "you're a man. It's the fault of this *sinvergüenza* (shameless woman)." He then took his little daughter by the hand and left the house.¹⁰ Guadalupe resumed her uninhibited ways, forming a liaison with a man called Ponciano. Later she is reported to have taken up with a Federal soldier.

Natalia's story is a sadder one. In 1929, the year her father died and the rebellion ended, she was taken in by a León couple named Agustín and María de la Luz Larrinue Gutiérrez. She was then about nine years old. That autumn, in September or October, she received her first communion in León's Templo de Los Angeles.¹¹ Natalia subsequently married, but was left widowed and penniless.

Though he was as male chauvinistic as might be expected, Victoriano had definite scruples in his dealings with women. All his paramours had been eager volunteers and (as Navarrete and Valdés would painfully learn) he took a poor view of men who attempted to conquer by force. Another aspect of his character—an unexpected gentleness—was also part of the legend. José Casillas speaks of his "nobility" and relates an incident that took place after the San Julian engagement, when the unwounded Federal prisoners were shot.

> Father Vega was very hard; [he] had an evil heart, a black heart, and it didn't hurt him to kill anybody. So he gave the order to kill that soldier [one of the Federal prisoners] and asked him if he had a final request. "I want to be killed by Victoriano El Catorce," said the soldier.
> Then they went to Victoriano and [repeated the soldier's request]....Victoriano said, "No, I won't kill anybody in cold blood. You shoot him."[12]

Victoriano walked away so he wouldn't have to witness the shootings.

Victoriano's magnanimity angered not only killers like Vega but, at times, even fair-minded men like Miguel Gómez Loza. Gómez Loza had ordered Victoriano to execute four collaborationist officials in the Guanajuato village of Piedra Gorda (later renamed Ciudad Manuel Doblado). When Victoriano seized the offenders he was set upon by a swarm of their relatives, weeping and begging for mercy. The prisoners were promptly released. Then he reported back to Gómez Loza, saying, "Yes, *licenciado* (lawyer) I arrested them and then let them go."

Gómez Loza flushed with anger. "Why did you do it?" he demanded.

"*Licenciado*," replied Victoriano, "you know how to read and write, and you know the legal codes. But what you don't know," he added, pointing to his muscular forearm, "is that the tears of the people I would have made widows and orphans fell on this very arm."[13]

Another incident took place before the rebellion, when Victoriano encountered a hometown enemy named Chon Campos on a country road. The two exchanged insults and went for their pistols. Predictably, Victoriano won. Then he felt a spasm of remorse: Campos had a wife. To his dying day Victoriano furnished food and financial assistance to his slain enemy's widow.[14]

THE PLOT AGAINST EL CATORCE

An examination of the events that led to Victoriano's death shows that each of the men involved in El Catorce's downfall had his motive. Gorostieta's pique against Victoriano stemmed from an affront to his gargantuan ego, but the affront was not delivered by Victoriano. The unwitting instrument of Gorostieta's murderous rage against El Catorce was an eccentric León priest named José Isabel Salinas. He was known, even to fellow Catholics, as "El Padre Loco." Father Salinas's two outstanding characteristics were an extravagant admiration for El Catorce and an equally extravagant sense of his own importance. Though Father Salinas had no connection with any official resistance organization, he was under the delusion that he had the authority to issue grades and commissions.

In early April of 1928, a few days after Martínez Camarena had been appointed interim governor by the Liga, two sisters from León by the name of Jasso arrived at the *cristeros'* Palmitos headquarters. They carried a sealed roll of papers from Father Salinas to Victoriano. The sisters were received by Martínez Camarena, who promised to deliver the roll to El Catorce, then in the field with his troops. Martínez did not break the seal.

Gorostieta arrived the following day and Martínez informed him of the Jasso sisters' visit. He promptly opened the roll and extracted an *oficio* (official memorandum) drafted by Father Salinas. The *oficio* nominated Victoriano brigadier general and commander of all forces in Los Altos. When he read the document Gorostieta flew into a violent rage. "Now he's really gone too far," he stormed to Martínez. "An illiterate brute, enjoying a fame he does not deserve, wants to usurp a post that I hold legitimately. I'm going to have him shot so the *sardos* will know who is really hitting them."[15] (Gorostieta apparently thought that Victoriano had put Father Salinas up to making his presumptuous proclamation.)

Though Gorostieta backed down from his plan of shooting Victoriano on the spot, Martínez is certain that he formed the conspiracy that destroyed him. Describing Gorostieta as "intellectually responsible for the murder of Victoriano Ramírez," Martínez states that he gave Father Pedroza an order to eliminate Victoriano.[16] Without questioning Martínez's good faith it must be remembered that, of all the *cristero* chiefs, he disliked Gorostieta the most. He detested him on ideological grounds (as a liberal, Mason, and anti-clerical) and personally for having removed him as interim governor and for having threatened him with execution.

Martínez's theory is disputed by another ex-*cristero* and close friend of Victoriano—Víctor López. López exculpates Gorostieta for complicity in Victoriano's death, explaining that Gorostieta realized what an adverse effect El Catorce's elimination would have on *alteño* morale. "This was a perverse deed," says López, "and Gorostieta was not perverse enough to do what the Federals had failed to accomplish in three years."[17]

Yet this theory seems to lean too far in the other direction. Even if Gorostieta never issued a specific order to have Victoriano killed, he did everything in his power to undermine him. These efforts even included slandering Victoriano to his own brother. Vicente, who had refused El Catorce's invitation to join in the armed movement, remained in the San Miguel area during the rebellion. "One time when I was in San Julián, General Gorostieta talked to me," recalls Vicente. "He said my brother didn't take care of his troops, that he was always going to La Mesa, Rincón de Chavez, San Juanico, one place or another, always involving himself with women."[18]

The accusation that Victoriano made love to the exclusion of making war is rejected by his supporters. They point out that he was the only major *cabecilla* who kept the rebellion alive in Los Altos during that dismal summer of 1927, when Pedroza was in hiding and Hernández and Vega in exile. That accusation was also rejected by one of Victoriano's military foes, General Miguel Z. Martínez, who commanded a Federal regiment in Los Altos. "El Catorce was killed by his own men! Jackasses! They cut off the viper's head and left the tail to me."[19]

Whether by accident or design, Gorostieta was absent from Los Altos when Victoriano was killed. When he returned to the region he made a remark that can be clearly interpreted as an effort to shift all the blame onto Father Pedroza. "I'm very sorry about what happened," he told an aide. "If I had been here it might not have been necessary to go to such an extreme. The final responsibility is General Pedroza's and he will answer for his actions in due time."[20]

Was Father Pedroza responsible for Victoriano's murder? One witness believes he was. According to Librada Gutiérrez de Hernández, a member of the family that sheltered Pedroza during the summer of 1927, Pedroza described Victoriano as a man who "carries off girls and rapes them at will;...this I cannot permit."[21] Such an interpretation is open to grave doubt, as it shows both Victoriano and Father Pedroza in an uncharacteristic light. Victoriano was never known to take women by force (he didn't have to), and he dealt sternly with those who did.

There is the possibility that Librada's memory may have been faulty. Did Pedroza specifically charge Victoriano with rape, or was he just making a general reference to his sexual magnetism and ever-active libido? Assuming the latter, it is inconceivable that Father Pedroza would plot against a man's life merely on grounds of excessive machismo. Though personally puritanical, he never made the foolish mistake—as did Luis Navarro in Michoacán—of playing the moral policeman among his troops. He checked looting and rape, to be sure, but this control was simply in line with his policy of maintaining good relations with the civilian population. Given his forbearance with Father Vega's industrious wenching, it is hardly likely that he would interfere with anyone else's pleasures in the cantinas and bordellos.

A more likely explanation is furnished by Father Salvador Casas, who attended the seminary with both Pedroza and Vega. He defines Pedroza's anti-Catorce stance as a matter of *política* (policy).[22] In his cool chess-player's head Pedroza saw Victoriano as an irritant—an inconvenient person who hampered the movement by greatly antagonizing a number of its key members. No doubt he considered the matter carefully, weighing Victoriano's role as nuisance and irritant against his popularity and combat record. Then something clicked in his orderly mind and the answer came tumbling out of the slot: Victoriano must go.

With Father Vega the motive was simply envy. He was as courageous as Victoriano and, as an educated man, probably a better tactician. Yet he never came close to winning the love and respect that Victoriano inspired among his men. All feared Vega and many must have looked askance at the alacrity with which he shared their carnal pleasures. Though not puritanical themselves, they did have an *alteño* standard of how a priest should behave; the ascetic Pedroza was far more popular among the troops than the libertine Vega.

Mario Guadalupe Valdés and Heriberto Navarrete had the same grievance against Victoriano. (If Valdés was also a Federal spy, then he would have had a double reason for wanting to destroy Victoriano.) Valdés and Navarrete were posted to the San Miguel regiment in October 1928. Both men had the rank of major, and Valdés assumed the duties of adjutant. Gorostieta's written order to Valdés, dated 12 October 1928, contained a sarcastic entry that "Colonel Ramírez has numerous social relationships that limit the fulfillment of his duties."[23] This jibe was in line with Gorostieta's campaign of denigration against Victoriano.

It wasn't long, however, before Valdés and Navarrete began to develop social relationships of their own. They were greatly drawn to the two pretty sisters of Victoriano's current mistress, but attraction was not mutual and their attentions were icily discouraged. Undaunted, they pressed their claims more aggressively—so aggressively that the sisters complained to Victoriano about their unwelcome suitors. Victoriano was outraged—such behavior went against his ethic of voluntary cooperation. Finding Valdés and Navarrete, he seized them and knocked their heads together. Then he challenged them to a singular duel: himself against the two of them. Having witnessed his marksmanship in both target practice and combat, the mortified pair declined. From that moment on Valdés and Navarrete were totally committed to Victoriano's destruction.

Wounded egotism, icy calculation, envy, and physical plus psychological humiliation—these were the elements that motivated the men who destroyed Victoriano. Was there an actual conspiracy? Perhaps too much emphasis has been placed on whether a formal plot against El Catorce ever materialized; it may have been simply a meeting of minds. When five powerful men in an organization are united by furious antagonism against a sixth, this shared antagonism has a way of generating spontaneous pressure. Whether the product of an organized conspiracy or an *ad hoc* cabal, this pressure was moving events inexorably in one direction: toward the downfall of Victoriano Ramírez.

The first step was taken in January 1929, when Gorostieta relieved Victoriano as commander of the San Miguel regiment. Replacing him was Valdés, who was promoted to lieutenant colonel. Victoriano was placed under the direct authority of the brigade commander (Pedroza) and allowed an escort of six men. Though Valdés now commanded San Miguel, he was not satisfied with merely displacing his rival. Victoriano, still enormously popular, was a threat to his position and pride as long as he lived.

The first attempt on Victoriano's life was made on 7 March; it was preceded by a campaign of intimidation against the overwhelmingly pro-Catorce population of San Miguel. On 6 March a Valdés partisan named J. Jesús Jiménez came to San Miguel with two hundred men and, for the first time, began exacting money from the townspeople by force. This was done with "great rudeness and threats"; the *sanmiguelenses* were told that their homes and shops would be burned and their families taken hostage if they did not contribute.[24] Jiménez, himself from San Miguel, had formerly been Victoriano's secretary, but they had had a falling out, and he was later accused of being one of El Catorce's murderers. Jiménez and his men left town at midnight.

The following morning El Catorce arrived in San Miguel with great enthusiasm. At 1500 Valdés arrived with sixty men. In a boisterous mood, they began drinking and looting. This was too much for Victoriano. Though he knew he was in danger, he came out with his tiny escort and reproached Valdés. Valdés's response was to disarm the escort. He also tried to disarm Victoriano but the latter refused to hand over his weapons.

Then Valdés took another tack. Feigning friendliness, he asked Victoriano to join him for a *merienda* (supper) at the house of a local lady named Mercedes Jiménez de Jiménez. Though Victoriano came, he refused to eat or drink, fearing he might be poisoned. Seeing that hostility was mounting, he decided to leave. As he went out the door Valdés followed him, pistol in hand. Waiting outside was one of Victoriano's men, his first cousin Primitivo (Primo) Ramírez. When Primo saw Valdés stalking Victoriano he fired two shots at him. Both missed. Then Jesús Jiménez came out of the house and fired at Primo, killing him instantly. Victoriano managed to escape but had to do so on foot. He didn't have time to mount his magnificent horse, Chamaco, and the animal fell into the hands of Valdés.[25]

A different version of the incident is given by Navarrete. He claims it was Victoriano's men who were drinking, looting, and terrorizing the populace. If this is true, the reign of terror was carried out by just eighteen individuals—six of the original escort plus twelve who had been added by Victoriano.[26] Navarrete also states that it was Victoriano who issued the dinner invitation. During dinner, he continues, a loud argument broke out between Victoriano's men and Valdés's (both groups were standing guard outside the house). Valdés came out to calm the disputants and it was then that Primo Ramírez [presumably at Victoriano's instigation] fired at him. Navarrete was not in San Miguel at the time and admits that his information came from Valdés.[27]

Following Victoriano's escape Valdés announced a 2,000-peso reward for his apprehension, dead or alive. Though the sum must have seemed a fortune to the hard-pressed *san-miguelenses,* nobody gave Victoriano away (strange behavior for people who were allegedly robbed and terrorized that afternoon by Victoriano's men). He hid that night in the house of friends and the following day went to San Julián to seek the aid of Miguel Hernández and one of his officers, a priest named Miguel Pérez Aldape. They pledged their support, and Victoriano left for San Juan de los Lagos. There he visited the Church of the Sanctuary and gave thanks to the Virgin for saving his life.[28]

On 9 March another of Valdés's followers, José María Arias, came to San Miguel to look for Victoriano. Arias had ten men with him.[29] But El Catorce had returned to the San Julián regiment, where he felt safe with such friends as Hernández, Víctor Lopez, and Father Pérez Aldape. Four days later Hernández, following a meeting with Gorostieta near San Julián, prepared to set off for Tepatitlán with his regiment. Here the entire brigada was massing for an attack on Guadalajara. On that day Victoriano made the most fateful decision of his life: he would accompany the San Julián regiment to Tepatitlán. The decision was made against the advice of all his supporters and friends.

Leandro Padilla, a former San Julián captain, recalls that "when we left San Julián, General Miguel Hernández again said to Colonel Victoriano Ramírez, 'It would be better if you stayed while we go and come back,'...but Colonel Ramírez said that he would not stay; he was anxious to speak to the *jefes*."[30]

José Robledo, who knew many of the persons involved (though he was not an active participant in the *cristiada*) recalls this conversation between Victoriano and a friendly priest:

> It was Father González or Father Pérez Aldape, I don't remember which.... Then the father told him, "They're going to kill you; I know it well, they're going to kill you."
>
> Then [Victoriano] said, "No, they're not going to do anything. They're my *compañeros*. How could they kill me? No, they won't kill me."
>
> And the father insisted, "They're going to kill you. Look: leave and I'll leave with you. They're going to kill you for sure."
>
> And then Victoriano said, "No, padre, they're not going to do anything." He armed himself to leave and on arriving in Tepa they seized him.[31]

Concepción Alcalá recalls the advice of her friend, Marina Casillas, to El Catorce: "Don't go, Victoriano; all your enemies are there and something bad could happen to you."[32] Victoriano was not to be dissuaded. A trusting, ingenuous man, he thought it was simply a case of justifying himself to Fathers Pedroza and Vega. He planned to file a complaint against Valdés, citing the *merienda* incident and the theft of his horse. He did not then know that the two priests were as dedicated to his undoing as Valdés himself.

As a forerunner of things to come, a second attempt on Victoriano's life was made on 15 March. José María Arias, who had come looking for him on the ninth with ten men, was still in San Miguel. He had sent the men back to Tepatitlán, declining to accompany them on grounds of illness. His real reason for staying was that he knew the San Julián regiment would be passing through San Miguel on the way to Tepatitlán. Correctly guessing that Victoriano would be with Hernández, he thought he might have a chance to kill him. The regiment arrived on 14 March, receiving a wild welcome from the townspeople. The loudest cheers were reserved for Victoriano. At 1030 the following morning San Julián began to move out of town. Its destination was Capilla de Guadalupe, the final stop before Tepatitlán. As the regiment was riding out, Arias, rifle in hand, positioned himself behind a column. From this vantage point he had a good shot at Victoriano's back. But he was spotted by some townspeople and had to abandon the attempt.[33] Now fearing for his own life, Arias slipped out of town and rode off at full gallop.

Two more efforts were made to dissuade Victoriano from going to Tepatitlán. On 15 March, with the column on the way to Capilla de Guadalupe, Father Pérez Aldape again begged him to go back to San Julián. But Victoriano refused, insisting that he would vindicate himself with Pedroza and Vega.[34] The following day, with the column only a few miles from Tepatitlán, Hernández made a final plea. He even offered a twenty-five man escort if El Catorce would return to San Julián. Stubbornly, Victoriano shook his head. Hernández then knew there was no longer any way he could save his friend.[35]

At noon of the 16th the San Julián regiment rode into Tepatitlán. Leading the column were three men—General Miguel Hernández in the center, Colonel Pérez Aldape on the right, and Colonel Victoriano Ramírez on the left. Immediately a cry went up from people lining the streets. "Allí viene El Catorce (Here comes El Catorce)!" they shouted. As the regiment approached the town hall, which served as brigade headquarters, its progress was observed by another man: Father Pedroza. On seeing Victoriano he barked an order to Navarrete: "Bring a typewriter here immediately." Pedroza dictated an *oficio* directing that Colonel Ramírez was to be disarmed and confined to a cell in the town hall. Navarrete, accompanied by a six-man detachment, was to deliver the message personally to General Hernández.[36]

VICTORIANO'S ARREST

Hernández's strategy was to appear reasonable and accommodating but at the same time to protect Victoriano's interests. Quickly, silently, he read the *oficio*. Then he, Victoriano, and Víctor López accompanied Navarrete and his men to headquarters and began to climb the stairs. It was not until they reached the second floor that Hernández broke the news. "Victoriano," he said, "I have an order from General Pedroza that you are to surrender your weapons. Don't do anything rash. Give them to me and I'll speak in your behalf." Victoriano, believing Hernández was influential enough to save him, handed over a .45 and a small Mauser. Hernández passed them over to Navarrete, saying, "Colonel Ramírez is at your disposal, Major."[37] Victoriano was then taken downstairs and locked in a cell. To add a macabre touch, he was led to confinement through a dining hall where the brigade's officers were about to enjoy a lavish banquet.

Following the banquet, a court-martial was held; the accused was not present. Father Pedroza presided as judge, Valdés acted as prosecutor, and Agustín Sanchez (one of the civil chiefs in Los Altos) as defense counsel.[38] Navarrete was a witness for the prosecution; Hernández and Pérez Aldape were defense witnesses. Father Vega, in a rather anomalous position, functioned as a glorified court recorder, but with the authority to "clarify testimony of witnesses and statements of fact."[39]

There were three charges against Victoriano—insubordination, misappropriation of funds, and plotting against the life of Mario Valdés. A fourth was dropped; it was so flimsy that it would have made the prosecution look ridiculous. Valdés, not knowing Victoriano was illiterate, had forged letters purporting to be treasonable correspondence between El Catorce and Federal General Miguel Z. Martínez. When interviewed after the rebellion, Martínez denied that he had ever had any communication with Victoriano.[40]

The result of this proceeding was very strange: thanking the others for their "efficient collaboration," Pedroza simply announced that he "would personally take a decision and act accordingly." Bewildered, Sánchez, Hernández, and Pérez Aldape left.[41] In the meantime, Víctor López was doing what he could to save Victoriano. Excluded from both the banquet and court-martial, he had been given orders to confine the entire San Julián regiment to barracks. Not a man was to leave; food was to be sent in. Having obeyed the order, López went to visit Victoriano. He asked El Catorce why he had been imprisoned; he didn't know. At this point an unidentified major politely asked López to leave. López hesitated but Victoriano himself urged him to go, asking that he work on his behalf and see Hernández. López went upstairs but saw that all the doors were locked—the court-martial was then in progress. He waited until 1900, taking a brief recess to eat, and then Hernández came out. Declining to speak until they were out of the building, Hernández made the gloomy observation that "it will be very difficult to save Victoriano."[42]

Fearing the worst, some of Victoriano's friends decided to take matters into their own hands. At 2100 Captain Leandro Padilla encountered Father Pedroza. Pedroza told him it had been decided that Victoriano would remain under arrest during the Guadalajara attack and then be freed and made garrison commander in Atotonilco or Ayo el Chico.

Two hours later a delegation of San Julián officers ran into Father Vega. Demanding Victoriano's release, they requested in the name of the entire regiment that he be assigned to Hernández's command. Vega replied that they were not to worry; Victoriano would be released the next day and assigned to his own regiment. Reassured, the officers returned to barracks.[43]

THE MURDER OF EL CATORCE

Shortly after midnight the San Julián regiment received orders to march on Zapotlanejo—Federal troops had been reported in the vicinity. As the column set off, the men saw a car with no headlights approaching them. It could be coming from only one direction—the cemetery. Obviously a body had just been left there. A chill of apprehension swept the ranks: had Victoriano been done away with?

The answer came the following day. Having been told by local campesinos that a Federal column was approaching, San Julián had dug in at Paredones, a village about halfway between Tepatitlán and Zapotlanejo. Then a courier arrived with two *oficios*. The first ordered San Julián to suspend the advance and return to Tepatitlán. The second, bristling with arrogance, announced that anyone who objected to the sentence passed on Victoriano Ramírez would be shot. When the regiment arrived in Tepatitlán, Hernández was officially informed that Victoriano was dead.[44]

There are several versions of how he died. Navarrete states that after the court-martial (no exact time is mentioned) Father Pedroza handed "an *oficio* to Colonel Vega, as Chief of the Garrison, that Colonel Victoriano Ramírez should be shot before dawn of the following day."[45] Vega, in turn, designated

Lieutenant Refugio Cholico of the Ayo regiment to organize a firing squad. Navarrete continues:

> Cholico, having formed the firing squad just before dawn, tried to open the thick wooden door.... Removing the lock he found that Victoriano had barred the door with beams he had found inside. The soldiers began to hit the door with an improvised battering ram while Cholico stood two paces behind with a cocked rifle. When the door gave way they say that Victoriano leaped out and tried to struggle with Cholico but the latter fired at the colonel, mortally wounding him in the chest.[46]

The words "they say" indicate that Navarrete was not present at Victoriano's execution and heard about it from other sources.

Navarrete's statement is contradicted by the written accounts of Víctor López and Concepción Alcalá and an oral one by Crescencio Martí, a Brigada veteran who stood guard at the town hall the night Victoriano was killed. López and Alcalá both state that El Catorce was stabbed to death in his place of confinement. Martí supports this view, adding that he was one of the guards friendly to Victoriano who were relieved at 2200 by a detachment of Valdés's men. Shortly after the change of guard a priest was admitted to Victoriano's cell. He was Father José Guadalupe Loza, a member of the Guadalajara diocese operating clandestinely in the *cristero*-controlled countryside.[47] Then the door opened again: Victoriano's killers (or killer) had arrived.

How many were there? Before the publication of a series of articles by *IMPACTO* (a weekly Mexico City news magazine), there were three main suspects—J. Jesús Jiménez (his former secretary), José María Arias (who had earlier tried to shoot him in the back), and Refugio Cholico. But *IMPACTO* suggests that two more men may have participated in the killing. One was allegedly Trinidad Martínez, godson of José Guadalupe Gutiérrez, son of the family that sheltered Father Pedroza during the 1927 *reconcentración*. Gutiérrez states that Martínez was originally a "good boy" but was corrupted by Cholico, another native of the Atotonilco region. It is possible that Cholico induced Martínez to join Victoriano's assassination squad. On the other hand, Martínez may merely have been boasting to his godfather. Gutiérrez admits that Martínez was his sole informant, and no other chronicler has linked him to Victoriano's murder.

The fifth killer is said to have been a man named Martín Díaz. He was firmly believed to be so by a namesake and self-appointed avenger of El Catorce, Victoriano Ramírez "El Chivero (The Goatherd)." This view was not shared by Father Salvador Casas. "Martín Díaz was a humble rancher from Lagos de Moreno," states the *cristero* archivist. "He had absolutely nothing against Victoriano and would have no reason for wanting to kill him."[48]

Father Casas and his close friend, Rafael Martínez Camarena, spent years trying to get at the truth about Victoriano's death. Their task was complicated by the fact that the accounts of Víctor López and Concepción Alcalá agree only in the particular that he was stabbed rather than shot. Of that there is no doubt. El Catorce's body was seen by two eyewitnesses— his brother and the Tepatitlán graveskeeper. "They didn't shoot him," said Vicente Ramírez, adding that the corpse bore three knife wounds.[49]

But who wielded the knife—or knives? Here is Concepción Alcalá's account:

> "...When he had confessed he told the priest [Father Loza] to give him absolution because he felt his enemies were coming to kill him. This was so because J. Jesús Jiménez and José María Arias entered at that moment. Seeing them, El Catorce stood and crossed himself. The priest tried to intervene in his favor but his efforts were useless. Seeing them give him the first cut in the arm, which he had raised to defend himself, and the second in the neck, he pronounced absolution and left so he would not have to witness such cruelties. Then they stabbed him in the heart and cut off his head...."[50]

Víctor López, in a briefer statement, writes that "it is said the material author of the crime was an individual named Cholico, resident of a place near Atotonilco el Alto."[51] López also affirms that El Catorce was killed by *arma blanca* (cold steel).

Like Navarrete, Alcalá and López received their information from unidentified third parties. The former was in San Miguel el Alto during the assassination and the latter with the

San Julián regiment. Both Father Casas and Martínez Camarena believed the López version to be more accurate. Two eyewitnesses—Vicente Ramírez and the Tepatitlán gravekeeper—confirm that the head was not severed from the body. The Alcalá version is further damaged by Father Casas's statement that Arias, who belonged to the San Gaspar regiment, was not in Tepatitlán at the time of the murder.[52]

Could Cholico alone, even though armed, have succeeded in overpowering a man as powerful as El Catorce? At the time of his arrest Victoriano was suffering from a severe bronchial ailment. The debilitating effect of his illness would have made things easier for a man who was healthy, armed, and probably younger. (Victoriano was thirty-six at the time of his death and Cholico, a low-ranking officer, may have been barely out of his teens.)

How about Martínez and Díaz? Their participation seems unlikely. Had five men taken part in the butchery, Victoriano's corpse would certainly have borne more than three wounds seen by witnesses. Martínez, who ended his life a bandit, was known as a braggart and could have been quite capable of falsely claiming that he was one of the killers. The possibility that Díaz was involved is slightly plausible, based largely on the fact that Victoriano's avenging namesake was so convinced of his guilt. Or was he? An explanation that cannot be ruled out is that El Chivero had a personal grudge against Díaz and was using revenge for El Catorce as a convenient pretext to eliminate him.

So we are left with one probable suspect (Cholico), two possibles (Jiménez and Arias), and two doubtfuls (Martínez and Díaz). The only certainty is that Victoriano, after trustingly believing he could get justice by presenting himself in Tepatitlán, paid for his trust by being slaughtered like an animal.

At least three of the presumptive assassins died violently—two in that same year of 1929. J. Jesús Jiménez was killed by Victoriano Ramírez "El Chivero" in July. With Jiménez out of the way, the Goatherd set out to track down Martín Díaz. He spotted him one afternoon at a Tepatitlán bullfight but lost him in the crowd. Then this dedicated avenger became himself a victim of revenge. The men who gunned him down were believe to be in the pay of Romulo Jiménez, father of Jesús.

Martín Díaz also failed to last out the year. Though his killer was known to be a man named Victorio de Anda, there are two versions of the killing. *IMPACTO* states that de Anda was Díaz's *compadre* and that the murder stemmed from a personal quarrel. This explanation was rejected by Father Casas. Since the two men were from different communities (Díaz from Lagos de Moreno, de Anda from San Juan de los Lagos), it is unlikely that they would have been united by a bond of *compadrazgo*. Father Casas believed de Anda was a Federal bounty hunter who befriended the simple-minded Díaz, invited him to a meal at his house, and then treacherously murdered him.[53] The murder took place during the period when former *cristero cabecillas* were being indiscriminately slaughtered to prevent another outbreak of the rebellion. As the leader of a local band, Díaz would have been fair game.

Trinidad Martínez joined a gang of brigands after the rebellion and was killed by a Federal patrol near Ayo in 1935. The fates of Arias and Cholico are unknown.

Of the men who masterminded Victoriano's downfall, Gorostieta, Pedroza, and Vega outlived him by only a few months. All died violently. Valdés and Navarrete fared better. The former escaped from Los Altos not only with Victoriano's horse but with a cash box containing the regimental funds. He had a meeting with Federal General Saturnino Cedillo, who gave him a car in exchange for the horse.[54] Then he went to Mexico City where he immediately made himself available to the government's security apparatus. His function was that of a "finger man": he aided police and military intelligence in tracking down ex-*cristeros*.[55] The late Aurelio Acevedo, who lived in Mexico City and was for many years editor of the *cristero* veterans' monthly, stated that Valdés in those days was a frequent visitor to a Masonic temple. It was one thing for Gorostieta and his liberal, anti-clerical colleagues to be Masons but quite another for a young man of supposedly impeccable Catholic antecedents who joined the rebels under Liga auspices. His actions tend to reinforce views that Valdés was a spy from the beginning.

Navarrete, after resuming his engineering career, entered the Society of Jesus in 1933. In line with the Jesuit tradition of intellectual accomplishment, he became active as a teacher and writer. Among his works are four books on the *cristiada*.

Though the Brigada de Los Altos continued to fight—and fight well—its morale was dealt a crippling blow by Victoriano's murder. It is not true, as has been claimed, that Hernández disbanded his forces after the El Catorce affair and refused to continue serving under Gorostieta and Pedroza. San Julián took part in a number of key actions in the last part of the war, including Poncitlán-Puente Grande and San Francisco del Rincón. But Hernández displayed almost paranoid suspicion in subsequent dealings with Gorostieta, Pedroza, and Vega. On 26 March (1929) he was asked to go alone to the Cerro del Aguila for a meeting with Pedroza, Vega, Valdés, and Navarrete. Hernández brought the entire regiment. When asked why he had disobeyed orders he replied that he feared a government ambush. He was then ordered to dismiss his bodyguard and attend a private conference. He refused, saying he trusted his bodyguard in everything. The bodyguard stayed.[56]

Victoriano's martyrdom contributed immeasurably to his legend. In a lyric tribute. Víctor López eulogized

> ...this man, El Catorce, celebrated for his valor and his deeds, who donated that valor to the cause of Christ and his Church from the first of January 1927, to the seventeenth of March 1929...who was behind the victory at San Julián...who made the Federals bite the dust at El Camaleon and La Cacayaca...who remained in the field with a reduced number of men after the first *reconcentración* when other chiefs fled the region and dispersed their troops...who refused the surrender offers of Generals Garza and Limón...who became a legend, a terror to his enemies, and the valued friend of all *cristeros*...[and who suffered] a pantomime of justice, after an arrest made easy by the trust and good conscience of the man arrested...[and who met] an ignominious death at the hands of those who stained his name with his innocent blood."[57]

Victoriano continued to be a legend in his homeland in the early 1980s, even among a younger generation of *sanmiguelenses* that knew next to nothing about the *cristiada*. His grave is unmarked [the remains are said to have been stolen], there is no monument to him, and no street bears his name. Yet his fame has been kept alive by such men as José Pedroza Ramírez, a blind street singer and guitarist who knows twenty-one *corridos* (street ballads) about Victoriano. People of all ages listen intently to the sightless troubador as he begins one of them:

> *Voy a cantar un corrido*
> *Me encomiendo a San Francisco*
> *Que a Victoriano El Catorce*
> *Lo queria todo Jalisco.*

> I'm going to sing a *corrido*
> I commend myself to St. Francis
> That Victoriano El Catorce
> Was loved by all Jalisco.

Poncitlán

The Cristero Ardennes

DESPITE THE DEMORALIZATION caused by the El Catorce affair, Gorostieta decided to launch his most ambitious offensive at the height of this divisive controversy. He had good reason for doing so. On 3 March 1929 the factional volcano that had been simmering finally erupted when a group of disgruntled generals, supported by several state governors, declared against the government. The insurgents, all followers of Obregón, correctly surmised that Calles's aim was to continue as strong man of Mexico and rule through a series of puppet presidents. Though many of the conspirators held high ranks, they were not members of the inner circle—as they would have been had Obregón lived. The "Renovators," as they called themselves, saw power within their grasp. They reached for it.

Supreme commander of the rebellion was General José Gonzalo Escobar, chief of military operations in Coahuila. Three other regional commanders who backed the rising were Generals Francisco Manzo in Sonora, Francisco Urbalejo in Durango, and Jesús Aguirre in Veracruz. Other prominent insurrectionists were Roberto Cruz (ex-police chief in Mexico

City), Gilberto Valenzuela (former secretary of *gobernación*), and the governors of Durango, Sonora, and Chihuahua.

On 3 March the rebels issued a proclamation, the so-called Plan de Hermosillo. In a conglomeration of mixed metaphor and purple rhetoric, it denounced Calles as "the Jew of the Mexican Revolution who insists on remaining on the throne of the Caesars at all costs." The manifesto attributed the present sorry state of affairs to "bastardly passions, unchained ambitions, and cynical and criminal impostures [that have] turned the government and its institutions into a school of mercantilism, corruption, and baseness."[1]

A PACT WITH THE RENOVATORS

The rising led by Escobar had an excellent chance of success. The insurgent generals commanded about twenty-five thousand men, over a third of an army already burdened down with fighting the Catholics.[2] The *cristero* factor had not been overlooked by the Renovators. Though a number of the new rebels, Urbalejo in particular, had fought bitter battles against the Catholics, past enmity was subordinated to present expediency. Two weeks before the rebellion Gorostieta had authorized a meeting between two Liga representatives (the Chávez Hayhoe brothers) and Escobar. A pact was concluded specifying that a measure of religious liberty would be restored and the ratings of the Guardia Nacional recognized by the Renovators.[3] Escobar also promised to finance *cristero* efforts to purchase ammunition in Sonora and the southwestern United States.[4]

The Escobar rising sent a thrill of hope through *cristero* ranks. Optimism was particularly high in Los Altos. Townspeople who had suffered a hated occupation awoke one morning to find the Federals gone. Tepatitlán and San Miguel el Alto were abandoned overnight and, in the hills overlooking Arandas, soldiers of the Brigada de Los Altos saw the garrison decamping with every scrap of its impedimenta. To avoid *cristero* attacks, all government units moved out in heavy column formation.[5] The Federal presence in Jalisco was reduced to a token force, consisting of a 600-man garrison in Guadalajara and an *agrarista* unit in the eastern suburb of Tlaquepaque.[6] The rest of the state belonged to the *cristeros*. As units of the Brigada de Los Altos occupied Tepatitlán, San

Miguel el Alto, and Arandas, they were welcomed with delirious enthusiasm that rivaled the liberation of Paris.

There was one man, however, who did not view the situation brightly: Enrique Gorostieta. Despising the *escobaristas* as a band of "unscrupulous generals and discredited politicians," he thought the rising would at best gain only a temporary advantage.[7] His long-range view was decidedly pessimistic. In a letter to Aurelio Acevedo, dated 31 March 1929, he made these comments: "Instead of having improved, our situation has deteriorated with the military *pronunciamientos*.... The movements in the north are in danger of suffering the same fate as the one in Veracruz. [Aguirre's rising had already been put down.].... After their defeat the Turk [Calles] will turn on us again. He will come with many men, highly motivated and proud of their victories."[8]

He agreed to a temporary alliance, but with many reservations. Fewer political bedfellows have ever been stranger—and less compatible—than the *cristeros* and the *escobaristas*. Adopting a policy of *"juntos pero no revueltos* (together but not mixed)," the *cristeros* refused to come under the *escobarista* command and insisted that they should have numerical superiority whenever conducting joint operations.[9] It was almost as if Gorostieta's men feared contamination by being too closely associated with such an openly careerist movement.

Gorostieta's pessimism was immediately given substance by events in Mexico City. Confirming his adversaries' views of him as a power behind the throne, Calles came rushing out of retirement and took over as Secretary of War and Marine. Everywhere, loyal troops were rushed into action. Aguirre, the Veracruz conspirator, was the first to fall. Abandoned by some of the units he considered loyal, he fell back on the Isthmus of Tehuantepec with a depleted force. Captured on 20 March, he died before a firing squad the next day.[10]

With its southern flank secure, the government was free to face north. Manzo, the rebel commander in Sonora, had been assigned to move down the west coast in the direction of Guadalajara. Should he penetrate Jalisco, then a *cristero* fief, the new rebels would be able to link up with the old and march on Mexico City through the *bajío*. Manzo got no farther than Mazatlán, where he was stopped by Federal Generals Carrillo and Rico. By 25 March his forces were falling back into Sonora.[11] The loyalists scored successes on other fronts, with

Generals Juan Andreu Almazán and Eulogio Ortiz entering Monterrey on 7 March and the *escobaristas* abandoning Durango on the fourteenth.[12]

As their fortunes declined, the Renovators began reneging on their commitments to the *cristeros*. Having promised to pay for ammunition, Escobar told Chávez Hayhoe, the Liga representative, that there were enough Catholics in Mexico to enable the *cristeros* to pay for their own cartridges.[13] Relations between the two factions, never cordial, now became icy. Gorostieta stigmatized Escobar as a man "who robs banks and abandons the field," while Acevedo complained that the *escobaristas*, had they wanted to, could have given the *cristeros* "entire trainloads of munitions."[14]

Faced with this situation, Gorostieta decided to launch his grand offensive. It was now or never. If he waited while the *escobaristas* went down to certain defeat he would face, as he had foreseen, a revitalized Federal army fresh from victory over the military rebels. He had to make hay while the sun shone—and the sun was setting fast. His objective was Guadalajara. In spite of *cristero* successes since the bleak summer of 1927, the rebels had never been able to occupy a major population center. Capture of Mexico's second most important city would be both a military and propaganda victory. The Guardia Nacional, established in Guadalajara, could no longer be dismissed as a collection of bandits and back-country bushwhackers.

With Jalisco stripped of Federal troops, Guadalajara was a prize that seemed ripe for the taking. The city's diminished garrison, defeated in attempts to make sorties, was now more prisoner than occupier. Every night rebel patrols penetrated Tlaquepaque and Zapópan (both suburbs) and even the city itself. They were especially active in the eastern Libertad sector, the one nearest to Los Altos.[15]

Gorostieta's plan was to deploy the Brigada in a two-pronged attack against the city. The initial objective was Poncitlán, a town on the south bank of the Santiago River about thirty miles southeast of Guadalajara. Poncitlán was a railhead and this was the key factor in Gorostieta's calculations. A four-regiment task force would seize a passenger train from Mexico City, overwhelm the escort, and ride into Guadalajara. In the meantime, the rest of the brigade would cross the river at Puente Grande, about sixteen miles northwest of Poncitlán and about the same distance due east of Guadalajara. The mission of the second group was to engage the cavalry regiment protecting Guadalajara while main force units rode into the capital by train.

DEGOLLADO AND THE GRAND OFFENSIVE

Scheduled to join in the attack was General Degollado's División del Sur. To work out details, Gorostieta summoned Degollado to Los Altos. There is confusion as to the exact date of the meeting, caused mainly by an error in Degollado's memoirs. He states they conferred around the end of April, but this time is impossible because the operation they were planning took place a month earlier. The date can be narrowed down to between 18 and 23 March, because the battle of Cocula, in which Degollado participated, ended on the eighteenth while the Guadalajara attack was launched on the twenty-third.[16]

So effective was the *cristero* Fifth Column in Guadalajara that Degollado came right through the city to meet Gorostieta. Traveling by horseback he left La Mora, the División del Sur's headquarters, and made his way to the village of Santa Cruz de las Flores, about twenty miles south of Guadalajara. There he called on an old comrade from the "U" who briefed him on conditions in the city. On entering the capital he had a close call. As he was riding north he encountered a southbound car filled with secret policemen. Apparently suspecting something, they made a U-turn and began following him. At that moment a cry went up—the gigantic Corona market, a midtown landmark, was in flames! Forgetting Degollado, the policemen leaped into their car and sped off to the disaster.[17]

Degollado spent the night at the house of a staunch Catholic family named Gómez Tejada. There he conferred with Luis Beltrán Mendoza, the Liga representative, who was operating freely in the friendly atmosphere of Guadalajara. The next day Beltrán took Degollado to Colonia Oblatos, an outlying section only a short distance from the Santiago River. Waiting for them was a courier from Gorostieta, a girl identified only as María Luisa. Posing as a campesino couple, Degollado and the girl made their way unmolested to the west bank of the river. Though the region was safe from *callistas,* crossing presented a problem. Here the river cut through a deep gorge, and the only way to cross was in a crude basketlike contrivance attached to a cable. Degollado describes the crossing as one of the most terrifying experiences of his life.[18]

It was dark when Degollado completed the crossing and, to his chagrin, he encountered none of Gorostieta's men. María Luisa guided him to a cave where they passed an anxious night. The next day they were met by two riders from the Brigada and taken to Gorostieta.

At the meeting between the chiefs Degollado displayed the two most salient aspects of his complex personality— continuing self-doubt and very real military aptitude. He began by requesting that a professional soldier take over command of his division, insisting that he knew nothing of military matters. Gorostieta denied the petition, citing the División del Sur's impressive record in two years under his leadership. Degollado then applied for a six-month leave, pleading fatigue and insisting that he needed a complete rest. Gorostieta not only rejected this request but informed Degollado that his authority had been extended to cover *cristero* forces in Michoacán.

That there was a basis for Gorostieta's faith in Degollado is proved by what happened next. After hearing a situation report on the División del Sur, Gorostieta produced a large map of Jalisco. Informing Degollado of the impending attack on Guadalajara, he asked him how he would deploy his forces in the operation. After the usual disclaimers of military expertise, Degollado asked Gorostieta if he could borrow the map for half an hour. He would study it and try to come up with an idea. Gorostieta agreed and Degollado took the map into the shade of a nearby tree. In exactly half an hour he returned and began his exposition.

Since Degollado never carried out his plan, it is not necessary to review it in detail. It should be noted, however, that it was an eminently sound one, combining a firm grasp of basic tactics with the sophistication that would later become characteristic of counterinsurgency and commando operations. One regiment would cut off rail access from Tequila and Etzatlán, where Federal detachments guarded the railway. Three others would mount the main assault, entering the city from the southwest and through the northwestern sectors of Atemajac and Zapópan. This action would be coordinated with the east-west movement of the Brigada de Los Altos. In the meantime, smaller units would be formed into special attack teams and sent to knock out telegraph and power installations. Degollado also displayed a knowledge of street fighting. Troops entering the city would be instructed to avoid open streets, where the Federals had set up machine guns at key intersections. Instead, they would advance through houses and over rooftops, striking at the machine gun posts from protected positions.

When Degollado finished, Gorostieta looked at him in amazement. "Did you conceive this plan in just thirty minutes?" he asked.

"No, señor," replied Degollado, "I've been thinking about it and studying it for some time. I was just waiting for a chance to present it."[19]

Degollado's disclaimer did nothing to diminish Gorostieta's admiration. Giving him an *abrazo,* he congratulated him on his frankness and excellent presentation. After covering a few minor matters, the chiefs adjourned.

The next day Degollado was on the way back to his command. Again he passed through Guadalajara and, again, his passage reflected the strength of *cristero* influence in the city. He spent the night with two schoolteachers, maiden sisters named Carvajal. Their house was less than thirty yards from the Federal barracks. In the morning he was on his way to Cocula by car. The vehicle belonged to a family named Castillo. Accompanying Degollado, who was driving, was the mother and two daughters. Though the car was once stopped by police, it was a purely routine check. Believing Degollado to be the family chauffeur, they let the party pass unmolested. That night he was back at his headquarters.[20]

That Degollado never attacked Guadalajara was due to a sudden resurgence of Federal strength in western Jalisco, especially along such key access routes as the Guadalajara-Mazatlán railway and all highways leading to Guadalajara from the west and southwest. Operations against Manzo had been so successful that sizable contingents of Federal troops could be diverted to relieve Guadalajara from the west. This move frustrated two of Degollado's main objectives: to cut the rail lines to Tequila and Etzatlán with one regiment and mount a three-regiment drive on the capital along the Cocula-Guadalajara highway. While southern Jalisco was still under *cristero* domination, the western part of the state had reverted to Federal control. It was no longer possible for the División del Sur to attack Guadalajara from the southwest.

Though Degollado's failure may have cost the *cristeros* Guadalajara, his colleagues held no rancor against him. For all his modesty, Degollado was never known to lack courage and his ideological dedication to the *cristiada* was total. He was simply faced with an impossible situation. Had he coordinated his attack with that of the Brigada de Los Altos, hurling himself against the well-defended western approaches to Guadalajara, the result would have been a suicidal bloodletting. On 13 May (1929) when Degollado's wife was arrested in Guadalajara, Gorostieta sent his colleague a warm message of condolence.[21] Later, after Gorostieta had been killed, the Liga named Degollado chief of the Guardia Nacional.

THE BATTLE

Though other events have been more publicized, Poncitlán–Puente Grande was unquestionably the most decisive engagement of the rebellion. It was the *cristeros'* Ardennes offensive—a last-ditch Battle of the Bulge, with a salient aimed at Guadalajara just as the Germans had groped for Antwerp. Had the rebels succeeded in taking Guadalajara, the insurrection might have gone on for years. Gorostieta feared the peace faction in the hierarchy and the American mediators as much as he did his enemies in the field. Such a show of force as the capture of Guadalajara would seriously, perhaps fatally, weaken the efforts of the peacemakers and enormously strengthen the hand of the Liga and such hawkish bishops as Manríquez, Lara y Torres, and González Valencia.

Every regiment in the Brigada took part in the assault. On 22 March 1929 the attackers assembled in Zapotlanejo, which served as a staging area for the operation. They moved out during the day and by nightfall were in position opposite both their objectives. The four regiments detailed to seize the train were Gómez Loza I, Gómez Loza II, San Miguel, and Carabineros de Los Altos. (Since Poncitlán was in the operational zone of the Carabineros, this unit would play a key role in the attack.) The other regiments—Ayo and San Julián—formed the Puente Grande force.[22]

At Poncitlán the river flows west to east and parallels the course of the railroad. About fifteen miles west of Poncitlán it begins curving north, and by the time it reaches Puente Grande the flow is directly north-south. The river's curve meant the *cristeros* were deployed at right angles to each other—the Puente Grande force facing west and the Poncitlán force south.

At midnight a small detachment from the Carabineros crossed the river and blew up a railroad bridge about three kilometers west of Poncitlán. The purpose of this maneuver was to delay the train during the attack. The bridge would then be repaired and the captured train ridden into Guadalajara.

The bridge was blown by 0200 and, in the pre-dawn hours, the Poncitlán force made its preparations. Since the train was not due until 0700, there was plenty of time. Conditions for the attack seemed ideal. The Santiago's north bank near Poncitlán rises somewhat, so the attackers would be able to fire at the train from an advantageous position. The military escort, consisting of 100 men, would rapidly be overwhelmed. Then the attackers would wade across the river and seize the train. The Carabineros would lead the crossing. They were familiar with the terrain and knew exactly where the river was most shallow.

Field headquarters was the chapel of a nearby ranch, the area's highest elevation. There, watching developments from the tower, were Fathers Pedroza and Vega. As dawn broke the two men began anxiously scanning the railroad tracks with high-powered binoculars. At 0700, right on schedule, a train whistle was heard from the direction of Ocotlán, an industrial town ten miles east. As the train pulled into Poncitlán, Pedroza and Vega fretted nervously. Had the engineer or escort commander noticed anything out of the ordinary? Then they sighed with relief—the train was starting up again. Only three kilometers—the distance to the blown bridge—stood between the *cristeros* and success.

As the train approached their observation post, the priests noticed something strange: it was considerably longer than the Mexico City–Guadalajara express. Then Vega gave a

sharp cry. "General!" he said to Pedroza. "This isn't a passenger train. Look at the perforated silhouettes on the cars.
It's a troop convoy and there are soldiers on every roof!"[23]

Pedroza and Vega scrambled down from the bell tower
and made for their horses. The soldiers on the river bank,
positioned on lower ground, still thought they were about to
attack a passenger train. They had to be warned at all costs.

It was too late. Even as they mounted their horses, the
priests heard a deafening sound from the river bank: the
cristeros had opened fire. Then they heard another sound—
quieter, but even more ominous. Down the track came the
squeal of another train whistle—and a second troop convoy
came into view. For the *cristeros* it was an incredible stroke of
bad luck. The two convoys were transporting troops of General Amarillas's division, fresh from victory over the *escobaristas* in Durango. The division had been reassembled in
Irapuato, an important railhead between Mexico City and
Guadalajara, and was on its way north to engage the remnant
of Manzo's forces in Sonora.

Though the rebels' initial fusillade caused heavy casualties, the Federals rallied quickly—too quickly, perhaps. Un-
derestimating the *cristeros'* strength, they formed up and
made an ill-advised charge across the river. At that time of
year, the height of the dry season, the Santiago is sluggish and
choked with water lilies. As they advanced through the
swampy, plant-infested water, the Federals were cut down by
the Brigada's sharpshooters. The attack was bloodily
repulsed.

Chastened but still full of fight, the *callistas* spread out in
linear formation on the south bank of the river. With their
superiority in numbers and firepower, it was only a matter of
time before the rebels ran out of ammunition. At this point,
conventional wisdom would have dictated that the *cristeros*
cut their losses and retire to Los Altos. Though neither Pedroza nor Vega was given to foolish gambles, this was one battle
that could not be lost. So they held their ground, hoping for a
miracle that would turn the tide against their stronger foe.

It was Father Vega who conceived the idea of a flanking
attack. At noon he ordered the San Miguel regiment to move
downriver to look for a suitable place to cross. Once on the
other side, they would be able to mount an attack from the rear

and roll up the *callista* right flank. The plan didn't work, however. Seasoned and battle-tested, the Federals observed San Miguel's downriver movement and matched it with one of their own. Anywhere the rebels tried to cross they found themselves up against determined resistance.[24]

By mid-afternoon Federal aviation had entered the battle. Several planes flew over *cristero* positions and dropped bombs. As usual, little damage was done and the rebels even managed to shoot down one of the attacking aircraft. The plane had swooped down so low that the pilot was killed by ground fire.[25]

As night fell the firing died down. Both sides dug in and the inevitable exchange of insults began across the river. "To-morrow you're going to see us on the other side, you *cristero* sons of whores," shouted a Federal soldier.

"Don't be too sure, you son of the devil," replied a *cristero*.

While most of the exchanges contained the usual ancestral aspersions, the Federals would sometimes jeer at the rebels' limited resources. "Aren't you out of ammunition yet, you starving coyotes?"

"At least we're not being kept by the gringos, you sell-out *callistas*."[26]

RETREAT TO LOS ALTOS

The *cristeros* were in fact running dangerously low on ammunition. Father Vega held a count that night and discovered that the Poncitlán force was down to twenty rounds per man.[27] After conferring with Father Pedroza, he ordered a retreat to Los Altos.

The Puente Grande regiments fared no better. Ironically, they failed for exactly the same reason as their comrades at Poncitlán. The two-train convoy that frustrated the Poncitlán *cristeros* contained only half of Amarillas's division. The leading half had passed the ambush point the night before and was in the Puente Grande sector when the two northern regiments attacked. Faced with the same unexpected opposition—and shortage of ammunition—the Puente Grande *cristeros* broke off the attack and joined the rest of the brigade in the dispirited trek back to Los Altos.[28]

Gorostieta had been in western Michoacán during the Poncitlán–Puente Grande action, organizing resistance in that crucial sector. If he was downhearted by the defeat, he concealed his disappointment. On encountering the Brigada, he immediately led it on a ninety-mile forced march across Los Altos and into Guanajuato, where he successfully attacked San Francisco del Rincón. He then established a north-northwest line from San Francisco to Lagos de Moreno to Encarnación de Díaz, to meet any invasion that might be coming down the main road from San Luis Potosí.[29] While some of these maneuvers—particularly the attack on San Francisco—were carried out for psychological reasons, Gorostieta had a good reason for wanting to seal off the northeastern entrance to the *cristero* heartland. The *escobarista* rebellion was drawing to a close and the war would soon be returning to Los Altos.

The battle that sealed the military rebels' fate was fought at Jiménez, in southern Chihuahua, between 29 March and 3 April 1929. One of the bloodiest in Mexican history, it was the only one in which air power was used on both sides.[30] It ended in complete defeat for the Renovators, with *escobarista* leaders abandoning their beleaguered troops and falling back on Chihuahua City and Ciudad Juárez. At the same time, Cárdenas and Carrillo continued successfully to press Manzo in Sonora. Outfought and discouraged, he fled to the United States on 12 April.[31] While Escobar hung on until 4 May, his rebellion was effectively ended after Jiménez. He spent the last three months in the border town of Nogales, issuing bombastic *pronunciamientos* but ready to cross over to safety at any moment. It wasn't too long before Escobar crossed still another border. Facing bigamy charges in the United States, he turned up in Canada on 20 May.[32]

Though Gorostieta's darkest predictions had come true, he tried hard to discern a ray of light. Attempting to derive consolation from the Guadalajara failure, he reflected that *cristeros* "have a horror of cities because girls will immediately come out and flirt with the soldiers."[33] He went on to conjure up a picture of troops dispersed throughout the city, enjoying civilian hospitality, and then being surprised by the enemy in that disorganized state. "These cities that (the Federals) have abandoned are a greater curse than Capua was for Hannibal," he concluded.[34]

At this point urban temptations should have been the least of Gorostieta's worries. With the *escobaristas* defeated, the issue would now be decided on the red soil and rolling plains of Los Altos. Not since the earliest days of the rebellion, when Calles airily told Barba González that the fighting would be over in three months, had the government underestimated the importance of the region. Los Altos was the dragon's head; cut it off and the rebellion would die. And now, its forces flushed with victory and at maximum strength, the government was ready to make the effort.

The End
in Los Altos

PREPARATION BY THE FEDERALS for the Los Altos offensive began as early as 27 March 1929, even before the *escobaristas* had been smashed at Jiménez. On that day Portes Gil's office announced that a division was being outfitted in San Luis Potosí and would be used exclusively against the *cristeros*. Known as the División del Centro, it was commanded by the *potosino* warlord General Saturnino Cedillo. Because of the scarcity of Federal troops, most of whom were fighting Escobar, two-thirds of Cedillo's 12,000-man force was composed of agraristas.[1] But these were not ordinary members of the breed. While the average rural militiaman was a dispirited *peón*, contemptuously used by the Federals as cannon fodder, these *agraristas* were Pretorians from Cedillo's private army—tough, experienced, and motivated.

The División del Centro entered Jalisco at the beginning of April and advanced unopposed to Lagos de Moreno, a distance of forty miles. Here Cedillo split his force into three columns. One boarded a train and moved off in a north-western direction toward the towns of Santa María de En-medio and Encarnación de Díaz. Its mission was to engage the

San Gaspar regiment and drive a wedge between the Brigada de Los Altos and the Quintanar troops in the "Three Finger" zone. A secondary goal was to relieve *cristero* pressure on a remnant of the 74th Regiment that had been left in Santa María and Encarnación.[2]

A second column, comprising the extreme left of Cedillo's force, knifed southward toward Arandas in a course paralleling the Guanajuato-Jalisco border. Its objective was also twofold: to seal off Los Altos from friendly elements to the east and to reduce such longstanding rebel strongholds as the area around Unión de San Antonio and San Diego de Alejandría.[3]

The center column—a main force unit of 6,000 men—advanced straight down the old royal road to Tepatitlán and Guadalajara. While the other groups were to seal off Los Altos, this one was a dagger thrusting directly into the *alteño* heartland. Most of the Federal soldiers, including a general, had been assigned to this strong center.[4]

GENERAL CEDILLO'S STRATEGY

General Cedillo's strategy in the Los Altos campaign was just the opposite of previous Federal commanders. Under Ferreira and Figueroa the Federals had always advanced up and down main roads and in groups of never less than 300 men.[5] Faced with a slow-moving, roadbound enemy, the rebels either scattered into small groups and melted away or, if they were strong enough, stood and fought. With Cedillo all this changed. An experienced *guerrillero*, he scrapped the search-and-destroy tactics of his predecessors and replaced them with the brand of counterinsurgency he had learned so well in the Huastecan hills of his native state. Splitting his left and right wing into small groups—none larger than 100 men—he penetrated into regions of the *alteño* plateau that had never seen an enemy at close hand. But he wasn't foolish enough to let any of these groups get too isolated. Should 100 *callistas* be jumped by 200 *cristeros*, sounds of firing could bring other units to the rescue within minutes.

An even more radical departure from past procedure was Cedillo's treatment of civilians and captured *cristero* militants. Looting, rape, torture, and summary execution of civilians were strictly forbidden. Also halted were the hated *reconcentraciones*. For the first time in three years the suffering people of Los Altos found themselves treated like human beings. To a population so war-weary, this humane policy raised hopes that a Federal victory would not necessarily be accompanied by a Carthaginian peace.

Most astounding was the treatment now being meted out to war prisoners. Until Cedillo's arrival, captured *cristeros* were exterminated like vermin. A dramatic example of the new policy was the case of a rebel officer captured while visiting his ranch. In former times he would have been shot on capture, his lands despoiled and, in all probability, his wife gang-raped. Expecting cruel retaliation and sudden death, he was astounded to find his enemies behaving with the benevolence of social workers. Cedillo's officers, comporting themselves like the most decorous of guests, apologized to the officer's family and politely escorted him to Arandas. There he was taken before Cedillo and granted a long interview. The conversation ended with Cedillo's placing him at liberty, allowing him to retain his pistol, and giving him fifty pesos. In return, the officer had to give his word of honor that he would never again take arms against the government. He kept his word, took up life as a peaceful rancher, and no amount of coaxing by former comrades could get him to rejoin the *cristeros*.[6] Bit by bit, Cedillo's honey was beginning to erode *alteño* intransigence that had proved so impervious to the vinegar of Ferreira and Figueroa.

But there was still plenty of hard fighting ahead. The first sharp action took place on 4 and 5 April and involved Cedillo's right wing, the column charged with investing Encarnación de Díaz and cutting off the Brigada de Los Altos from the Quintanar troops in Zacatecas. As noted, a remnant of the 74th Regiment was garrisoning Encarnación and the village of Santa María de Enmedio, about fifteen miles southeast and on the same rail line. The Santa María force numbered 120 while the Encarnación detachment was down to 80 men.[7] On the night of the fourth a trainload of *agraristas* pulled into Encarnación. At that moment the San Gaspar Regiment made a daring night attack from the west and cut the railway just outside the town's limits. While the *agraristas* were detraining, 50 of the Federals attempted a sortie but were driven back into town by the *cristeros*.[8] By now the *agraristas*, white-shirted like the *cristeros*, had joined in. The similarity in dress produced a confused situation in which Federals fired upon *agraristas* and *agraristas* on each other. The *cristeros* might well have taken Encarnación had not sounds of firing alerted the Federal force in Santa María. Saddling up, they immediately rode off to the aid of their beleaguered comrades. Of four rebel squadrons deployed against Encarnación, two had to peel off and face the new threat from the south. By now dawn was breaking and the Federals and *agraristas* were no longer firing on each other. Threatened with envelopment, their ammunition running low, the *cristeros* broke off the battle and began an orderly retreat in a southwesterly direction.

For the *cristeros*, the Encarnación action was a tactical success but a strategic disaster. San Gaspar had brutally punished the combined Federal-*agrarista* force at a cost, according to rebel sources, of only three men.[9] Yet its failure to recapture this vital railhead gave Cedillo an important base and enabled him to realize his objective of cutting off the Los Altos *cristeros* from their Zacatecas allies. The Brigada de Los Altos and the Brigada Quintanar, those elite units that had so successfully complemented each other, would never work together again.

Cedillo's eastern column was also making progress. The advance from Lagos de Moreno to Arandas, a distance of sixty miles, was accompanied by an intense aerial leaflet campaign.[10] Though the pamphlets preached peace and conciliation, their effect was at times negated by sporadic violations of Cedillo's policy. Josefina de Arellano, wife of a *cristero* captain fighting in the field, was seized in her house in San Julián. With her was her brother-in-law, Silverio, a rebel lieutenant who was catching a few days rest. He was shot immediately and she was dragged off to the town jail. Since de Arellano had induced a Federal soldier, Juan Torres, to desert and join the *cristeros*, she was considered a dangerous enemy. However, after questioning her briefly, Cedillo ordered her release. As she was preparing to leave, this handsome *alteña's* good looks attracted the attention of some *agraristas* guarding the jail. Shouting ribald messages of endearment, they hinted broadly that they would soon be visiting her home. Angry and frightened, Josefina requested an audience with Colonel von Merck, a German mercenary serving on Cedillo's staff. She described her plight and von Merck gave orders that any man molesting her would be shot. Furnishing her with an escort to her house, von Merck gave her some food and the sum of fifty pesos.[11]

Cedillo's left continued its advance toward Arandas and by late April the Brigada de Los Altos had been cut off from its eastern allies, the 4,000-man Brigada de La Cruz that operated in northern Guanajuato and Querétaro.[12] The only friendly troops still in contact with the Los Altos *cristeros* were contingents in northeastern Michoacán. But these contacts were becoming increasingly tenuous. With the Escobar rebellion virtually over, more and more Federals were returning to the *cristero* theater of war and occupying points along the Jalisco-Michoacán border.

It was at this low ebb that the *cristeros* turned around and won their greatest victory of the war. Ironically, it was a completely meaningless one. The March defeat at Poncitlán-Puente Grande was far less publicized and infinitely more decisive than this engagement. With the failure to recapture Guadalajara the rebels had lost their last chance of winning the war, but they were still capable of winning battles. This one, appropriately, was won in the red-clay city that was the symbol and epicenter of *alteño* Catholicism: Tepatitlán.

FATHER VEGA AND THE BATTLE AT TEPATITLAN

The engagement at Tepatitlán on 19 April 1929 involved the 3,000-man advance guard of Cedillo's center column and 900 *cristeros*. The rebel contingent comprised the two Gómez Loza regiments and two squadrons of the San Miguel force. In command was that supremely gifted tactician, Father Vega. The Federal spearhead, stiffened by 500 soldiers and led by General Rodríguez, had been advancing slowly but steadily down the old royal road from Lagos de Moreno to Tepatitlán. Resistance had been light, restricted mainly to sniper fire.[13] Cedillo's policy of conciliation—coupled with counterinsurgency tactics—had been sufficiently successful to convince him that time was now ripe for a death blow to the *cristiada* in Los Altos. While his left and right columns—advancing in wild, roadless country to the east and west—continued to operate in small formations, his center bunched up on the main road and reverted to conventional frontal tactics.

This new ploy could more correctly be defined as search-and-negotiate than search-and-destroy. The advance was accompanied by a leaflet bombardment and the approach to towns along the way was preceded by the entry of couriers.

These emissaries bore not threatening ultimata but courteous messages requesting cessation of hostilities and the cooperation of civil officials. On the afternoon of the eighteenth one of these couriers rode into Tepatitlán's main plaza and encountered a group of *cristero* officers. Handing them a message, he requested that they take it to the chief of rebel forces in the city. That man was Father Vega.[14]

The decision to give battle in Tepatitlán had been reached two days earlier, at a meeting between Gorostieta and Vega near San José de Gracia. Half-banteringly, half-seriously, Gorostieta wanted to know "what kind of colonels we have in the Brigada de Los Altos who haven't yet been able to stop the *agraristas* from San Luis?"[15] His bantam-cock pride offended, Vega retorted hotly that colonels existed to receive orders from generals. Should he be directed to engage the *agraristas* in force, Gorostieta could rest assured that he wouldn't stand around with his arms folded.

Gorostieta then designated Tepatitlán as the battle site, expressing confidence in the outcome because he considered one *alteño* the equal of five *agraristas*. Agreeing, Vega vowed that any *agrarista* daring to enter the city would pay with his life. He described the trajectory of the enemy advance and assured Gorostieta that his Gómez Loza regiments, reinforced by the two San Miguel squadrons, would send Cedillo reeling north. Gorostieta offered to send a message to Father Pedroza requesting the detachment of either the Ayo or San Julián regiments. With confidence bordering on contempt, Vega refused the offer, bragging that he would eat up the *cedillistas* with the forces he had.

It was in this mood that Father Vega received the courier's message on the afternoon of the eighteenth. Grinning broadly, he called over a low-ranking noncommissioned officer. "Can you write?" he asked. The man admitted to marginal literacy and Vega directed him to answer the message. He was to reject the offer, signing himself "chief of the *cristeros* in Tepatitlán." It was a clever psychological stroke. The note, resembling the scribble of a first grader, must surely have bloated the already dangerous overconfidence of the Federals. Not only would they be facing a ragged and numerically inferior foe, but one led by a barely literate campesino.[16]

Even cleverer was Vega's battle plan. One regiment, Gómez Loza I, was left in Tepatitlán as bait for the Federals.

Numbering 300 men and led by Gabino Flores, this unit would be deployed exclusively as a sniper force. While 70 men were posted in church steeples and flat roofs overlooking the main plaza, the remainder took up positions on a low hill at the northern entrance to the city. Vega's plan was to draw the *cedillistas* into the center of town, wear them down with sniper fire for two or three hours, and then attack with the cavalry he was holding in reserve.[17]

This reserve consisted of Gómez Loza II, led by Cayetano Alvarez, and the two San Miguel squadrons. The former was poised southwest of Tepatitlán, while the latter covered the northeastern approach. Their orders were to stay in place until they received a written message from Vega to engage the *cedillistas* attacking Gómez Loza I.

In the attack the Federals followed a time-honored custom: keep the Army in reserve while using the *agraristas* as cannon fodder. Five hundred soldiers formed a rear guard at a ranch called Las Colonias.[18] The *agraristas* had their hands full against Vega's well-entrenched snipers. Their numerical superiority was offset by the *cristeros'* terrain knowledge and marksmanship.

While Tepatitlán exploded with sounds of battle, men of the reserve force were getting increasingly restive. Their unease was not assuaged by the taunts of nearby campesinos, who mistook obedience to orders for cowardice. "*Qué!*" they cried. "Aren't you going to give a hand to your comrades who have been fighting since dawn?"[19]

It was almost 0700 when the couriers arrived from Vega. The cavalry units were to mount an immediate attack on the city, flanking the *callistas* and cutting them off to the rear. As the San Miguel squadrons advanced, they came upon a ranch barely a kilometer from the town limits that served as Vega's command post. The priest, waiting on the road, halted them momentarily. Deciding on a modification of his original plan, Vega detached fifty men from the main body of attackers. Realizing that he didn't have enough ammunition to completely destroy the *cedillistas*, he decided to drive them back from the city and use the fifty-man force to harass them on their retreat north.

The men who received this order were Heriberto Navarrete, chief of the fifty-man detachment, and Mario Valdés, who would lead the remainder of the San Miguel effectives into Tepatitlán. Giving Navarrete and Valdés an *abrazo*, Vega promised the embrace would be repeated at 1000 in the Tepatitlán plaza—in celebration of a *cristero* victory.[20]

He was partially right. The main San Miguel force, joined by Gómez Loza II, struck the *agraristas* from two directions. Surprise was complete. So swift and crushing was the attack that General Rodríguez, who had accompanied the *agraristas* into Tepatitlán, decided on a hasty retreat to avoid encirclement.[21]

What had been a battle became a butchery. In their pell-mell flight many *agraristas* were cut down as they choked a narrow bridge leading out of town. On reaching the road north, the fleeing remnant was subjected to murderous fire from Navarrete's harassing force. Others, cut off from the main body, holed up in isolated farms and ranches for a last-ditch fight. So confused was the situation that the 500 Federals at Las Colonias were not even committed to the battle. By 1000, true to Father Vega's prediction, the rebels were in complete command.

But that *abrazo* was never repeated. At the very moment of victory, as church bells rang wildly and a carnival atmosphere pervaded the plaza, a somber message came to a group of jubilant *cristero* officers. Father Vega, mortally wounded, was making his last confession to Tepatitlán's parish priest.

What had happened was this. Following the *agraristas'* flight, Vega rode into the city to congratulate Gabino Flores, commander of Gómez Loza I, on his brilliant holding action. Flores informed Vega that a 100-man enemy force had holed up at a nearby ranch belonging to Quirino Navarro, the collaborationist mayor. The Federals, fearing they would be executed, had refused an invitation to surrender. Since they were well-entrenched, with an excellent field of fire, Flores suggested that no attack be made until nightfall. Rejecting this advice, Vega assembled a group on the spot and made for the ranch immediately. Pistol in hand, he was leading the attack when a bullet struck him in the head. He was taken back to town and lived just long enough to make his confession.[22]

Father Vega's death raised a mystery that still endures in the early 1980s: from what direction did the fatal shot come? Officially he was felled by a Federal bullet; yet it is significant that Vega's war party against the Navarro ranch contained a number of soldiers from the San Miguel regiment. It is widely believed in Los Altos that the real killer was a San Miguel trooper, angered by Vega's role in the downfall of El Catorce.[23]

Vega's death was a disheartening blow to the *cristeros*. For all his failings, this flawed priest was a remarkable leader of men. Without a day of formal military training he consistently held his own against the Mexican Army's ablest professionals.

Cedillo recaptured Tepatitlán three days later. Discouraged by Vega's death and low on ammunition, the *cristeros* abandoned the scene of their greatest victory.[24] But the Brigada was by no means finished. Cut off from friendly forces to the east and west, driven out of every sizable population center in Los Altos, Pedroza's men remained masters of the countryside. Cedillo, stunned by the Tepatitlán defeat, now completely abandoned the tactics that had served him so well at the beginning of the campaign. As one of his own colleagues, General Carrera Torres, put it: "Cedillo came to Los Altos with a desire to fight as little as he could."[25] Seeing that sweet reason alone would never wear down the *alteños*, he now welcomed massive troop reinforcements made available by the collapse of the *escobaristas*. It was back to search-and-destroy—with the odds tilted against the *cristeros* as they had never been before. Supplementing Cedillo's seventeen *agrarista* regiments were fresh units, including three air squadrons, that bolstered the Federal presence to 35,000 effectives.[26] This increase in troops meant that the Federals enjoyed an advantage of five to one over the 7,000-man Brigada de Los Altos.

THE PEACE FACTION VS. THE MILITANTS

To add to problems in the field, the rebels now received a blow from another enemy: the dominant peace faction in the Mexican hierarchy. It was Portes Gil who prepared the ground for further negotiations. On 1 May 1929, in response to a question from a foreign correspondent, he exculpated the Catholic Church from any responsibility in the Escobar rebellion. Turning to the *cristero* conflict, he attacked individual Catholics who "dedicate themselves to acts of absolute banditry," but he contrasted these acts with those of "worthy representatives of Catholicism who counsel respect for law and authority." He concluded with the assurance that "the Catholic clergy, when they wish, may renew the exercise of their rites with only one obligation, that they respect the laws of the land."[27]

The peace-minded prelates were quick to respond to Portes Gil's initiative. On 2 May, in Washington, Archbishop Ruiz y Flores issued a correspondingly conciliatory statement. Hailing the President's words as "most important," he stated that "the decision to suspend worship was taken because the hierarchy in conscience was not able to accept laws *that are enforced* [italics added] in my country...."[28] The meaning was clear: the bishops were no longer requesting repeal of the repressive laws but only their more lenient application. Ruiz y Flores also stated that the religious conflict could be corrected by men of good will and that the Church was prepared to cooperate with the government for the well-being of the Mexican people.

The peace offensive was now in full swing. On 7 May Portes Gil commented favorably on the archbishop's reply, with special emphasis on the points that the religious problem could be solved by men of good will and that the Church was prepared to cooperate with the government in advancing the popular interest. U.S. Ambassador Dwight W. Morrow was a prime mover in the preparation of this statement. Not only did he suggest that Portes Gil respond to Ruiz y Flores, but the statement itself was almost identical to a draft Morrow had submitted to him.[29]

Taking their cue from Ruiz y Flores, other peace-minded bishops began intensifying their efforts to end the conflict. On 8 May Bánegas Galván of Querétaro issued a pastoral letter to his diocese which amounted to a blunt directive to seek a solution to the religious problem by peaceful means. This sentiment was echoed by two of the exiled prelates—Vera y Zuria of Puebla, residing in the United States, and Guízar Valencia, who arrived in Rome on 11 May.[30]

These efforts filled the militants with cold fury. The pacifist bishops, as they saw it, were proving a far more insidious foe than their enemies in the field. It was at this time that a split began to develop between Catholic and liberal-Masonic elements on the rebel side. The Catholic *cristeros* had joined the movement solely to defend the rights of the Church. But now the bishops were saying that the religious problem was about to be solved. Should this happen, the Catholics would have no further reason for fighting.

This was not the case with the liberal, anti-clerical, and Masonic officers who had joined the *cristeros* both before and after the *escobarista* rebellion. While the Catholic campesinos might conceivably be allowed to return to their farms and ranches, the Jacobin *cristeros* anticipated no mercy in event of a government victory. (Later, many were given refuge by Cedillo.) Already anti-Catholic by inclination, it wasn't difficult for these men to detest the hierarchy for its peacemaking efforts.

The fight-to-the-death faction found an eloquent spokesman in Gorostieta. Earlier on he had sardonically predicted that at the first tolling of church bells even the most militant Catholics would lay down their arms.[31] On 16 May, seeing his prediction in danger of coming true, he sent a bitter message to the directors of the *Liga* with a request that they forward it to the Episcopal Committee.

In this memorandum Gorostieta made no attempt to conceal his contempt for the bishops. He emphasized that it was the Guardia Nacional, not the hierarchy, who must resolve the conflict. For the bishops to attempt to make peace independently of the field forces would be unworthy and treacherous. To please the increasingly powerful non-Catholic faction among the rebels, Gorostieta pointedly reminded the prelates that there were broad issues of national freedom at stake as well as the rights of religion. As the manifesto progressed, Gorostieta's rhetoric became increasingly rancorous. Implicitly accusing the bishops of cowardice, he chided them for lapsing into quietism or meekly accepting exile. "Had they lived among the faithful; had they, like good pastors, run the risks that their flocks ran; had they even adopted a firm attitude, they would be truly worthy representatives of our people. But this was not so...."[32]

Gorostieta's animus against the prelates was echoed on a more basic level by Santiago Dueñas, Atotonilco *cristero* and major in the Ayo regiment. "Just tell us what to do, General," he said to Gorostieta. "If the fathers go against us we'll shoot them down."[33]

These were trying times for Gorostieta. His pique against the hierarchy was almost equaled by the harsh feelings he bore toward another group of influential Catholics—the directors of the Liga. Unlike the bishops, the *ligueros* were bitter-enders and strongly opposed a settlement from which they would be excluded. But this attitude did not matter to Gorostieta. There were, in his view, intransigents and intransigents. He, his campesino soldiers, and his nucleus of liberal-Masonic officers drew a firm line between themselves and comfortable Catholics who took dangerous stands in safe places. Moreover, there was the Liga's record of incompetence, heavy-handed meddling, and—as many believed—bad faith. (The Liga's prestige had never recovered from the disappearance of the 25,000 pesos sent to San Antonio by Gómez Loza.) As pressure mounted against the Guardia Nacional, so did Gorostieta's disillusionment with the "jackasses of the League."[34]

By the end of May (1929) the Brigada de Los Altos had broken up into small, semi-autonomous units. To keep resistance alive, Gorostieta decided on a journey to Michoacán. While there were even more *cristeros* in that wild state than in Jalisco, they were nowhere near as well organized. Of twelve thousand rebels operating in Michoacán, many were in isolated bands roaming in the high sierra or dense jungles along the coast.[35] There they served as regional self-defense forces, keeping local villages under rebel control but doing little to challenge mounting Federal pressure in the more populous and strategically important areas. Unlike the hard-pressed *alteños,* some of these Michoacán bands could go for months without seeing an enemy soldier.

Gorostieta's plan was to make more effective use of this relatively untapped source of manpower. To transform the Michoacán *cristeros* from back-country bush fighters into disciplined soldiers, he had induced a Federal general named Alfonso Carrillo Galindo to join his staff. Carillo would accompany Gorostieta's party to Michoacán and there take charge as chief of operations.[36]

On 1 June Gorostieta, accompanied by eighteen men, began his eastward journey toward the Michoacán border. The rainy season had come early that year and all day long his party had been buffeted by a cold, bone-chilling downpour. They had intended to spend the night at a friendly hacienda, but the presence of Federal patrols compelled them to sleep in the woods. The following morning, between 0900 and 1000, the party arrived at Hacienda del Valle, about eight miles southwest of Atotonilco. After breakfast, Gorostieta lay down to rest his eyes (he suffered from conjunctivitis).

Suddenly there were sounds of firing. It was between 1040 and 1100, and a detachment of Federals had been spotted in the vicinity of a small store that formed part of the hacienda. Leaping to his feet, Gorostieta shouted "Galdem!"* and rushed out the door, frantically calling for his horse.[37] He tried to mount but a volley of bullets killed the animal. As the horse fell it momentarily pinned Gorostieta's leg to the ground, but he wriggled free and made his way back to the hacienda's main building. Though two of Gorostieta's party managed to escape, he and the others were trapped inside the house, now completely surrounded.

Gorostieta knew the end had come. When one of his aides asked what they should do he replied: "Fight bravely and die like men."[38] As it turned out, he was the only one who followed his advice. Quickly reconnoitering the house, he found a door in the chapel that led out to a small orange orchard. He came through the door, guns blazing, and was cut down immediately. The rest of the party, numbering sixteen men, promptly surrendered and were taken to the Atotonilco city jail.

There is strong circumstantial evidence that Gorostieta was betrayed by a member of his party. The most comprehensive account of his last days is a thirteen-part serial in volume four of *DAVID*, the *cristero* veterans' publication. The author is José Guadalupe de Anda, one of the sixteen who were taken into captivity. De Anda states that on 29 May he had a meeting in Ocotlán with an engineer named Alfonso Garmendia. So fervent were Garmendia's protestations of allegiance to the rebellion that de Anda invited him to join Gorostieta's entourage. Possibly seeking to relieve himself of blame for what proved to be a disastrous error, de Anda explained that he had been "commissioned" (presumably by higher-ups in the movement) to initiate the meeting by calling on Garmendia at his hotel.[39]

On 5 June, three days after Gorostieta's death, de Anda, in captivity, began to develop suspicions about Garmendia.[40] On 7 July, in line with Cedillo's conciliatory policy, all surviving members of Gorostieta's party were set free. Loaded into trucks, they were taken to the railroad station. There de Anda

---

*This expression is probably an incorrect rendition of "Goddam!" (Gorostieta spoke English).

saw a familiar figure on the platform. It was Garmendia—in the uniform of a Federal colonel.[41]

As a renegade from the officer corps, General Carrillo Galindo faced certain death. He saved himself with a clever ruse. He had never, he insisted, gone over to the *cristeros*. His sole reason for being with Gorostieta (who was an old friend from the Military College) was that he had undertaken a mission to try to persuade the latter to surrender. It was only through incredible bad luck that he happened to be with Gorostieta that fateful day at Hacienda del Valle. Carrillo was persuasive enough to make Cedillo believe his story and he was also released.[42]

Though the government and the peace Catholics breathed deep sighs of relief over Gorostieta's death, the *cristeros* doggedly fought on. To succeed Gorostieta, the Liga named Jesús Degollado Guízar supreme commander of the Guardia Nacional. With customary modesty he at first declined the appointment, protesting that it was an act of "madness" and that the LNDLR had committed a "very great error."[43] Father Pedroza, he insisted, was far better qualified for the post.[44] But this was not to be. Degollado, who had ascended from civilian status to general, was clearly the Liga's man; besides, the *ligueros* never felt completely at home with the independent-minded Pedroza.

The Brigada's final hour was one of its finest. At the beginning of June (1929), on the eve of Gorostieta's death, the *cristero* forces in Los Altos had broken up into small units waging intermittent guerrilla warfare. Among pessimists there was talk of burying weapons, hiding horses, and suspending combat until Federal pressure had been relaxed.

Such defeatist thinking was completely alien to Father Pedroza's nature. His first act was to change the brigade's name—from Brigada de Los Altos to Brigada Enrique Gorostieta. On 6 June he sent a message to the Liga on occasion of Gorostieta's death. He assured the *ligueros* that, while serious, the loss was by no means fatal. Just as the rebels had recovered from the death of such leaders as González Flores and Gómez Loza, so would they be able to fill the void created by Gorostieta's loss.

Being hawks—albeit comfortably situated ones—the men of the Liga needed no special prodding to confirm that in their militant stance. On 12 June a reply was sent to Pedroza over the signature of Rafael Ceniceros y Villareal. Praising Pedroza's message as one that "vibrated with notes of patriotism and enthusiasm," it informed him of Degollado's appointment and expressed confidence in final victory.[45]

On 11 June Pedroza sent another message, this one addressed to Archbishop Ruiz y Flores, chairman of the Episcopal Committee. Though more tactfully worded than Gorostieta's bitter statement of 16 May, its thrust was the same: the higher clergy should not break faith with the Guardia Nacional by "making a pact with the tyrant." It concluded by reminding the bishops that they had sanctioned the legitimacy of armed defense three years earlier and imploring them not to "deliver your flocks to the executioner's knife."[46]

Though it is not known whether the message ever reached Ruiz, the point is academic. Pedroza never received an answer and was naive to suppose that he might. Ruiz and his colleagues were going out of their way to shake the "clerical fanatic" image. For them to enter into communication with a live, fire-breathing "clerical fanatic," a priest-general fighting the Federals in the field, would have been the height of folly.

Pedroza's activity in these last days was not confined to writing letters. Achieving a miracle of organization, he was able, in less than two weeks after Gorostieta's death, to transform the Brigada from a group of scattered guerrilla bands into a force capable of engaging the enemy in set battles. The first of these engagements took place on 15 June and fifteen more were recorded during a ten-day period between the eighteenth and the twenty-eighth.[47] These heroic efforts were to no avail, however. Even as the *cristeros* were performing prodigies in the field, their fate was being decided at higher levels. On 9 June Archbishop Ruiz y Flores and his leading associate, Bishop Pascual Díaz, arrived in Mexico City by train from the United States. The next twelve days witnessed a period of frenzied diplomatic maneuvering, with peace assuming the guise of an alluring but elusive temptress.

The prelates had two meetings with Portes Gil, a friendly one on 12 June and a tense, disconcerting one the following day. Like the bishops, the President faced pressure from hawks in his own camp. His nervous tension was hardly eased the following day when he received a telegram from one of the most intransigent anti-clericals, Veracruz governor Adalberto

Tejeda, who had previously served as secretary of *gobernación*. In rhetoric that sounds remarkably modern, Tejeda deplored the imminent return of the "pig clergy that wishes to renew its monstrous work of deforming the conscience and morality of the people."[48] Tejeda's jeremiad was accompanied by messages from labor and Masonic groups, urging a continuing hard line toward the clergy.

Had it not been for the efforts of influential foreigners, the *arreglos* (agreements) might never have been signed. The key figure was Ambassador Morrow. With the skill of a juggler he manipulated his contacts with the Mexican hierarchy, the Vatican, Portes Gil, and the American State Department. To avoid further friction between president and prelates, he himself prepared drafts for both sides and delivered them personally, suggesting that the parties refrain from meeting again until they had read and approved each other's statements. Other foreign peacemakers who helped speed the settlement were Manuel Cruchaga Tocornal, former Chilean ambassador to the United States, and Rev. Edmund A. Walsh, S.J., director of the Georgetown School of Foreign Service. Both men were in Mexico City during this crucial period, working closely with Morrow.

The agreement was announced on 21 June. It consisted of two statements, one by Portes Gil and a considerably shorter one by Ruiz y Flores. The President began by acknowledging assurances from the bishops that they were "motivated by sincere patriotism" and that they wished public worship to be resumed within the framework of the constitution and laws. It was not, he continued, the government's wish to "destroy the identity of the Catholic Church or any other, nor to intervene in any way in its spiritual functions."[49] The statement concluded with three points which can be interpreted as minor concessions to the Catholics. The first stipulated that registration of clergymen would apply only to those who had been named by hierarchical superiors; the second allowed religious instruction in churches, while forbidding it in schools; the third guaranteed all citizens, including members of any church, the right of petition for the reform, derogation, or enactment of any law.

Ruiz y Flores's statement was so brief that it can be reproduced almost in full:

Bishop Díaz and I have had several conferences with the President...and their results are set forth in the statement he issued today.

I am glad to say that the conversations have been marked by a spirit of mutual good will.... As a consequence of the statement by the President, the Mexican clergy will resume religious services in accordance with the laws in force.

It is my hope that the resumption of religious services may lead the Mexican people...to cooperate in all moral efforts undertaken for the welfare of all the people of the country.[50]

These statements brought about what three years of military action had failed to: the end of the *cristiada*. The rebellion terminated with neither a bang nor a whimper; it simply melted away in the wake of the *arreglos*.

THE FINAL DAYS

No war or rebellion ever ended less formally. There were neither victory parades nor surrender ceremonies. The word "surrender *(rendición)*" was not even used. As a sop to militant Catholics, it was announced that the existence of the Guardia Nacional would be terminated through a *licenciamiento*—general discharge.

There were, however, individual surrenders with *cristero* units yielding their arms to local Federal commanders. These affected but a minority of the fifty thousand men the rebels had mobilized.[51] According to Portes Gil, only fourteen thousand *cristeros* surrendered officially; the rest, believing the religious problem had been solved, simply went home.[52]

There was a departure from the script in Los Altos, however—one that took the form of a final spasm of violence. Of the charismatic *jefes* who had made their mark in that bloody land, only Father Pedroza remained. There had been a trickle of desertions from the Brigada when the *arreglos* were rumored; the trickle became a flood when they were officially announced. Though bitter, Pedroza was realistic. He had no alternative but to seek peace. At the end of June (1929) he entered into an informal agreement with Cedillo whereby both sides would suspend hostilities. Should *cristeros* and Federals encounter each other in the field they were to identify themselves by unit and go peacefully on their way.[53] Such an encounter took place on 2 July, on the road between Arandas and Jesús María. Unfortunately one of Pedroza's escort, a fifteen-year-old boy named Bartolillo, opened fire and wounded a Federal soldier. (Bartolillo later claimed he knew nothing of the Cedillo-Pedroza agreement.)[54] A fire fight ensued in which Pedroza was slightly wounded in the arm and taken prisoner. Transported to Arandas, he was first treated leniently. Lodged in a hotel, he spent part of the evening playing chess with the Federal commander, General Alberto Carrera.

The horror came the following day. A squad of soldiers called for Pedroza on the pretext that they were taking him to Federal military headquarters in Yurécuaro, but the column halted at the municipal graveyard. Knowing the end had come, Pedroza asked bitterly if his captors were going to kill him. One of the soldiers, a lieutenant named Varela, taunted him with lacking machismo. Hotly denying he was afraid to die, Pedroza protested that they should have notified him beforehand so he could be confessed. Varela's response was to push Pedroza through the graveyard gate. Flinging himself on Varela, the priest wrestled him to the ground with his good arm. In the ensuing struggle Varela managed to extricate his revolver and shoot Pedroza in the chest. His comrades then shot and clubbed the dying man, one blow from a rifle butt smashing his skull. The body was thrown into a shallow grave and hastily buried. In 1960 the remains were exhumed by *cristero* sympathizers and reburied in Arandas's Templo de San José.[55]

Father Pedroza's death greatly accelerated the dissolution of the Brigada. The campesino rank-and-filers went home to their farms and ranches. Most of the liberal-Masonic officers took refuge with Cedillo. The *potosino* strong man, a fellow non-Catholic, was known for his leniency toward ex-*cristeros*. As for the Catholic officers, mostly *acejotameros*, they dispersed as best they could. Of those imprudent enough to remain in Jalisco, many were hunted down and killed after the *arreglos*. The ones who left the state, however, generally managed to survive.

A case in point involves Major Heriberto Navarrete. Navarrete had just completed arrangements for surrender of the remaining arms and horses of the San Miguel regiment. He then called on General Figueroa, requesting a permit to carry firearms. As Navarrete entered Figueroa's office, the general was conferring with a man he immediately recognized. It was the collaborationist governor, Silvano Barba González. Barba left immediately and the interview between Figueroa and Navarrete began.

The general, in an affable mood, granted Navarrete's request and inquired about his plans. As Navarrete replied that he would settle in Guadalajara and resume his engineering studies, a look of incredulity came over Figueroa's face. "But, man, you're an innocent," he said. He explained that while Navarrete had nothing to fear from Federal military authority, it was a different story where a group of vindictive "little politicians" were concerned. "They will kill you soon," he insisted. "They will treacherously assassinate you."[56] Navarrete, if he valued his life, should leave Guadalajara immediately and go far away.

As Navarrete absorbed Figueroa's words, he began to contemplate the identity of these enemies. No figure loomed larger than that of the man who had just left the room. "Yo pensé en Silvano Barba (I thought about Silvano Barba)," he wrote in his memoirs.[57] Soon after, he left for Mexico City.

Degollado's official *licenciamiento* of the Guardia Nacional came on 12 August. But he was essentially "discharging" an employee who had already quit. This was especially true in Los Altos. The most celebrated unit in the *cristero* fighting forces ceased to function militarily with the Cedillo-Pedroza pact. With Father Pedroza's murder, the brigade disappeared completely. The lean lands, free of the three-year agony of war, now faced an uncertain future.

Aftermath

THE *ARREGLOS* THAT WERE SIGNED by President Portes Gil and Bishop Ruiz y Flores did little to end the Church's problems. By traducing their defenders in the field the prelates had hoped to ingratiate themselves with the central government, but this move proved to be a grave miscalculation.

Renewal of religious persecution began cautiously, but it rapidly escalated in tempo and severity. The two-year interval between the signing of the *arreglos* (21 June 1929) and June of 1931 saw a lull in anti-Catholic activity. Church services were being performed in large parts of the country, harassment of clergymen slackened, and a number of persons imprisoned for violating the *Ley Calles* were released.[1] It began to look as if the hierarchy's conciliatory policy had paid off.

This mini-thaw came to an abrupt end in the year marking the four-hundredth anniversary of the Virgin of Guadalupe. Possibly fearing a revival of devotional enthusiasm, the government began to crack down hard. Veracruz governor Adalberto Tejeda, second only to Tabasco's Garrido Canabal as Mexico's leading clerophobe, authorized a decree mandating a ratio of one priest for every 100,000 people—the same figure as in Tabasco. This affront was too strong even for the docile and blackmail-prone "holy bishop" of Veracruz, who suspended worship in his state.[2]

The situation worsened in 1932. In September, when Pope Pius XI complained that the government was not living up to the *arreglos*, President Abelardo Rodríguez accused the Pontiff of trying to foment rebellion. In October both the apostolic delegate and Archbishop Ruiz y Flores, the hierarchy's most pacific member, were deported from the country. Ruiz y Flores's offense had been to deny that the Pope was stirring up rebellion in Mexico.[3]

The Church's decline continued through 1933 and hit bottom during the next two years. By the close of 1935 it seemed as if Roman Catholicism would be buried as deeply by the followers of Calles as the Aztec religion had been by the followers of Cortés. Ruiz y Flores, in an agonized declaration from exile, stated that the Church had ceased to function.[4] Since the number of priests who could officiate legally had been reduced by 90 percent since 1925, the archbishop's statement was not far from the truth.[5] Another burden on the Church during this period was a constitutional amendment calling for establishment of a "socialist education" program—a measure that would arouse a fire storm of resentment throughout the Catholic regions of Mexico.

Even grimmer than renewal of religious persecution was the systematic assassination of former *cristeros*, particularly those who had risen to leadership positions. Should attacks on the Church provoke another rebellion, the government wanted to make sure that there were no men of capacity on hand to direct it. *Cristero* veterans were not given the two-year respite granted the Church; their extermination began immediately.

The first victim of the terror was Father Pedroza, executed less than two weeks after the *arreglos*. The same month witnessed the killing of three Guanajuato chiefs. Other 1929 victims were División del Sur generals Vicente Cueva, Lorenzo Arreola, and Carlos Bouquet and the commander of Gómez Loza II, Cayetano Alvarez.[6] Pedro Quintanar died on 14 June, under particularly grisly circumstances. Having fled to the border town of Ojinaga, Chihuahua, the sixty-nine-year-old man was trapped naked in a public bath and stabbed to death.[7] Before the carnage was finished, better than five hundred former officers, from lieutenants to generals, had lost their lives.[8] Surviving *cristero* leaders grimly agreed with Bishop Lara y Torres's view that more rebel chiefs died after the *arreglos* than during the war.[9]

THE SECOND *CRISTERO* REBELLION

This situation was the background to *la segunda*, the forlorn second *cristero* rebellion of the 1930s. "If the first stage of the *cristiada* (1926–1929) was a war of the poor," writes Jean Meyer, "the second was a war of the hopeless...."[10] The leaders of *la segunda* were not men fighting for the Church—whose leaders outdid each other in denouncing the new rebels—or even men fighting for their lives. Death was a foregone conclusion; the rebels of *la segunda* preferred the dignity of seeking it in combat rather than waiting to be assassinated.

The rebellion was so disorganized and sporadic that historians can't even agree on its dates. While most of the fighting took place between 1934 and 1937, violence began as early as 1932 and did not end until March, 1940, when Federico Vázquez was gunned down in the sierra of Durango.[11] The locus of *la segunda* differed somewhat from that of its predecessor. Puebla, Veracruz, and Sonora, dormant in the first *cristiada*, were active in the second. Jalisco and Michoacán, on the other hand, were relatively quiet. Except for a brief flareup of violence in 1935 and early 1936, Los Altos contributed nothing. Only Durango and Guanajuato remained constant, rising to about the same level of insurgency as they had before. Other states involved, to varying degrees, were Oaxaca, Tlaxcala, Sinaloa, Guerrero, Nayarit, Colima, Zacatecas, Morelos, and Querétaro. The "rebellion of the hopeless" was never able to attract more than seventy-five hundred militants, or about one-seventh the number who had risen in 1926 to 1929.[12] Adding to the rebels' difficulties was the fact that their enemies had available a vastly improved communications system. Many miles of paved roads had been built; telephone, telegraph, and radio facilities were far better than before; and military aviation functioned as an efficient adjunct to the movement of cavalry and infantry.

Another obstacle faced by the new *cristeros* was the un-wavering hostility of the Church. On 31 May 1932, after the first outbreaks of violence, Bishop Ignacio Plascencia of Zacatecas ordered priests in his diocese to withhold the sacraments from "chiefs and agitators, who must be considered not in a state to receive them because of their disobedience to ecclesiastical authority."[13] In the same year a Colima priest, Father Covarrubias, went so far as to order a penitent to repeat to military authorities information about rebel activity he had told in the confessional.[14] Other clergymen forbade the faithful to give the *cristeros* food, scorned them as bandits and rebels, and even repudiated the movement of 1926 to 1929.

The extreme right also opposed the rebellion. Guanajuato was the seat of the clerical-fascist *sinarquista* movement, and its members actively aided the government in hunting *cristero* bands in the Sierra de Agustinos.[15]

La segunda in Los Altos began and ended with the efforts of Lauro Rocha. In 1929 he had gone to Mexico City, where he pursued studies as a military veterinarian, first in the Colegio Militar and then in the Escuela Nacional de Veterinaria. Deeply disturbed by the renewed persecution, he returned to Los Altos in April of 1935 and went into rebellion, but he was able to raise only three hundred men, most of them veterans of the Ayo and Gómez Loza II regiments.[16] By the summer of 1936 he had come to the conclusion that military action was useless. "I don't believe I will last here much longer," he wrote to a friend. He complained that he and his men were living in "a completely hostile environment" and that an anti-*cristero* pastoral letter by Bishop (later Cardinal) José Garibi Rivera "has damaged us more than the government itself."[17] Rocha returned to Mexico City in late summer. Betrayed by an associate, he was murdered by Federal agents on New Year's Eve of the same year.[18] Thus ended the organized military effort in Los Altos.

THE *BRAGADOS'* REIGN OF TERROR

Exhausted by the first *cristiada*, mindful of the Church's hostility toward the second, most *alteños* abandoned the field and began concentrating on civil resistance to the hated socialist education program. Those who remained were not rebels but hoodlums masquerading as rebels. Feared and hated for their

cruelty, they had all of Father Vega's less pleasant characteristics and little of his military skill. Where the *cristeros* of 1926 to
1929 fought armed enemies of the Church, the *bragados*—as
they were called—concentrated on unarmed teachers who
administered the socialist education program. (The *bragados*
were so named because it was their custom to wear green
fringes around the neck bearing the legend "Down With Socialist Education!" These fringes were about the width of a
mule's "*bragadura* (crotch)."[19]

Considering the loathing it aroused, the most astonishing
feature of that program is how tame it seems by the standards
of the early 1980s. It began on 10 October 1933, when Article 3
of the Constitution was amended to read as follows:

> The education imparted by the State shall be a socialist one
> and, in addition to excluding all religious doctrine, shall com-
> bat fanaticism and prejudices by organizing its instruction and
> activities in a way that shall permit the creation in youth of an
> exact and rational concept of the Universe and of social life.

This bit of watered-down Marxism was the brainchild of Nar-
ciso Bassols, Abelardo Rodríguez's Minister of Public Education. Bassols might have gotten away with the amendment
had he not made the error of extending his reforming zeal into
another—and more sensitive—area. What really inflamed
the Catholics was his plan to introduce sex education courses
into the school curriculum. Bassols first got the idea from a
1930 resolution adopted in Lima, Peru, by the Sixth Pan American Welfare Congress. It recommended that schools in Latin
America introduce courses in physiology and hygiene. This
suggestion was supplemented by a list of proposals presented
to Bassols's ministry in 1933 by the Mexican Eugenic Society.
Pointing to the high incidence of unwanted births and venereal disease among girls of poor families, the Society advocated a specific program of sexual education. Far from being
radical, it was based on a standard physiology text used in the
United States.[20]

The program's relative innocuousness was completely
obscured by those loaded words—"sexual education." It was
the label, not the content, that provoked the mindless reaction
that followed. Street demonstrations were accompanied by
wild rumors—partly inspired by the Church—about "sex in

schools." Of lip-smacking prurience, these reports accused teachers of using nude models in class and even of seducing their students. Archbishop Pascual Díaz, abandoning his quietist role, was emboldened to the point of ordering parents to keep their children out of secondary schools and threatening to excommunicate offending teachers.[21]

Faced with such frenzied opposition, the government was forced to backtrack. Bassols tried to soften the impact of his program by changing its name from "sexual" to "social" education. This cosmetic concession was not enough. Antagonism had reached such a fever pitch that Rodríguez was forced to offer up Bassols as a sacrifice. The education minister resigned in May 1934, but the program continued; only the name had been changed.

Resistance to socialist education in Los Altos faithfully followed the cultural norm of fanaticism uncomplicated by puritanism. In their holy fury against government teachers, the *alteños* paid scant regard to biblical teaching about the casting of first stones. Painted bordello girls vied with pious crones in denouncing "the whores of the government school," and all segments of rural *alteño* society were united in their zeal to "take out the Bolshevik rats and drag them through the streets."[22]

The "atheistic" teachers were hated in Los Altos far more than the Army—or even the *agraristas*—had ever been. The worst that had ever happened to these military foes was the shooting and stabbing that followed San Julián. Teachers, on the other hand, were routinely tortured and mutilated by the *bragados*. The most popular chastisement consisted of cutting off the ears of male educators and breasts of female ones. Another was for horsemen to lasso victims and drag them along the ground for extended periods of time. One such case occurred in the town of Villa de Refugio, Zacatecas. (This community is in the "Three Finger" zone, which is culturally a virtual replica of Los Altos.) One evening a young schoolmarm was seized by a band of riders and dragged in the dust for hours. When the body was discovered there was barely enough of her left to bury.[23] A contemporary writer, hostile to both Marxism and the Catholic Left, described the campaign against rural teachers as one that "reached a level of hysterical barbarism."[24]

Whether the victims lived or died pretty much depended on the whim of their tormentors. Some *bragados* thought that it was amusing to allow mutilated teachers to survive as figures of fun in communities where they had been spreading their "godless" doctrines.

Adding to the teacher's troubles was the fact that they received woefully little backing from the government. Local army garrisons were thoroughly corrupt and openly functioned as mercenaries for the rich. Such protection was beyond the teacher's means. The educators were also bitter about a system of priorities that placed them at the bottom rung of the ladder. "The government, when cutting its budget, always begins with us," said one rural maestro. "They'll pay the *marungos*, those health department employees who treat the whores, before they pay us...."[25]

Rural teachers were not the *bragados'* only victims. Catholic ranchers, *cristero* to the core, were also subjected to exactions "*pa' la guerra* (for the war)."[26] During the 1926 to 1929 period, Mario Valdés was the only *jefe* in Los Altos who shook down campesinos and poor townspeople. The others scrupulously followed the "Robin Hood" policy described by E.J. Bumstead, an American mining engineer kidnaped by the rebels and held for a 30,000-peso ransom: "If they stopped at a farm to eat they had to pay for their food, except in cases where the proprietor was a rich man."[27] In the first uprising El Catorce had ordered the execution of a man for stealing food and Father Pedroza had disciplined soldiers who compelled mule drivers on the Atotonilco road to pay tolls. The Los Altos *cristeros* of 1926 to 1929 had furnished a textbook case of the correct method to win over a civilian population.

This credit was quickly squandered by the *bragados*. Recalcitrant Catholics, regardless of economic status, were intimidated and bludgeoned into making contributions. If they refused, they were tortured or killed. The rich Catholics paid off or bought protection. As for the poor, they fared better than the schoolteachers only in that they were tortured selectively rather than indiscriminately. They were also spared the hideous mutilations practiced against the educators.

The *bragados'* cruelty and rapacity played a large part in bringing about their downfall. Having robbed themselves of the civilian support enjoyed by the *cristeros*, their position became increasingly precarious. For the first time, an *alteño* could give information to a local garrison commander without being considered a traitor.

Peace eventually came to Los Altos through a progression of events that dissipated the major causes of tension. The *bragados* frightened away the "atheistic" teachers, the military and civil defense forces broke the *bragados,* and the government relaxed its campaign against the Church.

CHURCH-STATE DETENTE

The relaxation process between the Church and the government began with Lázaro Cárdenas. Though he was the most radical president in Mexican history, he lacked the doctrinaire anti-Catholicism of such men as Calles, Tejeda, and Garrido Canabal. His goal was social revolution and—providing the Church didn't obstruct his political aims—he had no intention of being sidetracked into policies of sterile anti-clericalism. Though granting the right of communities "to break down the resistance of fanatics egged on by enemies of the Revolution," he held at the same time that "it is no concern of the government to undertake anti-religious campaigns," adding that "hereafter there must be no more anti-religious propaganda in the classrooms."[28]

The Catholics received another bonus on 9 April 1936, when Plutarco Elías Calles was expelled from Mexico by Cárdenas, his one-time follower. Though as anti-clerical as ever, Calles had been moving steadily to the right. He soured on land reform, flirted with fascism, and was found reading a Spanish translation of *Mein Kampf* the night he was arrested.[29]

The Church's fortunes continued to improve under Manuel Avila Camacho, Cárdenas's successor. Declaring himself a religious believer, Avila Camacho changed Article 3 of the Constitution in such a manner as to virtually emasculate it of anti-Catholic content. The most significant section of the new version read as follows:

> The education that the State imparts shall tend to develop harmoniously all the faculties of the human being and shall develop in him a love of country and a consciousness of international solidarity, independence, and justice. Freedom of belief...shall be maintained by complete freedom from any religious doctrine and, based on the results of scientific prog-

ress, shall struggle against ignorance and its effects, servitudes, fanaticism, and prejudices.[30]

The final remnant of socialist education was discarded in 1942, when the entire concept was scrapped in favor of a campaign to wipe out illiteracy.[31]

The end result was a return to the pre-Calles condition of Church-State détente: the oppressive laws remained on the books in 1982, but little effort was made to enforce them. Catholic schools were thinly disguised as private institutions, religious holidays were observed in both public and private schools, nuns went about in a modified habit, and one occasionally might see a priest publicly wearing clerical garb.

In the 1970s there was an interesting change in the nature of anti-clericalism. Once an exclusively leftist phenomenon, much of it began to come from the Right. The new confrontation was between old revolutionaries who had become comfortable and radical Catholics. A leading spokesman for the former was the journalist and writer Rodrigo García Treviño, who discerned a sinister new trend he identified as *católicomunismo* (Catholic Communism). Prominent in García's demonology was the Society of Jesus ("Those tonsured Socialists") whom he saw as "promoters...of another *cristero* rebellion."[32] Among members of the hierarchy García viewed with special loathing was Sergio Méndez Arceo, the pro-Castro "red bishop" of Cuernavaca. This distaste was expressed on a more primitive level during one of Méndez Arceo's visits to Rome. Seized by a band of Italian ultra-clericals, the bishop was roughed up and daubed with red paint.

Deepening antagonism between secular Right and clerical Left during the late 1970s and early 1980s gave the Mexican Communist Party (Partido Comunista Mexicano) a golden opportunity to fish in troubled waters. The PCM favored constitutional reform designed to relax restrictions against churchmen in politics. This represented a 180-degree turn: while far leftists favored virtual extermination of the Church in the 1920s and 1930s, in the early 1980s they wanted the statutes changed to allow their radical Catholic allies a greater share in the political process.

These shifting tides of ideology have made little impression on the ranchers and campesinos of Los Altos. They have remained as indifferent to the blandishments of the Méndez

Arceo progressives as they were to the clerical-fascist *sinar-quistas* in the 1930s and 1940s. All the *alteños* ever wanted was to practice their religion in peace. With the relaxation of anti-Catholic persecution, their objective was attained.

By 1982 the image of Los Altos as a center of militant Catholicism had faded and once again been replaced by the pre-*cristiada* stereotype—one of bristling machismo, dashing *charros*, fiery tequila, stunning women. The flow of Los Altos into the mainstream of Mexican history began and ended with the *cristiada*. Having occupied center stage with this magnificent witness to their faith, the people of the red-clay country again withdrew into the cocoon so finely and tightly spun by the imperatives of their unique culture.

ABBREVIATIONS IN NOTES

ACG Archives of René Capistrán Garza
ASC Archives of Father Salvador Casas
AMC Archives of Rafael Martínez Camarena
ARF Archives of Antonio Ríus Facius
NARS U.S. National Archives and Records Service
PASM Parochial Archives of San Miguel el Alto

Notes to Chapters

THE LEAN LANDS: A PROFILE

1. Information furnished by DETENAL *(Dirección General de Estudio del Territorio Nacional).*

2. Luis Pérez Verdía, *Historia particular del estado de Jalisco,* vol. 1, p. 257.

3. Ibid., pp. 259 and 262.

4. J. Jesús González Martín, "Feria de abril en Tepa," p. 4.

5. Jean Meyer, *La Cristiada,* vol. 3, p. 31.

6. José Guadalupe de Anda, *Los Bragados,* passim.

7. Charles C. Cumberland, *Mexico: The Struggle for Modernity,* p. 127.

8. Pérez Verdía, vol. 2, p. 83.

9. Ibid., vol. 2, pp. 525–26 and vol. 3, p. 252.

10. Ibid., vol. 3, p. 123.

11. Ibid., p. 239.

12. Ibid., p. 252.

13. Ibid.

14. González Martín, p. 4.

15. Meyer, *La Cristiada,* vol. 2, p. 34.

16. Ibid., p. 38.

17. Ibid., p. 54.

18. Josephus Daniels, *Shirt Sleeve Diplomat,* p. 40.

19. Meyer, *La Cristiada,* vol. 2, pp. 95 and 97.

20. U.S. Department of State Records, Report No. 24, NARS, File 812.00/14266.

21. Jim Tuck, "The Primitives," pp. 285 and 287.

22. Father Salvador Casas to author.

23. Meyer, *La Cristiada,* vol. 3, p. 284.

24. J. Guadalupe de Anda, *Los Bragados,* p. 58.

25. Agustín Yáñez, *The Lean Lands,* p. 279.

26. Ibid., pp. 280–81.

27. Nikolai Larin, *La Rebelión de los cristeros,* p. 208.

28. Meyer, *La Cristiada,* vol. 3, p. 13.

29. Ibid., p. 84.

30. Ibid., p. 284.

31. Ibid., p. 75.

32. Ibid., p. 74.

33. *El Machete,* 27 September 1927.

THE MAESTRO AND HIS PUPILS

1. David C. Bailey, *¡Viva Cristo Rey!,* p. 40.

2. Ibid., p. 40.

3. Meyer, *La Cristiada,* vol. 2, p. 98.

4. Bailey, p. 41.

5. Efrén Quezada, "Anacleto González Flores, verdadero maestro," p. 276.

6. Heriberto Navarrete, *Por Dios y por la patria,* p. 23.

7. Ibid., p. 24.

8. *DAVID* 5:329.

9. Ibid.

10. Ibid., pp. 329–30.

11. Bailey, p. 41.

12. Navarrete, *Por Dios,* p. 87.

13. Ibid., p. 89.

14. Meyer, *La Cristiada,* vol. 2, p. 146.

15. Ibid., p. 147.

16. Navarrete, *Por Dios,* pp. 110–11.

17. Ibid., p. 114.

18. Bailey, p. 109.

19. Miguel Gómez Loza to Miguel Palomar y Vizcarra, 21 December 1925, *DAVID* 4:153–54.

20. Father Heriberto Navarrete to author.

21. Navarrete, *Por Dios*, p. 120.

22. Ibid., p. 122–23.

23. Ibid., p. 123.

24. Ibid., pp. 124–25.

25. Ibid., pp. 34–35.

26. Ibid., p. 88; Bailey, p. 155.

27. "Datos biográficos del general Lauro Rocha G.," pp. 207–8.

28. Navarrete, *Por Dios*, pp. 51–52.

CALLISTA CHALLENGE, CATHOLIC RESPONSE

1. John W. F. Dulles, *Yesterday in Mexico*, pp. 611–21.

2. Bailey, p. 34; Meyer, *La Cristiada*, vol. 2, pp. 105–10.

3. Memorandum from Ernest Lagarde, French Chargé d'Affaires in Mexico City, to Quai D'Orsay, 18 September 1926, NARS, File 812.414, p. 12.

4. Ibid., p. 13.

5. Ronald Atkin, *Revolution! Mexico 1910–20*, p. 152.

6. Bailey, pp. 47–48.

7. Ibid., pp. 49–50.

8. Ibid., p. 50.

9. Ibid., p. 51; Meyer, *La Cristiada*, vol. 2, p. 148.

10. Bailey, p. 52.

11. Ibid. pp. 51–2; Meyer, *La Cristiada*, vol. 2, p. 148.

12. Bailey, p. 52.

13. Ibid., p. 16; Meyer, *La Cristiada*, vol. 1, p. 58.

14. Alicia O. de Bonfil [Alicia Olivera Sedano], *Aspectos del conflicto religioso de 1926 a 1929*, pp. 112–13.

15. Bailey, p. 55.

16. Antonio Ríus Facius, *La Juventud católica y la revolución mejicana: 1910–1925*, p. 45.

17. Meyer, *La Cristiada*, vol. 1, p. 84.

18. Ibid., p. 62.

19. Bailey, p. 56.

20. Antonio Ríus Facius, *Méjico cristero*, pp. 50–53.

21. Luis Rivero del Val, *Entre las patas de los caballos*, p. 27.

22. Bailey, pp. 44–45.

23. Ibid., pp. 230–31.

24. Memorandum from Lagarde to Quai D'Orsay, NARS, p. 67.

25. Bailey, p. 78.

26. Ibid., p. 79.

27. Meyer, *La Cristiada*, vol. 2, pp. 289–90.

28. Confidential political report from Dudley G. Dwyre, U.S. Consul in Guadalajara, to Secretary of State, 6 August 1926, NARS, File 812.404/560.

29. Meyer, *La Cristiada*, vol. 2, p. 290.

30. Ibid.

31. Navarrete, *Por Dios*, p. 111.

32. Ibid., pp. 112–13.

33. Meyer, *La Cristiada*, vol. 2, pp. 290–91.

34. Ibid., p. 291.

35. Ibid.

36. Ibid.

37. Bailey, p. 82.

38. Meyer, *La Cristiada*, vol. 1, p. 105.

39. Ríus Facius, *Méjico cristero*, p. 94; Navarrete, *Por Dios*, p. 103–5; Report from Dwyre to Secretary of State, NARS.

40. Ríus Facius, *Méjico cristero*, pp. 94–95; Navarrete, *Por Dios*, p. 103–5; Report from Dwyre to Secretary of State, NARS. The consular report put the number of prisoners at 500.

41. Report from Dwyre to Secretary of State, NARS.

42. Meyer, *La Cristiada*, vol. 1, p. 107; Ríus Facius, *Méjico cristero*, p. 95.

43. Aurelio Acevedo and Vicente Viramontes, "El general Quintanar," pp. 1–5; and Ríus Facius, *Méjico cristero*, p. 95–99.

44. Ríus Facius, *Méjico cristero*, p. 100; Bailey, p. 88.

45. Bailey, p. 89.

46. Ibid.

47. Ibid.

48. Ibid.; Ríus Facius, *Méjico cristero*, p. 102.

49. Alfonso Trueba [Martin Chowell], *Luis Navarro Origel: el primer cristero*, pp. 90–91.

50. Ríus Facius, *Méjico cristero*, p. 127.

51. Ibid., pp. 307–9; and Trueba, pp. 137–41.

52. Francisco Campos, "Santiago Bayacora, Durango," pp. 130–32; José Gallegos, *La Persecución religiosa en Durango*, pp. 31–32.

53. Ríus Facius, *Méjico cristero*, pp. 128–30 and 199–202.

54. Meyer, *La Cristiada*, vol. 1, p. 111.

55. Ríus Facius, *Méjico cristero*, p. 144.

56. Ibid., p. 145.

57. Meyer, *La Cristiada*, vol. 1, p. 113.

58. Ibid., p. 87.

59. Ibid., pp. 87–88.

60. Jesús Degollado Guízar, *Memorias*, pp. 33–36.

61. Ibid., p. 45–47.

62. Ibid., pp. 93–100.

63. Meyer, *La Cristiada*, vol. 2, p. 296.

64. Bailey, p. 94.

65. Ibid., p. 95.

66. Ibid., p. 96.

67. Ibid., p. 97.

68. Ibid., p. 98.

69. Ibid., pp. 98–99.

70. Ibid., p. 99.

71. Ibid., p. 107.

72. René Capistrán Garza to author.

73. Bailey, p. 121.

74. Ibid., pp. 121–34; Ríus Facius, *Méjico cristero*, p. 208.

75. Thirteen-page memorandum prepared by René Capistrán Garza, *Documentos secretos de la revolución cristera*, 14 November 1928, ACG, pp. 8–9.

76. Ríus Facius, *Méjico cristero*, original draft reprinted on p. 141.

LOS ALTOS IN FLAMES

1. Meyer, *La Cristiada*, vol. 1, p. 132; Manuel Ramírez de Olivas, "Más Noticias de don Nicho Hernández," pp. 30–32.

2. Josefina Arellano, "Narración histórica de la revolución cristera en el pueblo de San Julián, Jalisco.

3. Concepción Alcalá, *Diario de San Miguel el Alto*, pp. 11–12; and Víctor Ceja Reyes, "El Catorce lo llamaron," p. 33.

4. Ceja Reyes, "El Catorce lo llamaron," p. 33.

5. Meyer, *La Cristiada*, vol. 1, p. 134.

6. Víctor López Díaz, "Origen del movimiento en Jalpa de Canovas," pp. 30–31.

7. Ibid., p. 31.

8. Meyer, *La Cristiada*, vol. 1, p. 131.

9. "Informe sobre lo que yo sé del Padre Aristeo Pedroza," ARF. Statement prepared in 1956 by Father Antonio Alba, who attended the seminary with Father Pedroza.

10. Ibid.

11. Ibid.

12. Ibid.

13. Jean Meyer, *Apocalypse et révolution au Mexique*, pp. 184–85.

14. Father Salvador Casas to author.

15. Meyer, *La Cristiada*, vol. 1, p. 48.

16. Alfonso Taracena, *La Verdadera Revolución mexicana*, vol. 12, pp. 187–88; and de Bonfil [Olivera Sedano], *Aspectos del conflicto*, pp. 184–85.

17. Navarrete, *Por Dios*, p. 173.

18. Heriberto Navarrete, *Los Cristeros eran así*, pp. 1–19.

19. Navarrete, *Por Dios*, p. 233.

20. From tape recorded narration by Rafael Martínez Camarena.

21. Father Antonio Alba, *Informe*, ARF.

22. Meyer, *La Cristiada*, vol. 1, p. 134.

23. Tape by Martínez Camarena.

24. Silvano Barba González, *La Rebelión de los cristeros*, pp. 155–56.

25. Meyer, *La Cristiada*, vol. 1, p. 134.

26. Ibid., p. 171; José Marquez M., "San Julián," p. 205.

27. Barba González, p. 161.

28. Tape by Martínez Camarena.

29. López Díaz, "Origen del movimiento," pp. 126–28.

30. Ibid., p. 127.

31. Ibid., p. 128.

32. Ibid., pp. 127–28.

33. Ibid., p. 128.
34. Ibid.
35. Ibid.
36. Jesús García, "Combate de Cerro Blanco, Jalisco," p. 328.
37. José Márquez, "San Julián," p. 205.
38. López Díaz, "Memorias de Víctor López," p. 143.
39. José María Camarena, "Ampliación de datos del combate de San Julián, Jalisco," p. 261.
40. Marquez M., p. 206.
41. Ibid., p. 206.
42. Ibid.
43. Bailey, p. 154.
44. *IMPACTO,* no. 1375 (July 17, 1976):134.
45. Ceja Reyes, "El Catorce lo llamaron," p. 41.
46. Ceja Reyes, "Crueldades de cristeros," p. 42.
47. Meyer, *La Cristiada,* vol. 3, p. 261.
48. Ibid.
49. Ibid.
50. Taracena, vol. 12, p. 187; Meyer, *La Cristiada,* vol. 1, p. 173; Tape by Martínez Camarena; Carleton Beals, *Mexican Maze,* pp. 307–8.
51. Meyer, *La Cristiada,* vol. 1, p. 173.
52. Tape by Martínez Camarena.

REPRESSION AND *RECONCENTRACION*

1. Meyer, *La Cristiada,* vol. 1, p. 170.
2. Ibid., p. 171.
3. Ríus Facius, *Méjico cristero,* pp. 169–70.
4. Ibid., p. 169.
5. Heriberto Navarrete, *En las Islas Marías,* p. 32.
6. Ibid., p. 34.
7. Ibid.
8. Ibid., p. 35.
9. Ibid., p. 36.
10. Ibid.
11. Ríus Facius, *Méjico cristero,* p. 175.
12. Ibid.

13. Ibid., p. 177.

14. Ibid., p. 178.

15. Colonel Alexander MacNab to President Emilio Portes Gil, Military Intelligence Division Report 2657, 25 February 1929, NARS; J. Meyer, *La Cristiada*, vol. 1, p. 164.

16. Meyer, *La Cristiada*, vol. 1, p. 175.

17. Ibid.

18. Bailey, p. 188.

19. Beals, *Mexican Maze*, pp. 316–17.

20. Ibid., pp. 19–20.

21. Carleton Beals, "Civil War in Mexico: How It Strikes an Observer," p. 166.

22. Meyer, *La Cristiada*, vol. 1, p. 177.

23. Ibid., pp. 175–76.

24. Ibid., p. 177.

25. *Excelsior*, 25 May 1927.

26. Confidential political report from U.S. Consul Dudley G. Dwyre to Secretary of State, 26 May 1927, NARS, File 812.404/799.

SUMMER OF DESPAIR, AUTUMN OF HOPE

1. Tape by Martínez Camarena.

2. Navarrete, *Por Dios*, p. 137.

3. Ibid.

4. Ríus Facius, *Méjico cristero*, p. 221; and Bailey, p. 153.

5. Ríus Facius, *Méjico cristero*, p. 221.

6. Alberto María Carreño, *el Arzobispo de México*, p. 342–43; Bailey p. 152.

7. Ríus Facius, *Méjico cristero*, pp. 223–24.

8. Tape by Martínez Camarena.

9. Alcalá, *Diario*, p. 20.

10. Concepción Alcalá, "Efemérides de Los Altos," p. 183.

11. Ibid.

12. Ibid.

13. Ibid., p. 195; López Díaz, "Memorias," p. 272.

14. Tape by Martínez Camarena.

15. López Díaz, "Memorias," p. 258.

16. Tape by Martínez Camarena.

17. Ibid.

18. Tape by Martínez Camarena.

19. Navarrete, *Por Dios,* pp. 176–79; Tape by Martínez Camarena.

20. Navarrete, *Por Dios,* p. 178.

21. Ibid., pp. 177–78.

22. Salvador Camarena [pseud.] "Organización del movimiento cristero en la región de Los Altos, Jalisco," p. 120.

23. Tape by Martínez Camarena; Bailey, p. 155.

24. Tape by Martínez Camarena.

25. Ibid.

26. Meyer, *La Cristiada,* vol. 3, p. 165.

27. Gomez Loza papers, ASC.

28. Ibid.

29. Cecilio E. Valtierra, "Memorias de mi actuación en el movimiento cristero," pp. 116–18.

30. Meyer, *La Cristiada,* vol. 3, p. 167.

31. Tape by Martínez Camarena.

32. Meyer, *La Cristiada,* vol. 3, pp. 168–69.

33. Rafael Martínez Camarena and Father Salvador Casas to author.

34. Tape by Martínez Camarena.

35. Ibid.

36. López Díaz, "Memorias," p. 273; Ríus Facius, *Méjico cristero,* p. 250.

COLLABORATION AND RESISTANCE

1. "La Collaboration," *Historia Hors Serie,* no. 39 (Jan., 1975):15–87, 94–136, 140–46.

2. Rebecca West, *The Meaning of Treason,* p. 103.

3. Oral testimony of several witnesses.

4. Ríus Facius, *La Juventud católica,* p. 160.

5. Barba González, pp. 105–6.

6. Ibid., pp. 135–36.

7. Ríus Facius, *La Juventud católica,* p. 159–60.

8. Ríus Facius, *Méjico cristero,* p. 69.

9. Alicia O. de Bonfil, *La Literatura cristera,* pp. 17–18.

10. Barba González, p. 36.

11. Ibid., p. 37.

12. Ibid., p. 36.

13. Meyer, *La Cristiada*, vol. 3, p. 41.

14. Father Casas to author. The same information was recorded in Heriberto Navarrete's *El Voto de Chema Rodríguez*, pp. 9–19. In this work, described by the author as "totally historical," only the names of minor figures were changed for narrative effect. The identities of Víctor Contreras, the collaborator, and Chema Rodríguez, who vowed to kill him, are authentic.

15. Father Casas to author; Heriberto Navarrete, *El Voto de Chema Rodríguez*, p. 15.

16. Alcalá, *Diario*, p. 19.

17. Ibid., p. 41.

18. Ibid., p. 55.

19. Ibid., p. 64.

20. Ibid.

21. Ibid., pp. 67 and 69.

22. Gómez Loza Decree No. 1, Article VII, ASC.

23. Rivero del Val, *Entre las patas*, p. 239.

24. Meyer, *La Cristiada*, vol. 3, p. 37.

25. Ibid. p. 97.

26. *Informador*, 26 February 1927.

27. Meyer, *La Cristiada*, vol. 3, pp. 167–68.

28. Ibid., p. 171.

29. Ibid., p. 110.

30. Ibid., p. 118.

31. Ibid., p. 121.

32. Ríus Facius, *Méjico cristero*, p. 225.

33. Meyer, *La Cristiada*, vol. 3, p. 121.

34. Ibid., p. 124.

35. U.S. Department of State Records, 29 March 1929, NARS, File 812.00/Jalisco 51.

36. Meyer, *Apocalypse et révolution au Mexique*, pp. 11–12.

37. Meyer, *La Cristiada*, vol. 3, p. 128.

38. Enrique de Jesús Ochoa [Spectator], *Los Cristeros del Volcán de Colima*, vol. 1, pp. 363–66.

39. Meyer, *La Cristiada*, vol. 3, p. 128.

40. Meyer, *The Cristero Rebellion*, p. 137.
41. Meyer, *La Cristiada*, vol. 3, p. 122.
42. Ibid., p. 123.
43. Ibid., p. 132.
44. Ríus Facius, *Méjico cristero*, pp. 226–27.
45. Beals, *Mexican Maze*, pp. 20–21.
46. Navarrete, *Los Cristeros*, p. 81.
47. Ibid.

GOROSTIETA: THE *CAUDILLO* AS LIBERAL

1. Meyer, *La Cristiada*, vol. 1, p. 199.
2. Father Salvador Casas to author.
3. Meyer, *La Cristiada*, vol. 1, p. 202.
4. Ibid.
5. Ignacio Muñóz, *Verdad y mito de la revolución mexicana relatado por un protagonista*, vol. 4, p. 270.
6. Meyer, *La Cristiada*, vol. 1, p. 200.
7. Ibid., vol. 1, p. 83.
8. Ibid., vol. 3, p. 22.
9. Bailey, p. 171; de Bonfil [Olivera Sedano], *Aspectos del conflicto*, p. 196–97.
10. de Bonfil [Olivera Sedano], pp. 147–49.
11. "Información de la jefatura de Jalpa, Zacatecas," p. 40.
12. Meyer, *La Cristiada*, vol. 1, p. 215.
13. Ibid.
14. Ibid., p. 83.
15. Bailey, pp. 187–88.
16. Ibid., p. 188.
17. Navarrete, *Por Dios*, pp. 176–81.
18. Aurelio Acevedo, Response to a letter from Salvador Camarena [pseud.], *DAVID* 4:120.
19. Tape by Martínez Camarena.
20. René Capistrán Garza to author.
21. Statement on Gorostieta drafted by Rafael Martínez Camarena on 12 December 1951, AMC.
22. Rafael Martínez Camarena, "Reinhumación de los restos del Padre Pedroza," p. 139.

23. Tape by Martínez Camarena.

24. Ibid.

25. Meyer, *La Cristiada*, vol. 3, p. 123.

26. Taracena, vol. 14, p. 8.

27. Tape by Martínez Camarena.

28. Ibid.

29. Meyer, *La Cristiada*, vol. 3, p. 162.

30. Navarrete, *Por Dios*, p. 155.

31. Ibid., p. 159.

32. Ibid.

33. Ibid.

34. Meyer, *La Cristiada*, vol. 1, p. 82.

35. Ríus Facius, *Méjico cristero*, p. 224.

36. Bailey, p. 234.

37. Meyer, *La Cristiada*, vol. 1, p. 68.

38. Ríus Facius, *Méjico cristero*, pp. 351–52.

39. Ibid.

40. Bailey, p. 230.

41. Meyer, *La Cristiada*, vol. 2, p. 332.

42. Manuel Ramírez de Olivas, "Recuerdos de un cristero," p. 210.

43. Meyer, *La Cristiada*, vol. 1, p. 265.

44. Dwyre to Secretary of State, 2 March 1928, U.S. Department of State Records, NARS, File 812.00/Jalisco 4.

45. Meyer, *La Cristiada*, vol. 1, p. 244.

46. Ibid.

47. Ibid.

48. Taracena, vol. 14, p. 79.

49. Meyer, *La Cristiada*, vol. 1, p. 245.

50. Ibid., pp. 245–46.

51. G-2 Report 1394, Military Archives Division, NARS.

52. Bailey, pp. 177 and 227.

53. Meyer, *La Cristiada*, vol. 1, p. 269.

54. *Excelsior*, 16 December 1929.

55. Meyer, *La Cristiada*, vol. 1, p. 270.

56. Ibid., pp. 282–83.

57. Text of circular announcing third *reconcentración, Excelsior,* 7 January 1929.

58. Meyer, *La Cristiada,* vol. 1, p. 284.

59. Ibid., p. 263.

60. Ibid., p. 276.

61. Ibid., p. 273.

62. G-2 Report 2025.293/1778, Military Intelligence Division, 7 November 1928, NARS.

63. James W. Wilkie, *The Mexican Revolution,* p. 102.

64. Meyer, *La Cristiada,* vol. 1, p. 285.

65. *Excelsior,* 14 February 1929.

66. Dwyre to Secretary of State, 7 January 1929, U.S. Department of State Records, NARS, File 812.00/Jalisco 40.

THE EL CATORCE AFFAIR

1. Father Salvador Casas to author.

2. Navarrete, *Por Dios,* pp. 183–84.

3. *IMPACTO,* no. 1395 (December 11, 1976):34.

4. Ibid., no. 1373 (July 3, 1976):41.

5. Ibid.

6. *IMPACTO,* no. 1394 (December 4, 1976):58.

7. Ibid.

8. Navarrete, *Por Dios,* p. 186.

9. PASM.

10. Meyer, *La Cristiada,* vol. 3, pp. 221–22.

11. Father Salvador Casas to author. He officiated at the ceremony.

12. *IMPACTO,* no. 1376 (July 24, 1976):41.

13. Meyer, *La Cristiada,* vol. 3, p. 222.

14. *IMPACTO,* no. 1395 (December 11, 1976):34.

15. Correspondence from Rafael Martínez Camarena to Fr. Salvador Casas, 18 August 1959, AMC.

16. Ibid.

17. López Díaz, *El Escuadrón,* p. 100.

18. *IMPACTO,* no. 1396 (December 18, 1976):43.

19. Meyer, *La Cristiada,* vol. 3, p. 223.

20. Navarrete, *Por Dios,* p. 221.

21. *IMPACTO*, no. 1393:33.
22. Fr. Salvador Casas to author.
23. Meyer, *La Cristiada*, vol. 3, p. 222.
24. Alcalá, *Diario*, p. 56.
25. *IMPACTO*, no. 1383 (September 18, 1976):46.
26. Navarrete, *Por Dios*, p. 197.
27. Ibid., p. 198.
28. Alcalá, *Diario*, p. 56.
29. Ibid., p. 57.
30. *IMPACTO*, no. 1385 (October 2, 1976):36.
31. Ibid.
32. Ibid., p. 35.
33. Alcalá, *Diario*, p. 56.
34. Ibid.
35. López Díaz, *El Escuadrón*, p. 94.
36. Navarrete, *Por Dios*, p. 205.
37. Ibid., p. 207.
38. Fr. Salvador Casas to author.
39. *IMPACTO*, no. 1387 (September 16, 1976):31.
40. Meyer, *La Cristiada*, vol. 3, pp. 222–23.
41. *IMPACTO*, no. 1387 (September 16, 1976):31.
42. López Díaz, *El Escuadrón*, pp. 95–96.
43. Ibid., p. 94.
44. Ibid., pp. 97–98.
45. Navarrete, *Por Dios*, p. 209.
46. Ibid., p. 212.
47. Fr. Salvador Casas to author.
48. Ibid.
49. *IMPACTO*, no. 1397 (December 25, 1976):27.
50. Alcalá, *Diario*, p. 59.
51. López Díaz, *El Escuadrón*, p. 98.
52. Fr. Casas to author.
53. Ibid.
54. Meyer, *La Cristiada*, vol. 3, pp. 222–23; Fr. Casas to author.
55. Fr. Casas to author.
56. López Díaz, *El Escuadrón*, pp. 103–4.
57. Ibid.

PONCITLAN: THE *CRISTERO* ARDENNES

1. Taracena, vol. 15, pp. 27–28.
2. Meyer, *La Cristiada,* vol. 1, p. 286.
3. de Bonfil [Olivera Sedano], *Aspectos del conflicto,* p. 225.
4. Bailey, p. 244.
5. Navarrete, *Por Dios,* p. 196.
6. Barba González, p. 183; Larin, p. 228.
7. Meyer, *La Cristiada,* vol. 1, p. 287.
8. Ibid., p. 289.
9. Ibid., p. 288.
10. Ríus Facius, *Méjico cristero,* p. 357; Taracena, vol. 15, pp. 43–44.
11. Taracena, vol. 15, p. 47.
12. Ibid., pp. 32 and 38.
13. Bailey, p. 244.
14. Meyer, *La Cristiada,* vol. 1, p. 288.
15. Ibid., p. 299.
16. Degollado Guízar, pp. 194–206.
17. Ibid., p. 208.
18. Ibid., p. 210.
19. Ibid., pp. 218–20.
20. Ibid., p. 224.
21. Meyer, *La Cristiada,* vol. 3, p. 124.
22. Juan Rizo, "Datos proporcionados por Juan Rizo," pp. 73–74; Navarrete, *Por Dios,* pp. 213–19.
23. Navarrete, *Por Dios,* p. 215.
24. Ibid., p. 217.
25. Ibid., p. 218.
26. Ibid.
27. Bailey, p. 250.
28. Navarrete, *Por Dios,* p. 218.
29. Meyer, *La Cristiada,* vol. 1, p. 301.
30. Taracena, vol. 15, p. 55.
31. Bailey, p. 244.
32. Taracena, vol. 15, p. 111.
33. Meyer, *La Cristiada,* vol. 1, p. 300.
34. Ibid.

THE END IN LOS ALTOS

1. Meyer, *La Cristiada*, vol. 1, p. 301.
2. Manuel Ramírez de Olivas, "Combate en Encarnación, Jalisco," p. 380.
3. Meyer, *La Cristiada*, vol. 1, p. 302.
4. Ibid.
5. Navarrete, *Por Dios*, p. 235.
6. Ibid., pp. 236–37.
7. Ramírez de Olivas, "Combate," p. 380.
8. Ibid.
9. Ibid., p. 381.
10. Arellano, Chapter 13.
11. Ibid.
12. Meyer, *La Cristiada*, vol. 3, p. 108.
13. Navarrete, *Por Dios*, p. 221.
14. Ibid., p. 224.
15. Ibid., p. 222.
16. Ibid., pp. 224–25.
17. Bailey, pp. 250–51; Agustín Ramírez, "El Combate de Tepatitlán," p. 163.
18. Navarrete, *Por Dios*, p. 227.
19. Ibid., p. 225.
20. Ibid., p. 226.
21. Bailey, pp. 250–51.
22. Navarrete, *Por Dios*, pp. 229–30.
23. Meyer, *La Cristiada*, vol. 1, p. 303.
24. Bailey, p. 251.
25. Meyer, *La Cristiada*, vol. 1, p. 303.
26. Ibid., p. 304.
27. Bailey, p. 253.
28. *New York Times*, 3 May 1929.
29. Bailey, p. 256.
30. Ibid., pp. 260–61.
31. Meyer, *La Cristiada*, vol. 1, p. 320.
32. Ibid., vol. 1, p. 318.

33. Navarrete, *Por Dios,* p. 240.

34. Tape by Martínez Camarena.

35. Meyer, *La Cristiada,* vol. 3, p. 108.

36. José Guadalupe de Anda, "Últimos Días del general don Enrique Gorostieta Jr." p. 114.

37. Ibid., p. 170.

38. Ibid.

39. Ibid., p. 139.

40. Ibid., p. 285.

41. Ibid., p. 320.

42. Ibid., p. 236.

43. Degollado Guízar, p. 231.

44. Ibid., p. 233.

45. Aristeo Pedroza, "Manifiesto del General Aristeo Pedroza," pp. 90–91.

46. J. Meyer, *La Cristiada,* vol. 2, pp. 337–38.

47. Military Intelligence Report 2657-670, 30 June 1929, and Report G 605/194, 28 June 1929, NARS.

48. Meyer, *La Cristiada,* vol. 2, p. 339.

49. Bailey, p. 280.

50. Ibid., p. 312.

51. Meyer, *La Cristiada,* vol. 1, p. 60.

52. Emilio Portes Gil, *Autobiografía de la revolución mexicana,* p. 574.

53. Navarrete, *Por Dios,* p. 265.

54. Ibid., pp. 265–66.

55. Martínez Camarena, "Reinhumación," pp. 137–40; Taracena, vol. 15, p. 162.

56. Navarrete, *Por Dios,* p. 269.

57. Ibid., p. 270.

AFTERMATH

1. Bailey, p. 292.

2. Ibid., p. 295.

3. Leopoldo Ruiz y Flores, *Recuerdo de recuerdos,* p. 102.

4. Wilfrid Parsons, S. J., *Mexican Martyrdom,* p. 268.

5. Bailey, p. 296.

6. Meyer, *La Cristiada*, vol. 1, p. 345. (Cayetano Alvarez was erroneously listed as Gabino Alvarez, who was killed in May 1928.)

7. Acevedo, pp. 1–5.

8. Meyer, *La Cristiada*, vol. 1, p. 346.

9. Bailey, p. 294.

10. Meyer, *La Cristiada*, vol. 1, p. 367.

11. Ibid., p. 377.

12. Ibid., p. 359.

13. Ibid., p. 360.

14. Ibid., p. 370.

15. Ibid., pp. 377 and 381.

16. Lauro Rocha, "General Lauro Rocha," pp. 181–84.

17. Correspondence from Lauro Rocha to Guadalupe Gutiérrez, 7 March 1936, ASC.

18. "Datos biograficos del general Lauro Rocha G.," pp. 207–8.

19. de Anda, *Los Bragados*, p. 38.

20. James W. Wilkie and Albert L. Michaels, *Revolution in Mexico*, p. 201.

21. Ibid., p. 200.

22. de Anda, *Los Bragados*, p. 21.

23. William Weber Johnson, *Heroic Mexico*, p. 394.

24. Rodrigo García Treviño, *El Católicomunismo*, p. 47.

25. de Anda, *Los Bragados*, p. 100.

26. Ibid., p. 83.

27. Meyer, *Apocalypse*, p. 95.

28. Charles C. Cumberland, *Mexico: The Struggle for Modernity*, p. 284.

29. Johnson, pp. 416–17.

30. Charles C. Cumberland, p. 291.

31. James W. Wilkie, *The Mexican Revolution*, p. 88.

32. García Treviño, p. 39.

Annotated
Bibliography

ARCHIVES

Archives of Antonio Ríus Facius (ARF)
    México, D.F.

Archives of Rafael Martínez Camarena (AMC)
    Guadalajara, Jalisco

Archives of René Capistrán Garza (ACG)
    México, D.F.

Archives of Father Salvador Casas (ASC)
    Guadalajara, Jalisco

Parochial Archives of San Miguel el Alto (PASM)
    San Miguel el Alto, Jalisco

U.S. National Archives and Records Service (NARS)
    Washington, D.C.

OTHER SOURCES

Acevedo, Aurelio, and Vicente Viramontes. "El general Quin-
    tanar." *DAVID* 3:1–5.

Alcalá, Concepción. *Diario de San Miguel el Alto.* Guadalajara:
    Editorial DAVID, 1970.
———. "Efemérides de Los Altos." *DAVID* 4:146–383.

Alcalá, Concepción *(continued)*
The diary of an ardent *cristero* partisan living under Federal occupation in her home town. Events are recorded in minute detail and, considering the author's sympathies, in a communiqué style that is surprisingly laconic.

Arellano, Josefina. "Narración histórica de la revolución cristera en el pueblo de San Julián, Jalisco." Handwritten manuscript in ASC.

An account of life by a *cristero* partisan under Federal occupation. More emotional and less informative than that of Concepción Alcalá.

Atkin, Ronald. *Revolution! Mexico 1910–20.* London: Panther Books, 1972.

An able presentation of the revolutionary decade that preceded the *cristiada,* anecdotal in style without yielding to triviality.

Bailey, David C. *¡Viva Cristo Rey! The Cristero Rebellion and the Church-State Conflict in Mexico.* Austin: University of Texas Press, 1974.

A scholarly and lucid work that focuses more on high-level maneuvering behind the *cristiada* than it does on the rebellion itself.

Barba González, Silvano. *La Rebelión de los cristeros.* México, 1967.

Barba González, an *alteño* by birth, was Federal governor of Jalisco during the *cristiada.* In this disingenuous memoir he attempts to conceal an early career of Catholic activism before he became a government partisan. Yet Barba was the only highly placed Federal who correctly gauged the revolutionary potential of Los Altos; for these perceptions his book has value.

Beals, Carleton. *Mexican Maze.* New York: Lippincott, 1931.
———. "Civil War in Mexico: How It Strikes an Observer." *The New Republic* (July 6, 1927):166–69.

Though anti-clerical and leftist, Beals was the first American writer to challenge the propagandist version of the *cristeros* as reactionary peasants in the service of the landowners and Catholic hierarchy. He observed the rebellion at first hand.

Camarena, José María. "Ampliación de datos del combate de San Julián, Jalisco." *DAVID* 2:261.

Camarena, Salvador [pseud.]. "Organización del movimiento cristero en la región de Los Altos, Jalisco." *DAVID* 4:120.

Campos, Francisco. "Santiago Bayacora, Durango." *DAVID* 2:130–32.

Carreño, Alberto María. *El Arzobispo de Mexico: excmo. sr. don Pascual Díaz y el conflicto religioso*. 2nd ed. México: Ediciones Victoria, 1943.

The author, a law professor and promoter of the Unión Nacional plan, was secretary and close friend to Bishop Pascual Díaz. He defends Díaz against charges of betraying the Catholic resistance movement.

Ceja Reyes, Víctor. "El Catorce lo llamaron." *IMPACTO* (July 14, 1976):41.
———. "Crueldades de cristeros." *IMPACTO* (Nov. 7, 1976):42.

(See annotation under *IMPACTO*)

Cumberland, Charles C. *Mexico: The Struggle for Modernity*. New York: Oxford University Press, 1968.

An incisive account of Mexico's aspirations to achieve social justice and fulfill her destiny from pre-Columbian times to the presidency of Gustavo Díaz Ordaz. Relevant to this study are sections on the relaxation of church-state tensions under Cárdenas and Avila Camacho.

Daniels, Josephus. *Shirt Sleeve Diplomat*. Chapel Hill: University of North Carolina Press, 1947.

Daniels, the country editor who served as ambassador to Mexico under Franklin Roosevelt, was a leading exponent

Daniels, Josephus *(continued)*
and practitioner of the Good Neighbor policy. Belying the folksy style are shrewd insights into Mexico's revolutionary process: he played a major role in forestalling U.S. intervention during the oil expropriation crisis. Daniels also maintained ties with church leaders and moved tactfully to ease anti-Catholic repression.

"Datos biográficos del general Lauro Rocha G." *DAVID* 7: 207–8.

DAVID. Official *cristero* veterans' publication, appearing monthly between 1952 and 1968.

This publication was edited by the late Aurelio Acevedo, a *cristero* regimental commander during the rebellion. Though an invaluable reference source for obscure events, it should be emphasized that the contributors were all dedicated *cristeros* and their emotional bias does not make for objective reporting. Relevant selections are listed individually throughout this bibliography.

de Anda, José Guadalupe. *Los Bragados*. 3rd ed. México: Imprenta Vega, 1976.
———. "Ultimos días del general don Enrique Gorostieta Jr." *DAVID* 4:38–321.

Two works by a disillusioned *cristero* who became a Federal senator. The first, thinly disguised as a novel, focuses on the atrocities of the *bragados,* sadistic bandits of the 1930s masquerading as religious rebels. The second is a gripping account of the last days of General Gorostieta.

de Bonfil, Alicia O. [Alicia Olivera Sedano]. *Aspectos del conflicto religioso de 1926 a 1929*. México: Instituto Nacional de Antropología e Historia, 1966.
———. *La Literatura cristera*. México: Instituto Nacional de Antropología e Historia, 1970.

Aspectos is the first major work by a Mexican author in which the *cristiada* is viewed impartially and as history. It covers both the church-state conflict and the rebellion. *La literatura* is a fascinating compendium of *cristero* songs, prayers, and poems, along with an analysis of pro- and anti-*cristero* works.

Degollado Guízar, Jesús. *Memorias de Jesús Degollado Guízar, ultimo general en jefe del ejército cristero.* México: Editorial Jus, 1957.

This memoir is by the last commander-in-chief of the rebel forces. While vague and inaccurate on dates, this is still a valuable work. It shows how an unassuming druggist, totally lacking military experience, developed into a skilled commander. Degollado was also the most humane and chivalrous of the *cristero* leaders.

DETENAL. *Dirección General de Estudio del Territorio Nacional.* Federal agency specializing in geographic studies.

Dulles, John W. F. *Yesterday in Mexico: A Chronicle of the Revolution, 1919–36.* Austin: University of Texas Press, 1961.

A fine account of the tense years between the fall of Carranza and accession of Cárdenas. Of particular interest are portions relating to the anti-religious frenzy unleashed in Tabasco under the Garrido Canabal dictatorship.

Excelsior. Mexico City daily. 1926–1929.

El Machete. 27 September 1927.

Gallegos, José. *La Persecución religiosa en Durango.* México: Editorial Jus, 1965.

A forty-page pamphlet by a *cristero* sympathizer; the most detailed account available of the events that led to and precipitated Trinidad Mora's rising in Durango.

García, Jesús. "Combate de Cerro Blanco, Jalisco." *DAVID* 2:328.

García Treviño, Rodrigo. *El Católicomunismo.* México: Ediciones Sociopolíticos, 1970.

García Treviño *(continued)*
A conservative anti-clerical's attack on what he discerns as an unholy alliance between Marxism and the Catholic left.

"General Lauro Rocha." *DAVID* 7:181–84.

Gómez Loza, Miguel. Letter of Dec. 21, 1925, from Miguel Gómez Loza to Miguel Palomar y Vizcarra. *DAVID* 4:153–54.

González Martín, J. Jesús. "Feria de abril en Tepa." April, 1977.

Documentary pamphlet printed in conjunction with regional *alteño* fair in Tepatitlán. Useful background information for those interested in traditional culture and folkways of Los Altos.

IMPACTO. Weekly México City news magazine.

From June to December, 1976, this publication ran a twenty-six-part report on the life, legend, betrayal, and murder of Victoriano Ram írez. Written by V íctor Ceja Reyes, the series was meticulously researched and is of inestimable value to students of the *cristiada* in Los Altos.

"Información de la jefatura de Jalpa, Zacatecas." *DAVID* 6:40.

Informador. Guadalajara daily. 1926–1929.

Johnson, William Weber. *Heroic Mexico.* New York: Doubleday, 1968.

A massive work, covering sixty years of modern Mexican history. Though the writing is superb and the material consistently interesting, there are several factual errors in sections relating to the *cristiada*.

"La Collaboration." *Historia Hors Series,* no. 39 (Jan. 1975) 15–87, 94–136, 140–46.

Special issue of a French historical bi-monthly devoted to exploring wartime collaboration. Twenty-three articles by sixteen authors.

Larin, Nikolai. *La Rebelión de los cristeros*. (Spanish translation, original in Russian.) México: Ediciones ERA, 1968.

The official Soviet version of the rebellion, as interesting for its wild inaccuracies as for its rigidly polemical tone. In one flight of fancy the author speculates that Father Vega, who didn't survive the war, and Miguel Darío Miranda, staunchly anti-*cristero* cleric who became primate of Mexico, were one and the same man.

López Díaz, Víctor. *El Escuadrón de Jalpa de Canovas, Gto., y el regimiento cristero San Julián*. Guadalajara: Editorial DAVID, 1970.
————. "Memorias de Víctor López: Actividades del grupo de Jalpa de Cánovas, Gto." *DAVID*, vol. 2, pp. 142–273.
————. "Origen del movimiento en Jalpa de Cánovas." *DAVID*, vol. 2, pp. 30–128.

Fast-paced, tightly written action narratives by a former *cristero* colonel. Shaky on dates.

Márquez M., José. "San Julián." *DAVID* 2:205.

Martínez Camarena, Rafael. "Reinhumación de los restos del padre Pedroza." *DAVID* 8:139.
————. Tape recording detailing his participation in the *cristiada*.

Martínez Camarena, friend and associate of Miguel Gómez Loza, succeeded him as *cristero* interim governor of Jalisco. Despite antagonism toward Gorostieta, who ousted him from his post, he remained a loyal supporter of the movement.

Meyer, Jean. *La Cristiada*. 3 vols. México: Siglo Veintiuno Editores, 1973.
————. *Apocalypse et révolution au Mexique*. Paris: Gallimard, 1974.
————. *The Cristero Rebellion: The Mexican People Between Church and State 1926–29*. New York: Cambridge University Press, 1976.

Meyer is by far the most prolific chronicler of the *cristiada* and the only one whose works on the subject have been

Meyer, Jean (*continued*)
　　translated into three languages. In the tradition of Carleton Beals, he rejects the *cristero*-as-white-guard stereotype and supports his thesis with impressive statistical evidence and fine, impassioned writing. His only weakness is a lack of impartiality, to which he freely admits. He originally approached the subject with a socialist and anticlerical bias but his investigations, coupled with warm friendships he has established with old *cristeros,* have transformed him into an ardent partisan.

Muñoz, Ignacio. *Verdad y mito de la revolución mexicana relatado por un protagonista.* México: Ediciones Populares, 1965.
　　A rightist liberal and Army colonel, Muñoz was both anticlerical and anti-revolutionary. He was a friend of Gorostieta and tried to dissuade him from taking over the leadership of a Catholic rebellion.

Navarrete, Heriberto, S. J. *Por Dios y por la patria.* 3rd ed. México: Editorial Jus, 1973.
　　———. *Los Cristeros eran así.* México: Editorial Jus, 1968.
　　———. *En las Islas Marías.* México: Editorial Jus, 1965.
　　———. *El Voto de Chema Rodríguez.* México: Editorial Jus, 1965.
　　Three non-fiction works about the *cristiada,* and a fourth—technically a novel—that is almost entirely historical. The author, a Jesuit and ex-*cristero,* has prepared material that is refreshingly free of hagiography or special pleading. In later years Navarrete came under attack for his role in the downfall of *alteño* folk hero Victoriano Ramírez.

New York Times. 1926–1929.

Ochoa, Enrique de Jesús [Spectator]. *Los Cristeros del volcán de Colima.* 2 vols. México: Editorial Jus, 1961.
　　Ochoa, a priest, was the brother of Dionisio Eduardo Ochoa, leader of the rebels in Colima. He served as a field chaplain with the *cristeros* but, unlike Navarrete, his view of them is rapturous and uncritical. The work's chief value is for its detailed coverage of a little-known theater of operations.

Parsons, Wilfrid, S. J. *Mexican Martyrdom*. New York: Mac-Millan, 1936.

The author, an American Jesuit editor, befriended René Capistrán Garza and for a time flirted with the idea of supporting his armed movement. But he fell out with Capistrán and ended as an ally of Bishop Pascual Díaz.

Pedroza, Aristeo. "Manifiesto del general Aristeo Pedroza." *DAVID* 6:90–91.

Pérez Verdía, Luis. *Historia particular del estado de Jalisco.* 3 vols. Guadalajara: n.p., 1952.

This noted historian's work contains the most complete coverage of the past allegiance of Los Altos to clericalism and conservatism. Indispensable as background material.

Portes Gil, Emilio. *Autobiografía de la revolución mexicana.* México: Institute Mexicano de Cultura, 1964.

A somewhat self-serving work by Calles's successor as president. To enhance his prestige, Portes Gil consistently downplays American contributions to the settlement ending the *cristero* war.

Quezada, Efrén. "Anacleto González Flores, verdadero maestro." *DAVID* 4:276–78.

Ramírez, Agustín. "El Combate de Tepatitlán: rectificación a Juan Rizo." *DAVID* 8:163.

Ramírez de Olivas, Manuel [pseud.]. "Más noticias de don Nicho Hernández." *DAVID* 5:30–32.
———. "Recuerdos de un cristero." *DAVID* 6:210.
———. "Combate en Encarnación, Jalisco." *DAVID* 7:380.

"Recordando al maestro Anacleto." *DAVID* 5:329.

Ríus Facius, Antonio. *Méjico cristero.* México: Editorial Patria, 1966.
———. *La Juventud católica y la revolución mejicana.* México: Editorial Jus, 1962.

Ríus Facius, Antonio (*continued*)
The "j" as opposed to "x" spelling in "México" (a form favored by Iberian-oriented conservatives) is a clue to this author's ideology. Though Rius's knowledge of the *cristiada* and Mexican Catholic activism is encyclopedic, his total commitment to traditionalism must ever be taken into account.

Rivero del Val, Luis. *Entre las patas de los caballos*. México: Editorial Jus, 1970.

A novel based on the diary of Manuel Bonilla, an ACJM militant who formed a rebel band in the Sierra de Ajusco near México City. Fast-moving and anecdotal; the author himself was an *acejotamero* turned *cristero*.

Rizo, Juan. "Datos proporcionados por Juan Rizo." *DAVID* 8:73–74.

Rocha, Lauro. "General Lauro Rocha." *DAVID* 7:181–84.

Ruiz y Flores, Leopoldo. *Recuerdo de recuerdos*. México: Buena Prensa, 1942.

A brief autobiography of the hierarchy's leading conciliator, published after his death.

Taracena, Alfonso. *La Verdadera Revolución mexicana*. Vols. 12–15. México: Editorial Jus, 1963.

Four volumes of this prodigious work on the Mexican Revolution deal with the church-state controversy and the *cristero* period. Taracena treats the *cristiada* objectively in a clear, chiseled style.

Thomas, Hugh. *The Spanish Civil War*. London: Pelican Books, 1968.

The definitive book on that tragic struggle and of interest as a secondary source.

Trueba, Alfonso [Martin Chowell]. *Luis Navarro Origel: el primer cristero*. México: Editorial Jus, 1959.

Navarro Origel, who was actually the second (after Pedro Quintanar) Catholic rebel to rise against the government. The author strains heroically to justify the alternately tyrannical and vacillating behavior that caused Navarro to be deposed and almost killed by his own men.

Tuck, Jim. "The Primitives: Catholicism's Submerged Third." *Catholic World* (Feb., 1967):284–87.

Valtierra, Cecilio E. "Memorias de mi actuación en el movimiento cristero." *DAVID* 4:116–18.

West, Rebecca. *The Meaning of Treason.* New York: Viking Press, 1947.

Wilkie, James W. *The Mexican Revolution: Federal Expenditure and Social Change Since 1910.* 2nd ed. Berkeley: University of California Press, 1970.

Wilkie, James W., and Albert L. Michaels, eds. *Revolution in Mexico: Years of Upheaval, 1910–40.* New York: Knopf, 1969.

The first of these works discusses President Avila Camacho's role in throwing out the socialist-cum-sexual education program. The second, a historical anthology compiled by Wilkie and Michaels, contains two relevant contributions by the former. One demonstrates how innocuous the concept of "sexual" education really was, while the other effectively challenges the view that church and state in Mexico were competing monoliths.

Yáñez, Agustín. *The Lean Lands (Las tierras flacas* in the original). Translated by Ethel Brinton. Austin: University of Texas Press, 1968.

The former governor of Jalisco and Secretary of Education was also a talented novelist and native of Los Altos. This work contains superb sketches of *alteño* life and culture.

Index